UN-CANADIAN:

ISLAMOPHOBIA IN THE TRUE NORTH

NIGHTWOOD EDITIONS

2019

UN-CANADIAN: ISLAMOPHOBIA IN THE TRUE NORTH

GRAEME TRUELOVE

Nightwood Editions
P.O. Box 1779
Gibsons, BC VON IVO
Canada
www.nightwoodeditions.com

COVER DESIGN: Topshelf Creative
TYPESETTING: Carleton Wilson

Canada

 Canada Council   Conseil des Arts
for the Arts   du Canada

 BRITISH COLUMBIA
ARTS COUNCIL
An agency of the Province of British Columbia

Nightwood Editions acknowledges the support of the Canada Council for the Arts, which last year invested $153 million to bring the arts to Canadians throughout the country.

Nous remercions le Conseil des arts du Canada de son soutien. L'an dernier, le Conseil a investi 153 millions de dollars pour mettre de l'art dans la vie des Canadiennes et des Canadiens de tout le pays.

We also gratefully acknowledge financial support from the Government of Canada and from the Province of British Columbia through the BC Arts Council and the Book Publishing Tax Credit.

This book has been produced on 100% post-consumer recycled, ancient-forest-free paper, processed chlorine-free and printed with vegetable-based dyes.

Printed and bound in Canada.

LIBRARY AND ARCHIVES CANADA CATALOGUING IN PUBLICATION

Title: Un-Canadian : Islamophobia in the true north / Graeme Truelove.
Names: Truelove, Graeme, 1983- author.
Identifiers: Canadiana (print) 20190127392 | Canadiana (ebook) 20190127422 |
ISBN 9780889713628 (softcover) | ISBN 9780889713635 (ebook)
Subjects: LCSH: Islamophobia—Canada. | LCSH: Muslims—Canada. |
LCSH: Muslims—Canada—Social conditions. | LCSH: Islam—Canada. |
LCSH: Canada—Ethnic relations. | LCSH: Canada—Race relations.
Classification: LCC FC106.M9 T78 2019 | DDC 305.6/9771—dc23

Contents

Let me not to the marriage of true minds
Admit impediments. Love is not love
Which alters when it alteration finds,
Or bends with the remover to remove.
O no! It is an ever-fixed mark
That looks on tempests and is never shaken

– William Shakespeare (from "Sonnet 116")

Foreword by Ihsaan Gardee, former Executive Director of the National Council of Canadian Muslims

IN A WORLD of rising extreme-right populism and anti-immigrant movements, Canada is often portrayed, and many rightfully perceive it to be, a beacon of human rights when compared with several other places in the world. At the same time, it cannot be argued that different groups, at different times in Canada's history, starting and continuing with its Indigenous populations, have not undergone the experience of being "othered" to varying degrees and with different impacts by those in positions of power and influence. Those who do not study history are doomed to repeat it, so recognizing this is the first step in working to prevent it from happening again.

Graeme Truelove's *Un-Canadian: Islamophobia in the True North* provides an excellent introduction to many of the issues related to Islamophobia and the varying experiences of Muslims in post-9/11 Canada. It should be required reading for sitting and aspiring politicians of all stripes, along with the bureaucrats and agencies charged with implementing their agendas and vision. Its exploration of the role that media plays is something that should encourage a lot of self-reflection based on the power that the fifth estate has to both mirror—as well as manufacture—the narrative in the public discourse. Anyone interested in gaining a better understanding of how Islamophobia, like other forms of hatred, continues to impact those who are (or are perceived to be) Muslims would do well to pay heed to the issues and challenges that Truelove successfully captures and distills.

While Islamophobia will likely not ever be eliminated, until the time when being a Muslim is considered to be an authentic representation of what it means to be fully Canadian, these challenges are likely to continue to grow, allowing those with personal, political or other agendas the ability to play upon the fears and ignorance of the unknown and the biases and hatred of some. We owe it to ourselves and to future generations to not simply acknowledge this, but also to be eternally vigilant and to actively take steps to address and combat hatred and xenophobia, regardless of its form or whom it targets.

– Ihsaan Gardee, former executive director of the National
  Council of Canadian Muslims

Introduction

St. Isaac Jogues is the most famous victim of "running the gauntlet" in Canada. The seventeenth-century Jesuit missionary was captured by Mohawk warriors and made to walk between two lines of armed captors who rained vicious blows down on him until he was near death. This was not a uniquely Mohawk practice—similar tortures have existed in the British army and navy and elsewhere in the world—but it is in the First Nations context that the ancient practice has become best known in Canada. That's probably because Jogues was later canonized by Pope Pius XI as the patron saint of Canada and became one of those the Catholic Church calls the "Canadian martyrs."

In a way, what happened to Jogues has been happening to newcomers here ever since.

On St. Patrick's Day, many Canadians with no Irish blood whatsoever like to wear green and, perhaps with a wink, lay claim to a heritage on the Emerald Isle. It's easy to forget that Irish immigrants were once looked upon as violent, Catholic fanatics who either refused to integrate or were incapable of it. Like French Canadians, Irish Canadians were looked down on as second-class citizens. "Speak white," they were told when they used their native tongues. For generations, both these ethnic groups ran the gauntlet of discrimination and prejudice before being accepted by mainstream Canada.

Canada's first prime minister, John A. Macdonald, argued against allowing Chinese Canadians the vote. He feared that they would swamp the voter rolls, win elections and foist their "immoralities" on the rest of the country. Once the Canadian Pacific Railway (CPR) was completed, the most dangerous work having been done by Chinese migrants, Macdonald's government instituted a "head tax" designed to limit further Chinese immigration to Canada. In years to come, violent riots targeted the Asian Canadians already here.

In 1914, the *Komagata Maru* docked in Vancouver carrying hundreds of Indian emigrants seeking a better life. Citing a technicality in Canadian law designed to prevent Indian immigration (a rule requiring ships to have made a non-stop journey from their point of origin before passengers were allowed to disembark), officials refused to allow the passengers off the ship. As weeks went by, Canadian authorities even limited the food and water allowed onto the cramped ship. After spring turned to summer, the *Komagata Maru* returned to India.

Ukrainian Canadians were interned during the First World War. German Canadians were, too. In the face of increasingly hostile anti-German sentiment, the largely German residents of Berlin, Ontario felt compelled to rename the town "Kitchener" after British military commander Herbert Kitchener. Perhaps if they demonstrated enough patriotism, they could avoid the discrimination those of German descent faced in Allied countries where even German dogs, like Dachshunds, were being abused for their apparent loyalty to the Kaiser.

The Canadian government once formally designated Italians as "non-preferred" immigrants. The Italian immigrant's "standard of living, his way of life, even his civilization seems so different that I doubt if he could ever become an asset to our country," attested the Commissioner for Overseas Immigration. When Italy declared war on Britain and France during the Second World War, within minutes the RCMP was given orders to arrest Italian Canadians who might be security threats. Hundreds were arrested and interned; none were ever charged. Other Italian Canadians were subjected to violence, verbal abuse, vandalism and discrimination. Some of those who might pass as non-Italian, such as lighter-skinned northern Italians, changed their names to hide their ethnicity.

Further wartime scapegoating targeted Japanese Canadians. After the Japanese attack on Pearl Harbour in 1941, the CPR fired its Japanese-Canadian employees. Other industries followed suit. Suddenly, having Canadians of Japanese descent living along the west coast was deemed a security threat. "No Japs from the Rockies to the seas," declared Liberal cabinet minister Ian MacKenzie. Thousands were interned in camps in the British Columbia interior. En route to the prisons, many were warehoused in livestock stalls.

Canada turned away the MS *St. Louis*, a ship carrying 907 German Jews fleeing the Nazi regime. The ship had already been turned away by the United States and Cuba, but there would be no safe haven in Canada, either. The decree reportedly uttered by a top-level Canadian immigration bureaucrat indicating the number of Jews Canada was prepared to take in—"None is too many"—was a death sentence. The *St. Louis* returned to Germany. Two-hundred and fifty-four of its passengers would be murdered in the Holocaust.

This was Canada. This was here. Few Canadians are aware that we had all-black segregated schools in this country, and that the last of them closed in 1983. We forget that slavery was legal for two hundred years in Upper and Lower Canada until it was banned throughout the British Empire—not through the efforts of altruistic Canadians, but through the efforts of an international cohort. We recall the Underground Railroad used by slaves to escape to northern US states and Canada, but not that some of those states had banned slavery before the British did, and that there was a time when slaves fled south from bondage in Upper Canada to freedom in Vermont and New York. We have trouble remembering these facts because they are incompatible with our self-image as an open, progressive and multicultural haven. Many of the groups once discriminated against have been successfully adopted into the mainstream, after all. It's hard to believe we ever did these things. But because it's so hard to believe, it's also difficult to recognize the pattern repeating.

Some reputable polls have shown that a majority of Canadians don't think Islamophobia exists in our country. It does. Given our history, that shouldn't be surprising. The targets of discrimination change over the years, but the message doesn't: You aren't one of us.

Today, that message is being sent to Muslims. This is not a book about what it's like to be a Muslim in Canada. With over one million Muslims in this country representing over sixty different ethno-cultural groups, that would be a difficult subject for one person to cover. This is a book about Canada, and about a gauntlet that's been run before. Islam's history in Canada has been punctuated by waves of discrimination, often coinciding with notable geopolitical events. This discrimination has taken the form of hate crimes, media stereotyping, prejudiced political rhetoric and populist laws seemingly designed to focus negative attention on non-citizens and foreign-born citizens. The application of these laws has been rife with prejudice against Muslims, and at times the rule of law itself has been abandoned. Serious, worrying consequences now threaten the relationship between Muslims and non-Muslims in Canada.

Canadians deserve to be proud of our progressive image, but not all of it is earned. This book is intended to help identify and confront those areas where we still divide the world into "us" and "them" and still force newcomers to run a painful gauntlet of discrimination before we eventually admit them, gradually and begrudgingly, into the ranks of trusted countrymen. Only once we recognize it as it is happening, not fifty years later when we read it in a history book, can the pattern of fear and exclusion finally end.

Welcome to Canada: Muslim Immigration before 9/11

IN 1854, LORD STANLEY, the man who would one day spend ten guineas on an ornate silver cup and donate it to the champion hockey team in the Dominion of Canada, was just thirteen years old. The first organized game of hockey, which would be held in Montreal and feature a wooden puck, was still decades away, but in that year a woman named Agnes Love gave birth to her son, James. As far as we know, he was the first documented Muslim born in Canada. This much is known of the family: they came from Scotland, were probably converts, and little James was named after his father. To understand Islam's place in Canada today, we need to understand just how deep its roots here are. In fact, they probably go back even further than the Love family.

In the 1700s, the slave trade was active in what would become Canada, and some 30 percent of African slaves were likely Muslim. Later, Europeans comprised the bulk of voluntary early Muslim immigration to Canada. Some early accounts suggest a warm welcome, reporting stories of "peddlers" being allowed to stay in people's homes overnight during heavy snowfalls. Most of them became farmers and businesspeople. They staked claims and sifted through endless sludge in the gold rush. They helped construct the CPR, the nation-building link binding East and West that has been called our "national dream." It's been said that Canada is a nation built by immigrants. This notion fails to recognize the crucial role of Indigenous peoples, but it does honour the extraordinary toil and achievement of people from around the globe that Canada represents. If Canada was built by immigrants, Canada was built by Muslims, too.

Of course racism is part of the story. The first Arabs to arrive in Canada, Muslims and Christians escaping conscription in the Ottoman Empire, arrived in 1882. Canadian officials called them all "Syrians" regardless of where they were from. In official correspondence in 1903, Superintendent of Immigration W.D. Scott wrote that the "Syrians" were "more of a nuisance than anything else to the residents of Canada." He grudgingly noted the financial success they had demonstrated, but concluded that "there is, however, a higher standard of citizenship than the mere ability to acquire dollars and cents... the Syrians are looked upon by the department as undesirable immigrants." In 1910, Canada began to restrict immigration: countries of origin were listed as either "preferred" or "non-preferred." What the lists looked like is not very surprising. The Ottoman Empire was "non-preferred," and immigrants from Africa were banned entirely. Immigration slowed, as many Muslims found more welcoming opportunities in the United States than in Canada. After the outbreak of the First World War, Muslim immigrants from Turkey were seen as enemy aliens, and many were sent back.

While there is racism in Islam's early history in Canada, it is also a story of success and strength. Even as immigration slowed, in many ways the descendants of earlier immigrants flourished. The first mosque in Canada, the Al Rashid mosque in Edmonton, opened in 1938. Newspaper accounts at the time indicate a curiosity, even excitement on the part of non-Muslims. "Many of the two hundred and fifty members of the Moslem community in the Edmonton district—most of them are Syrians—are expected to attend the service, and because it is anticipated that the capacity of the mosque will be taxed, invitations to only a few non-Moslems are being issued," noted the *Edmonton Journal*. The spelling of Muslim as "Moslem," now often considered offensive because of negative connotations in Arabic, was likely the result of ignorance, not malice. The paper seemed to expect its readers to be interested in attending, and indeed the mayors of Edmonton and Hanna both did. Over time, the Al Rashid mosque became a popular gathering place for both Muslims and non-Muslims as the Muslim community integrated. It probably helped that, when they had the opportunity, Muslims often chose to build their mosques near other places of worship, such as Christian churches. Sometimes they contributed financially to the churches, too. Years went by, and Islamic studies programs popped up at the University of Toronto and McGill. Families grew.

In the late sixties, Canada introduced a points system governing immigration, rewarding applicants who had certain education, skills and work experience rather than prioritizing those from certain countries of origin. This more-even playing field helped tremendously. The wave of Muslim immigrants that followed, from south and southeast Asia in the sixties and from east Africa in the seventies, was so well educated that University of Alberta professor emeritus of sociology Baha Abu-Laban has referred to it as a significant "brain drain" from the immigrants' ancestral countries. Contrary to the persistent myth that immigrants pose some sort of net cost to Canada, these Muslim immigrants were clearly a boon.

Canada's policy of official multiculturalism, adopted in 1971, prompted a further wave of Muslim immigrants, which has continued to this day. In fact there are now over a million Muslims in Canada. Illustrating just how ingrained and widespread Islam has become, in 2010, the Midnight Sun Mosque opened in Inuvik, Nunavut, at 29 Wolverine Road. There, in a part of the world that James Love, Jr. wouldn't have even imagined, the mosque started a food bank. In a distant, frozen part of Canada most Canadians will never visit, Islam is an integral part of the community.

How typical is this scenario? The vast diversity of Muslim communities makes analyzing their overall integration into the Canadian mosaic difficult. Some communities have integrated more easily than others, but there's a lot of data that tells a positive story. Rates of home ownership look strong and children of Muslim immigrants are successful in school. The numbers tracking women in the workplace are encouraging, too. Gender equality is an area in which some Muslim communities are regularly criticized for failing to integrate with the Canadian mainstream, but Muslim women are just as likely to have paid employment outside the home as women from other immigrant communities. "The bottom line is that assimilation is alive and well in Canada," wrote University of Toronto professor of sociology Jeffery G. Reitz. "Concerns about inassimilable Muslims are empirically unfounded."

Sometimes it's said that there is something inherent in Islam that prevents integration. It's been said before, about successive groups of newcomers, that while earlier immigrants were able to integrate, the latest group cannot or will not, but it's a false assertion. Some of this prejudice reveals a misunderstanding of what Islam is about. Muslim scholars confirm that, theologically, Islam is entirely compatible with modern Canadian society. In fact, according to Imam Dr. Zijad Delic in *Canadian Islam: Belonging and Loyalty*, Muslims are actively encouraged to embrace new cultures while remaining faithful to the principles of their religion. "This is, after all, how the true universality of Islam works: it consists in integrating the good, from wherever it may come," Delic wrote. "This recognition of universal good is what has made it possible for Muslims, without ethical contradiction, to adopt nearly every encountered culture as their own, from South America to the Indian subcontinent, through Eastern Europe, Asia, North Africa and many other regions. The same should be true for Canada."

Put that way, if Muslims face challenges integrating, it's not because of the theological tenets of their religion. However, despite Islam's long history in Canada, and the documented contributions made by Muslims, there has been a sense of unease about Islam's place here. As noted, there are over a million Muslims in Canada, but the actual number may be even higher than the number recorded by Statistics Canada. "Fear of stereotyping and other forms of discrimination such as Islamophobia cause a substantial number of Canadians to avoid identifying themselves as Muslim," wrote Delic.

There is discouraging data that helps explain that fear. By 2001, the Muslim poverty rate was a third higher than the national rate, despite a generally high rate of education and few language difficulties. Muslims tend to receive lower wages than their education might merit, and Muslim immigrants receive less recognition of work experience in their countries of origin than non-Muslim immigrants. Most disconcertingly, Muslims are the immigrant group most likely to report discrimination on the basis of ethnicity or culture. In *The Muslim Question in Canada: A Story of Segmented Integration*, Abdolmohammad Kazemipur wrote, "The data shows that, while Muslims are generally satisfied with their lives in Canada, they tend to report a lower level of trust towards the general population, a lower level of life satisfaction, and a lower level of participation in electoral processes than do other immigrant groups."

Over time, prejudice directed toward Muslims in Canada became subtler than the overt racism of government officials declaring "Syrians" to be "undesirable." According to Dr. David Goa of the University of Alberta, who has spent years doing field research with Muslim groups, the overthrow of the Shah and establishment of Iran as an Islamic Republic in 1979 could have offered a positive turning point, but it wasn't meant to be. "After the Iranian Revolution, I had a sense that, for a brief period of time, there was a bit of a shift in popular culture, in the media particularly, towards Islam. There seemed to have been a brief period where there was an opening to at least trying to understand a little bit about Islam, and not simply playing the fear card right off the bat," he said. "And then it seemed to me that, within a year or two, both Moscow and Washington realized they had a common enemy, so they circled the wagons."

Increasingly swept up in the broader global narrative, Canadian media told the predominant story that the Muslim world was dangerous and threatening. For example, in the eighties and nineties, a number of Western citizens were kidnapped in Lebanon, receiving extensive coverage in Canada. However, scant attention was paid to Canadians kidnapped elsewhere during the same period, including an engineer in Colombia, a nun in Lesotho, two businessmen in Brazil and two tourists in Cuba. "The occasional space given to these and other hostages paled in comparison to Canadian mass media's sustained coverage of the Beirut abductions," wrote Karim H. Karim in *Islamic Peril: Media and Global Violence*. It was an obsession that led to problematic reporting. A 1983 issue of *Maclean's* featured the image of a gunman captioned: "Islamic Amal gunman in Beirut," referring to the Lebanese Shia Muslim military movement. But *Maclean's* had it wrong. "The image seemed to fit the stereotypical model of a 'Muslim terrorist' so well that the editors appear to have overlooked that two crucifixes were hanging from the teenager's neck," wrote Karim. "Even though the gaffe could be excused as an 'honest mistake' in the rush to meet a deadline, it was undoubtedly made possible by the cultural stereotypes that exist in Northern societies about Muslims."

As the Cold War drew to a close and the threat of the Soviet Union faded, fear of Islam seemed to take its place. "A militant, Marxist, Islamic Middle East could be one of the most threatening things to world peace. We may have to face the inevitable consequences of pan-Arabism and pan-Islam and realize that, in one sense, all Arabia may be our enemy, and we simply cannot go on arming, equipping and encouraging any of these people," wrote Barbara Amiel, the journalist and future wife of media baron Conrad Black, in *The Ottawa Sun* in 1990. The constant barrage of media portrayals of scary, dangerous Muslims entrenched that image in the minds of many Canadians. Within months, as bombs fell on Iraq and the first Gulf War began, it became clear in Canada that a turning point had been reached after all.

* * *

"The Gulf War had more than just one front," wrote Zuhair Kashmeri in *The Gulf Within: Canadian Arabs, Racism and the Gulf War.* In 1990, Iraqi dictator Saddam Hussein ordered the invasion of Kuwait. When Canada joined the Americans in retaliation, the effects were keenly felt by Muslims in Canada. Suddenly, Canadians of Arab or Muslim background were identified with the enemy. "On the street, in workplaces, in schools, and in the media they became targets of ignorance, hostility and paranoia," Kashmeri wrote.

Peace groups and individual Canadians were allowed to criticize the government's decision to go to war, but when Muslims did it, they were demonized as extremists. Muslims were harassed and questioned about their religious beliefs by Canadian Security Intelligence Service (CSIS) agents and at the US border. The RCMP was called to a donut shop in Thornhill, Ontario to investigate reports of a "group of Arabs involved in lengthy discussions." There were incidents of men attacking women, and then ripping off their hijabs, throwing them on the ground and spitting on them. Families had bags of garbage thrown at their houses and received abusive phone calls in the middle of the night. An Edmonton man who made comments to the media in support of Hussein found a pipe bomb outside his townhouse. Attendees at peace marches in Hamilton were visited by security agents in their homes. London, Ontario schools that planned to hold a moment of silence for victims of the war faced a backlash from angry citizens denouncing the decision as unpatriotic. One London teacher forced her students, including one with relatives in an area being bombed, to write letters of support to Canadian troops. The child was distraught. "Please forgive me, but my teacher forced me to write this letter, and if any of our family is killed, I will never forgive myself," the girl told her family.

In Toronto, following reports of garbage and excrement being thrown at a mosque, the police officers called to investigate used the opportunity to gather information on local Muslims.

Kashmeri quoted anonymous Toronto officers who were dismayed by the actions of their colleagues: "You can't imagine how biased [some Caucasian officers] are toward Muslims. They even suspect Muslim officers on the force. And then you have the RCMP, which thinks there is a terrorist conspiracy at every mosque and in every Arab home," said one. "If you can only imagine the look on the faces of the people when we knocked on a door and then flashed our badges. Most of these were unsophisticated people who were trying to figure out their next month's rent, and here we walk in... without a warrant," said another.

For some Muslim immigrants, that experience was all too reminiscent of the frightening regimes they'd left behind. It took a toll. Montreal psychiatrist Dr. Mohammad Amin saw a dramatic increase in Muslim clients because of the war. "Fear is the one thing that has run through almost any person that I have been in contact with," he told Kashmeri. "That fear is actually very deep, and my assessment is that we are treated as outsiders in this country." Children were especially vulnerable to the psychological trauma brought on by the war and by the attitudes of fellow Canadians. In Winnipeg, thirty children were brought together for a group therapy session to address the bullying they'd endured since the war began. In Montreal, a similar session involved fifty children. As Kashmeri put it, for some kids, living in Canada during the Gulf War stole their innocence. Customs and Immigration announced there would be no visitor visas for Palestinians and Iraqis. "What they did not mention was that all one needed to have was an Arab or Muslim name to face this extraordinary scrutiny," wrote Kashmeri. In his view, the experiences of Muslims in Canada during the Gulf War set integration back by many years. "If all these actions did not amount to persecution and harassment, then the two words need to be redefined."

It's easily forgotten today by those who were not directly affected, but there was a certain climate of hysteria during the Gulf War. Sporting goods stores did brisk business in gas masks, schools bought anti-radiation pills and private security firms secured new contracts to protect businesses from terrorist attacks. Even after the conflict ended without any disasters befalling Canada, many Canadians tended to link Muslims with violence. In 1993 Canadian media reports emphasized religion when fundamentalists bombed the World Trade Center in New York City, but not when covering the armed standoff in Waco, Texas between US law enforcement and members of a Christian sect. Somehow it was accepted that the terrorists who had attacked the World Trade Center were representatives of Islam, while the Branch Davidians involved in the Waco conflict did not represent Christianity. That dynamic was repeated in coverage of belligerents throughout the world. By the late nineties, the hysteria brought on by the Gulf War had faded, and non-Muslim Canadians had moved on, more concerned with ensuring their personal computers were Y2K-compliant than with terrorism. But by the dawn of the new millennium, a certain, maybe unconscious, image of what Muslims were like became ingrained in the minds of many Canadians.

Then it all got much worse.

Sticks and Stones: Islamophobia in Canada

ON SEPTEMBER 11, 2001, nineteen members of al-Qaeda hijacked four passenger planes and committed a terrorist atrocity that shocked the world. In the West it provided a lens through which, in the coming years, everything from geopolitical events to domestic security to what songs could play on the radio would be viewed. Just weeks after the attack, American forces began bombing Afghanistan; not long after that, Canadian soldiers were on the ground fighting alongside Americans. Some of the aims of the war might have been laudable. The government promised soldiers would bring al-Qaeda terrorists to justice, free the Afghan people from the oppressive rule of the Taliban, promote democracy and gender equality, and win the hearts and minds of the Afghan people. In many ways, Canadian soldiers did just that. However, details that emerged about what else Canada and its allies were doing in Afghanistan were more disturbing. Some feared the so-called "War on Terrorism" was actually part of a war on Islam.

It didn't help that US President George W. Bush used the word "crusade" to describe the war, a term conjuring images of the bloody historical battles between Christians and Muslims. Some actions of Canada's allies also made it look like the war was yet another conflict between Christians and Muslims. "American soldiers spoke openly of God and avenging 9/11. Many of them wore crucifixes around their necks," wrote veteran British journalist Christina Lamb in *Farewell Kabul: From Afghanistan to a More Dangerous World*. Lest such anecdotal evidence be dismissed as sensational and unrepresentative, it's worth remembering that there are few Western journalists more credible than Lamb, who had been embedded with troops under fire in Afghanistan.

Incredibly, guns used by both Canadian and American soldiers in Afghanistan had Biblical inscriptions—references to the Gospel of John and Paul's second letter to the Corinthians—imprinted on their telescopic sights. After public criticism, the Canadian military conceded that the inscriptions were inappropriate and ordered them removed, but not until they'd been used by Joint Task Force 2 and a special operations unit from Petawawa. In the government, little happens without approval in triplicate. That these weapons had passed even the lowest level of approval is shocking. The fact that they were actually used beggars belief.

The notion that Canadian soldiers were only in Afghanistan to help build schools and train police officers was dispelled by General Rick Hillier. "We are not the Public Service of Canada. We are not just another department. We are the Canadian Forces, and our job is to be able to kill people," he said in 2005. Canadian Forces were at war. And of course, as in all wars, innocent people would die. The assessment of the war by then-president of Afghanistan Hamid Karzai was telling. At various times in his career, Karzai was criticized as being nothing more than an American puppet, but he had harsh words for Canada's allies. "This whole twelve years was one of constant pleading with America to treat the lives of Afghan civilians as lives of people," he told Lamb. "They did not work with me, they worked against me. They systematically waged a psychological war on our people. Did you know [American General David] Petraeus carried out 3500 bombardments? Three thousand five-hundred aerial bombs. That's unbelievable, shocking! Who were they trying to win the war against? The Afghan people?"

Meanwhile, international efforts to rebuild Afghanistan produced mixed results. "We didn't have a single computer in the Presidency—all we had was my laptop I had brought from the US. We didn't have a printer, so I would type documents then show them to the president on the screen, or the British or us ambassadors, then drive across town to an office with a printer," Karzai's chief of staff, Said Tayeb Jawad, told Christina Lamb. "We didn't even have a functioning toilet in the Presidency for guests coming in." With such a lacklustre commitment to development from the West, high-minded rhetoric about hearts and minds rang a little hollow. Rightly or wrongly, some Canadians came to believe that the war in Afghanistan was really about striking back at Muslim enemies who had attacked our ally.

While Muslims in Canada grieved the September 11, 2001 murders along with everyone else, they also feared they would pay the price for the actions of al-Qaeda. "I spent a few days after it happened in the mosques because it scared the hell out of the Muslims," says David Goa. Many Muslims kept their children home from school, afraid of the threats and assaults friends and family were already experiencing. In Edmonton, leaders of the Jewish and Christian communities concerned about a potential backlash targeting Muslims, went to the city's largest mosque to pray alongside Muslims as a deliberate, public gesture of solidarity. But for many Canadians, al-Qaeda and the enemies confronted by Canadian soldiers in Afghanistan were all they knew of Islam, and they became more and more suspicious. In 2001, an Ipsos-Reid poll showed that 27 percent of Canadians were suspicious of Arabs and Muslims from the Middle East. By 2002 that number was 35 percent. By 2006 an Environics poll showed that 51 percent of Canadians held a negative view of Muslims and Islam.

Media continued to play a role in shaping these negative perceptions. "A few media commentators brazenly categorized Muslims as a 'fifth column,' hiding sleeper cells amongst their midst. Others questioned their loyalty as Canadian citizens. Bordering on hate literature, some columns and national editorials dehumanized Muslims as a barbaric, murderous people," wrote columnist Sheema Khan in *The Globe and Mail*. This view of mainstream Canadian media is shared by Haroon Siddiqui, a former national editor of the *Toronto Star* and a regular commentator on Muslim issues. "The media have been unwitting, and sometimes not, partners in the spreading of this hatred and prejudice. I've been very critical of my colleagues sometimes. I say that, not as a Muslim, but as a journalist. It was beneath us to have done what we have done," he says. "The entire chain of [Postmedia] newspapers, starting with the *National Post*, and then the *Toronto Sun* chain, and in Quebec, the popular press, they use it as business model... Blowing up stories out of proportion. Finding Muslim terrorists under every canopy and every minaret. Bullshit, you know. And they really ought to be ashamed of themselves."

Repeatedly, Canadian media have filled the airwaves with stories of fringe militants, rarely clarifying just how unrepresentative these groups and individuals are. In October 2006, *Maclean's* published a 4800-word article by Canadian journalist Mark Steyn entitled "The Future Belongs to Islam." The following passage provides a flavor:

> ...of course, not all Muslims are terrorists—though enough are hot for jihad to provide an impressive support network of mosques from Vienna to Stockholm to Toronto to Seattle. Of course, not all Muslims support terrorists—though enough of them share their basic objectives (the wish to live under Islamic law in Europe and North America) to function wittingly or otherwise as the "good cop" end of an Islamic good cop/bad cop routine. But, at the very minimum, this fast-moving demographic transformation provides a huge comfort zone for the jihad to move around in.

Elsewhere in the article, Steyn wrote that the non-Muslim population in North America is being "supplanted remorselessly by a young Muslim demographic," as though Muslims should feel remorse for having children. Having a child is the most joyful, inspiring, humbling and human experience one can have. For a writer in an esteemed national publication to reduce that act of humanity to a cold act of demographic warfare is stunning. In another article, Steyn claimed that Europe would have a Muslim majority by the end of the century. "They've calculated that our entire civilization lacks the will to see them off," he wrote. Again, Steyn's use of language ("calculated") has a de-humanizing effect. It wasn't the only time Steyn preached on the topic. In one of his books, *American Alone: The End of the World as We Know It*, he expanded his theme: "The religion itself [Islam] is a political project—and, in fact, an imperial project—in a way that modern Christianity, Judaism, Hinduism, and Buddhism are not. Furthermore, this particular religion is historically a somewhat bloodthirsty faith in which whatever's your bag violence-wise can almost certainly be justified." The historically bloodthirsty pasts of other faiths are not explored. Giving Steyn a platform had an impact. Tragically, the Canadian journalist was cited by Anders Breivik, the Norwegian terrorist who murdered seventy-six innocent people as part of his quest to save Europe from the supposed threat of Islam.

Steyn's article wasn't a one-off. Students at Osgoode Hall Law School counted eighteen other articles in *Maclean's* they also considered to be Islamophobic. After a dismissive response from *Maclean's* editor Ken Whyte, they filed a complaint with several human rights commissions. While none viewed the articles as crossing the threshold into hate literature, Barbara Hall, Chief Commissioner of the Ontario Human Rights Commission, issued a stern rebuke to *Maclean's*: "By portraying Muslims as all sharing the same negative characteristics, including being a threat to 'the West,' this explicit expression of Islamophobia further perpetuates and promotes prejudice towards Muslims and others."

Rather than consider its own culpability in the demonization of Muslims, some Canadian media doubled down. On the CBC, the respected and popular commentator Rex Murphy suggested that Muslims focus their efforts on the human rights violations taking place in Muslim countries rather than complaining about their own treatment to human rights commissions in Canada. It was a ludicrous suggestion, akin to arguing that no man should avail himself of a human rights commission while so many other men were guilty of violence against women, or that no adult should when other adults were guilty of child abuse.

When Muslims have been the victims of prejudice, the response from the media has been, at times, dismissive. During a formal dinner at a Canadian Forces base in Nova Scotia in 2010, several soldiers entertained fellow troops with a skit they'd filmed featuring one of them in "brownface." Wearing a turban and fake beard and with brown makeup covering his face, he was a grotesque caricature of a Middle Eastern man. The heavily accented character, a taxi driver, implies that his taxi is actually a bomb and threatens to "hump" a goat. At a time when Canadian Forces were ostensibly winning hearts and minds in Afghanistan, the skit was far from funny.

But the *National Post* apparently disagreed. The newspaper treated the incident with a shrug, suggesting the CBC was trying to manufacture a controversy by reporting on the video. "I'm not saying 'cut them some slack,' exactly. But in the absence of any compelling case as to why I should swoon theatrically in outrage, I'm rather inclined to," wrote columnist Chris Selley, who suggested the skit was funnier than a CBC comedy. Selley himself was trying to be funny, injecting a little of the antipathy toward the public broadcaster that right-wing commentators are known for, but his glib response failed to acknowledge the deeply-offensive nature of the video. He wasn't alone in that: to some Canadians, the video was hilarious and they filled the comments section on the CBC's web article with supportive comments. The military, for their part, ordered an investigation, but Conservative defense minister Peter MacKay was in a forgiving mood. "These operations have proven

Canadian Forces members are Canadian heroes. And, like all of us, they are not infallible," he said. But the video had all the hallmarks of racism: the exaggerated accent, the character slurs, and of course, the makeup akin to the widely reviled "blackface" once used to mock people of African descent. The video deserved passionate condemnation from the media. It wasn't funny, and it wasn't funny to pretend it was funny.

Whether these examples of anti-Muslim sentiment are typical is a matter of debate. As noted, observers like Sheema Khan and Haroon Siddiqui have been harsh in their criticisms of the media. Others take a different view. "Not every Muslim will agree with me, but I think, generally speaking, the Canadian media tries very hard to be fair," says Alia Hogben, executive director of the Canadian Council of Muslim Women (CCMW). In support, she cites the refusal of most Canadian media to republish cartoons of the Prophet Muhammad originally published in the Danish newspaper *Jyllands-Posten*. Publication of the cartoons in Denmark sparked a firestorm of protests across the world. For many Muslims, the content of the cartoons was deeply offensive. Not only were the depictions of Muhammad insulting, but visual representations of Muhammad in general are avoided by Muslims (many believe they create a temptation toward idol worship, rather than the worship of God). Canadian media did the right thing by refraining to republish, despite pressure from some readers. Still there were outliers. Alberta-based *Western Standard* published them, and publisher and conservative commentator Ezra Levant decried other publishers' decisions not to: "Don't tell me the CBC respects religion. It's afraid of one religion," he said.

The CBC's decision not to publish wasn't about fear of reprisal, as the CBC would later articulate when defending a similar decision not to republish insulting cartoons of Muhammad published by the French magazine *Charlie Hebdo*. In response to these cartoons, terrorists burst into the *Charlie Hebdo* headquarters and opened fire, killing twelve staff members. Some people accused the CBC of

33

cowardice for refusing to show the cartoons in their coverage of the murders. But the CBC argued that the only reason to republish what the *New York Times* had also refused to republish, calling the cartoons "gratuitous insult," would be if it were impossible to tell the story without them. "I think the idea of cowardice is really interesting," said David Studer, the CBC's Director of Journalistic Standards and Practices. "My view is that remaining civilized and sticking to our principles is what defeats bad guys, not giving in to the emotion of the moment." It wasn't, as some claimed, censorship or fear; it was an exercise in self-limitation motivated by journalistic ethics. Nevertheless, this time Radio Canada, the *National Post*, Sun TV and several newspapers in Quebec did publish the cartoons, framing their decision as a defiant act in support of freedom of speech.

It is beyond question that journalists had the right to publish the cartoons, and that attempts to silence journalists through violence and intimidation should be resisted and condemned. The necessity of publishing the cartoons, though, is a matter of debate. To a large degree, the cartoons are juvenile. They add nothing to anyone's understanding of Islam's place in the world or of Muslims' place in Canada. If anything, republication highlighted a fault line between Muslims and non-Muslims. It offended many and gave others tacit permission to offend.

Much is revealed by terms used in the media. Consider the use of the term "Islamic terrorism." Terrorism is un-Islamic, and suggesting that the two terms could be complimentary, rather than contradictory, provokes questioning of all Muslims. Sheema Khan has argued that the word "jihad" should never have been used by media to describe the crimes of al-Qaeda. Jihad simply refers to a struggle for the betterment of one's self or society. Indeed, six of the most respected Muslim scholars in the world deemed 9/11 a "hirabah," a war crime under sharia law. "Once you call it Islamic, you've brought me into the picture even though I haven't done something wrong," Amin Elshorbagy, president of the now defunct Canadian Islamic Congress, told the *National Post*. Later, as the threat of al-Qaeda was supplanted by a group calling themselves the Islamic State of Iraq and the Levant (ISIL), Canadian media commentators unquestioningly took up the group's preferred name, again connecting "Islamic" with a group of vicious terrorists. Rather than dignifying the terrorists as Islamic, much of the Muslim world and some world leaders in the West call them "Daesh"—a name so hated by the group that they have threatened to cut the tongues out of anyone who utters it. If Muslims, who are among those most threatened by the group, dare to call them Daesh, surely Canadian journalists can, too.

This careless use of language had the effect of perverting what the Muslim faith is about, allowing it to become, as David Goa puts it, "colonized" by al-Qaeda in the minds of Canadians. Such language couldn't help but have an impact. In her Ph.D. dissertation, Baljit Nagra, now an assistant professor at the University of Ottawa, recounted evidence of Muslims in Canada losing their jobs in the aftermath of 9/11. "Dawoud [one of her interviewees], who was having difficulty finding a co-op work term, mentions that he suddenly 'began getting more interviews and job offers' when, at his career counsellor's suggestion, he deleted his involvement with Muslim organizations from his resume. Dawoud's experience illustrates how some Muslim Canadians feel compelled to conceal their Muslim identity when looking for work. In some instances, this entails altering their Muslim names." Italian Canadians old enough to remember looking for work during World War II can relate to such a story.

There are other sad stories of Islamophobic behaviour from Canadians after 9/11—of students whose prayer space was suddenly taken way, of shoppers ejected from stores, of girls in hijabs banned from soccer games and taekwondo tournaments—but in these stories, the victims return home, hurt, ashamed or angry, but at least in one piece.

Not everyone is as lucky.

* * *

The National Council of Canadian Muslims (NCCM) website has an interactive map powered by Google. You can pick a city and drag the map up and down, watching as streets disappear at the bottom of your screen while others appear at the top. There are little icons affixed to the maps. There is a map for each of the past five years. Each is peppered with those little icons, and behind each icon is a human being.

What the NCCM is tracking are anti-Muslim incidents: vandalism, hate propaganda, threats, verbal attacks, online attacks and physical attacks. Since 9/11, such attacks have become common. They include the mosques in St. Catharines and Montreal, which were firebombed within hours of 9/11; the mosque in Hamilton whose windows were broken four days after 9/11; and the mosques in Burlington and Mississauga, which were firebombed the following month. They include the medical resident in Montreal grabbed by the throat and spat on in an elevator; the fifteen-year-old Ottawa teenager who was asked if he was an Arab and then severely beaten; the woman and her mother first ejected from a store and then from the bus stop outside; the Calgary imam who was struck by a car, called a terrorist and then hit by the car a second time; the gunshots fired through the glass door of the Pickering Islamic Centre in broad daylight with people inside; and the woman in the Montreal Metro who was punched repeatedly in the face and told to go back where she came from. In Fort Saskatchewan, a large red crucifix was spray-painted on the wall of a Muslim prayer space. Four days later, the building was egged. On a few of the shards of eggshells left scattered about, some writing was still legible. The vandals had taken the time, in careful, kindergarten-teacher printing, to write "Fuck Allah!" on the eggs before they smashed them.

Most of the incidents are similar: taunts, vandalism (sometimes including swastikas or Christian imagery), firebombing (usually not very effectively) and assaults (usually by men against women). The cumulative impact of these incidents goes deeper than the bruises on the skin. Baljit Nagra recorded how Muslims, particularly women, avoided public places like shopping malls, grocery stores and public transit. "Yes, I was afraid, especially going out with my dad and with my mom because they distinctly look Muslim. My dad wears a little goatee beard and my mom wears the scarf," one of her interviewees told Nagra. "We had kind of resolved that if we had to go pick up something, we would go with either my brother or my father, so at least one of the men would be there." Another interviewee described never opening her bag on the subway for fear that even by checking her phone to see the time, she might draw attention to herself. That women have been targeted more often is partly a result of stereotypical images of Muslims. While Muslim men are often seen as barbaric and dangerous, Muslim women are often believed to be weak and oppressed, making them a more attractive target for cowards.

Not only Muslims have been targeted. Many of the vandals and thugs didn't really know who was and wasn't a Muslim. In their ignorance, they sometimes victimized non-Muslims who fit their assumptions of what Muslims looked like, how they behaved, or where they gathered. After 9/11, the Hamilton Hindu Samaj Temple was firebombed. Police concluded that the arsonists had mistaken it for a mosque. In Surrey, a billboard advertising a Sikh realtor had "Kill all Muslims" scrawled across it in black marker. "Sikhs have been living in fear of hate crimes since 9/11," reported *The Globe and Mail*. In addition to those victimized by mistaken identity, non-Muslim allies could be victimized, too. Italian Canadian lawyer Rocco Galati is one such example. "I've been getting death threats almost on a daily basis since 1997, ever since I've been representing members of the Muslim and Arab community," said Galati, then representing the Canadian Islamic Congress.

The Toronto Police Service Hate Crime Unit reported one hostile act against a Muslim in 2000. They reported fifty-seven in 2001.

Similarly dramatic increases were seen across the country, and in general, the trend continued throughout the next decade. It is worth remembering that Muslims are far from the only religious group being victimized; more hate crimes motivated by religion are still committed against Jews than against any other group. But even in years when attacks against other minority groups decreased, attacks against Muslims continued to rise. To help protect community members, the NCCM developed a community safety kit describing the rights people have when victimized by a hate incident, which they posted on their website and distributed to mosques.

Of course, the police can only record statistics for crimes that get reported to them. Statistics Canada estimates that two-thirds of hate incidents are likely to go unreported. "It really is the tip of the iceberg," said Amira Elghawaby, former communications director of the NCCM. The reasons are complicated. Many Muslims come from parts of the world where they have experienced brutality or corruption, and they have developed a deep-seated mistrust of police and other state authorities. They may also be unaware of their rights or wish to avoid potentially negative attention from neighbours or employers. It may seem counterintuitive to more-privileged Canadians, but sometimes vulnerable people don't want to rock the boat.

Unfortunately, when they do approach the police about a hate incident, many Muslims are disappointed with the response they receive from law enforcement officials. "As far as we can tell, hate crimes are often not taken seriously by the police, and where they are taken seriously, there almost has to be pressure for the police to even consider laying charges or taking any kind of steps to address the issue. So, there's a lot of malaise in our communities—that safety and public safety do not extend to our communities, and that we are, unfortunately, seen more as a threat than as communities to protect," Elghawaby explains.

She describes an incident in Ottawa in which a man stood on a Muslim woman's lawn and screamed obscenities about how all

Muslims should be killed. Scared, she phoned the police. An hour and a half later, they arrived. He was probably drunk, they told her, and she shouldn't worry about it. "She asked them to knock on his door, to scare him a bit, to let him know that he can't be making death threats against entire communities," Elghawaby says. They refused and said there was nothing they could do about it. After a letter from the NCCM, police followed up more vigorously but Elghawaby notes that it shouldn't take pressure from a national organization to get results. "This is very distressing, but not surprising, because we hear similar things across the country," she said.

A challenge for police is assessing whether a threat is real. Another challenge is assessing if a particular use of language is protected under freedom of expression, or if it has crossed the threshold into criminal hate speech. At times, while the NCCM and their legal counsel have been certain it has, police have not agreed. "There seems to be an uncertainty, a reluctance, a lack of clarity on the law. There's some kind of block there," Elghawaby said, noting that attorneys general should weigh in to provide further clarity for police. "Community members are simply losing faith in the process and losing confidence that their police services are going to protect them."

Meanwhile, far too much of the interaction between Muslims and police has been in the context of terrorism and national security. Elghawaby describes a meeting between the RCMP and Muslim women in which the women raised their concerns about a recent attack at a mosque. Violence from white nationalists and the extreme right is, after all, terrorism and a pressing national security concern. The RCMP responded that they were only there to talk about foreign-influenced extremism. The women's concerns about their own safety wasn't going to be on the agenda.

According to Elghawaby, there is a sense in Muslim communities that law enforcement isn't as engaged in countering threats when the victims, or potential victims, are Muslims. "That is actually leading to many of us feeling worried about our own personal safety when we hear about, for example, militias that are now forming in parts of the country, in Alberta and possibly parts of Ontario, of people saying, 'We're going to be carrying weapons, and—quote, unquote—monitoring mosques,'" she says. "We're not hearing the same level of concern [from police] that we're hearing about other potential threats to our collective security."

In response to these types of concerns, many police departments in Canada have devoted specific units to serve communities considered particularly vulnerable to hate crimes, including Muslim communities. "The [Vancouver Police Department] is dedicated to building relationships with specific communities, including the Muslim community," says Sergeant Jason Robillard of the Vancouver Police Department. The Vancouver Police Department has participated in several community forums and workshops with members of Muslim communities and has held a Police Board meeting in a local mosque. The Ottawa Police Service's David Zackrias, staff sergeant in charge of the Diversity and Race Relations unit, describes numerous outreach programs designed to build trust with Muslim communities. For example, the unit was a partner in organizing a three-month soccer league for newcomers to Canada which he describes as having been a big hit. He laments that, at times, the good work the police do in this area is overshadowed by negative stories. Getting the word out that police are there to help has been difficult. "There's a lot of people out there that don't know," he says.

Clearly, while the police deserve some criticism, they are also part of the solution. Negative experiences some Muslims have had with police should not be construed as a condemnation of the profession as a whole. In the same vein, using weaponry that promotes the idea of a Christian war against Muslims does not represent the true values of the Canadian Forces. Neither do the fools who dressed up in brownface represent the average soldier. Mark Steyn, the author of the *Maclean's* article that was debated before human rights commissions and the man who was quoted by Norwegian terrorist Anders Breivik, does not represent the average Canadian journalist. The cowards who would attack an empty mosque in the middle of the night do not represent ordinary Canadians. But there are enough acts of bigotry and hate to conclude that, even in this enlightened age, there are plenty of people who harbour extremely negative views of Muslims.

And a lot of them vote.

Let's Keep Talking About Niqabs: Islamophobia and Politics

ELITES. TALK TO different Canadians, and it will mean different things. To some it means Canada's richest and most privileged. To others it means our most educated, locked away in an ivory tower. An image that's becoming more and more pervasive, however, is the image of the political elite—the powerful insiders pulling strings in Centre Block on Parliament Hill, or at Queen's Park in Toronto, completely out of touch with the values, worries and dreams of average Canadians. To what degree that image is valid is a matter of debate, but it is incompatible with the fundamentally symbiotic relationship between politicians and voters.

Firstly, as many policy wonks have discovered, voters tend to choose politicians they can easily identify with. It's why politicians work so hard to seem like the sort of people you'd want to have a beer with. Secondly, once elected, politicians generally try to do what voters want because politicians generally want to get re-elected. So-called elites lose touch with average Canadians at their peril. It's Political Science 101.

As a result, the 338 members of parliament are a cross-section of society. Among them are doctors, lawyers, teachers, police officers, farmers and the former host of Canada AM. One of the 338 is engineer-turned-Liberal MP Omar Alghabra. "One of my life goals is to eliminate this perception that the political class is somehow foreign to the mainstream, that somehow a group of outside aliens has been planted into our public institutions. Our political class is an extension, a reflection, of our communities, of our society," says Alghabra. This means that if there's Islamophobia in

Canadian society, it's on Parliament Hill, too. Alghabra has given some thought to colleagues who might fit that bill. "Within the political class that appears to be less than friendly to Muslims, there are two different types. There's the informed segment, who perhaps, deep inside, doesn't really carry that hostility but may see that there's political traction to reinforcing that fear, exaggerating that fear, and then presenting oneself as the champion of defeating that fear," he explains. "And then there's another segment that is really part and parcel of the segment of society that is afraid."

So, if Canadians show politicians that there are voters among them with Islamophobic views, some politicians will make a calculation. Will anti-Muslim rhetoric or anti-Muslim policies translate into votes? Will those voters outnumber the voters who will be turned off by that kind of rhetoric? If so, they might choose to use that rhetoric and advance those policies—perhaps goaded by colleagues who genuinely share anti-Muslim views. The calculation is cynical and crass, but it would be naive to believe it doesn't happen. At the same time, it's unfair to suggest that Islamophobia on Parliament Hill can be blamed on ordinary Canadians. As critics of US President Donald Trump have pointed out, a leader can set a tone that creates a friendly space for bigotry. Emboldened by a sense that their views are more mainstream, bigots get even louder, which in turn suggests to politicians that there is yet more political capital to be gained in this way. Which came first is a chicken-and-egg question. They are mutually reinforcing. But it is clear that governments and politicians have contributed to a troubling public discourse about Muslims in Canada.

In some ways, politicians have worked to avoid inflaming anti-Muslim sentiment. After September 11, 2001, Prime Minister Jean Chrétien visited a mosque. NDP leader Alexa McDonough held a press conference with the Canadian Arab Federation and urged Canadians not to turn on their fellow Canadians. Years later, Prime Minister Stephen Harper hosted an iftar (a meal after sunset during Ramadan) at 24 Sussex, the prime minister's official residence. In 2015, the National Assembly of Quebec unanimously passed a motion condemning Islamophobia.

In other ways, politicians pandered to fear, ignorance and prejudice. In 2007, the town council of Herouxville, Quebec, a parish municipality with 1300 residents including only one family of recent immigrant descent, passed a Code of Conduct it expected newcomers to uphold through a signed contract. Among its commandments were:

> We would especially like to inform the new arrivals that the lifestyle that they left behind in their birth country cannot be brought here with them, and they would have to adapt to their new social identity...

> We consider that killing women in public beatings, or burning them alive are not part of our standards of life...

> We listen to music, we drink alcoholic beverages in public or private places, we dance, and at the end of the year we decorate a tree with balls and tinsel and some lights...

Six other municipalities signed the document. Not only did it assume the worst of immigrants by listing already illegal crimes; but it also attempted to officially designate what cultural activities were acceptable. And, while a Danish immigrant to Herouxville might have been disheartened by the apparent ban on festooning a Christmas tree with tiny Danish flags, as is commonly done in Denmark, there is little doubt as to whom the Code of Conduct really targeted.

"While no specific group was mentioned in this declaration, the listed 'undesired' values and practices were clearly perceived to be those associated with Muslim immigrants," wrote

Abdolmohammad Kazemipur. What's more, the Code of Conduct fit into a broader discourse that suggested it wasn't just the town council of Herouxville that felt this way. "Herouxville was not an aberration, but the canary in a mineshaft. Rather than smother the whiffs of racism, Quebec politicians pandered to the xenophobic fears of voters," wrote Sheema Khan in *The Globe and Mail*. A furious debate on the "reasonable accommodation" of minorities raged in the Quebec National Assembly, across the front pages of Quebec newspapers, and on popular television and radio talk shows.

The year 2007 was an election year in Quebec. Mario Dumont, leader of the opposition party Action démocratique du Québec, ran what has been called an anti-immigrant, anti-minority campaign focused particularly on Muslims. Seeing Dumont gaining in the polls shortly after the Code of Conduct was released, Quebec's Liberal Premier Jean Charest appointed a commission to study what "reasonable accommodation" should look like. The commission was led by prominent academics Gérard Bouchard and Charles Taylor. The Bouchard-Taylor Commission's public hearings provided a platform for what seemed like an unending stream of intolerant vitriol.

Quebeckers had enthusiastically adopted secularism since the Quiet Revolution in the sixties which freed them from the control the Catholic Church had exerted over Quebec society. For that reason, it was expected that Quebeckers might be uncomfortable with the overt displays of religion common among some religious minorities. But some of the complaints heard were simply farcical. One concerned citizen raised the issue of Benjamin Rubin, an Orthodox Jew who was a forward on the Gatineau Olympiques junior hockey team. Rubin, an unremarkable player who had scored only three goals the previous season, was requesting to skip games on the Sabbath. According to the complaint, such an accommodation was unreasonable: citizens demanded to see Rubin in skates on the Sabbath. Predictably, though, much of the anger voiced at the hearings was directed at Muslims. "This kind of 'reasonable-accommodation police' going around manufacturing crises within Quebec society is doing us all harm," stated Salam Elmenyawi of the Muslim Council of Montreal. "The Muslim community is at the receiving end of hate, anger, disgust and indignation, and it's damaging the social fabric of Quebec society."

Not all the concerns were fear-based. At times, concerns about women wearing head and face coverings, a common theme during the hearings, stemmed from a belief that women wearing such attire would only do so because of patriarchal oppression. Some of the activists objecting to head coverings appeared to be motivated by a genuine desire to provide equality to the women wearing them. The Quebec Council on the Status of Women, for example, called for hijabs and niqabs to be banned from the public service. Sheema Khan provided an instructive response in *The Globe and Mail*: "[The Council] is essentially telling Muslim women, 'We know what is best for you; you can't possibly wear that thing out of free will, and if you do, you are too oppressed to know any better.' Call it feminism on testosterone. Imagine telling that to [academic, activist and political candidate] Monia Mazigh, who fearlessly challenged three national governments and their security agencies. If the council has its way, Ms. Mazigh can never run for public office in her hijab, nor teach at a public university."

As election day approached, the hysteria was heightened when Quebec's Chief Electoral Officer, Marcel Blanchet, clarified that according to the law, women in niqabs were allowed to vote without removing their veils provided they made a sworn statement of their identity, brought identification, and someone who could vouch for them. It was the same process allowed for others who were unable or unwilling to show their faces, such as burn victims with bandages covering their faces. Vouching was also the standard procedure for other voters who didn't have photo identification, such as some homeless people. Blanchet wasn't creating new rules; he was simply announcing that his reading of the legislation provided that same right to women in niqabs. But in the divisive climate of Herouxville and the Bouchard-Taylor Commission, for many Quebeckers it was suddenly a scandal. Some Quebeckers threatened to wear Halloween masks to the polls. Blanchet received so many threats that he had to hire two personal bodyguards. Extra security was posted at Elections Quebec headquarters.

Election laws and officials are not just there to ensure the count is accurate, but to ensure the electoral process itself is fair and accessible. The threat of violence in an attempt to disenfranchise voters is a fundamental affront to democracy, exactly the sort of thing our institutions are meant to guard against. Blanchet was applying the law. Instead of coming to his defence, Jean Charest, Mario Dumont and Parti Québécois (PQ) leader André Boisclair all denounced Blanchet's decision and called for it to be overturned. Fearing unrest at the polls, Blanchet reversed his decision, and announced that women in niqabs would now have to remove them in order to vote. "I personally would have preferred not to have to [reverse the decision], but my priority is to ensure that everything will run normally, and that a few, or many, crazies won't show up to cause trouble Monday," he said.

"If the Chief Electoral Officer needs two bodyguards, imagine the woman in a niqab, how many guards she's going to need to guard her, at a polling station or even on a street today," said Salam Elmenyawi. According to Elmenyawi, the number of eligible voters wearing niqabs was small, and those who did wear them probably had no objection to lifting their veil in private with a female official. The public controversy was completely unnecessary. But now, she noted, the environment had become so toxic she doubted any veiled women would be brave enough to show up to vote.

A similar stir was caused later that year when Elections Canada announced that women in niqabs would be allowed to vote in the upcoming federal by-elections. Conservative, Liberal and Bloc Québécois MPs called for the decision to be reversed, but Elections Canada steadfastly continued to apply the law. "Common sense is being trumped by political correctness. It's the kind of thing that results in ordinary people just shaking their heads," said Conservative MP Peter Van Loan, the minister responsible for Elections Canada. Following the by-elections, Van Loan introduced a bill that would force women to remove their veils at polling stations. However, the bill still allowed voters to vote with only an oath and two pieces of non-photo identification. As *The Globe and Mail* put it, the additional requirement for a woman in a niqab to show her face would prove only that she had a face. "This illogical reasoning strongly suggests that the only reason for the amendment to the Act is to target an already besieged and vulnerable minority group," wrote Natasha Bakht in *Belonging and Banishment: Being Muslim in Canada.*

Despite the hysteria of the public hearings, the Bouchard-Taylor Commission's report, released in 2008, took a more balanced approach. While the report did recommend a ban on religious attire for public servants in coercive roles like judges or police officers (a recommendation Taylor has since repudiated), it also concluded that "the right to freedom of religion includes the right to show it." It recommended that Jews and Muslims get time off to celebrate religious holidays, and that prayer space be made available in schools, airports, jails, hospitals and other public places. Rather than banish signs of religiosity from the public sphere, as so many were advocating, the report took the position that public displays of religion were a social good that helped citizens become familiar with other cultures and prevented people from being marginalized. However, it was the public hearings, not the report, that would become the Commission's legacy.

Many of the same issues were raised again in 2013 when PQ Premier Pauline Marois, who had since come to power, proposed a so-called "Charter of Quebec Values." Her charter would go much further than Bouchard and Taylor's recommendations. Not only would the charter make it mandatory for everyone to leave faces uncovered when providing or receiving public services, but it

would also ban overt displays of religion by government employees including teachers, hospital workers, police officers, judges and
public daycare workers (elected members of the national assembly would be exempt.) The ban would include hijabs, niqabs,
burqas, turbans, kippahs and "large" crucifixes (small crucifixes
were acceptable). The proposal was likely unconstitutional, and
the PQ government never enacted it, but a poll by SOM, one of
the largest pollsters in Quebec, showed that the proposed ban
was supported by nearly seventy percent of Quebeckers. Federal
NDP leader Thomas Mulcair put Marois' proposal in context. In
his view, it was just a government with a slim minority posturing
ahead of an inevitable election: "Last year I remember being asked
to react when Madame Marois mused, in time for the provincial
election, about having language tests to run in a municipal election.
Of course, it was absurd, and I said they'd never do it. And guess
what? It was absurd, it was illegal, unconstitutional and, of course,
they never did it. But she provoked the reaction she wanted," he
said, and now she was doing it again. "She was sending a signal—a
low frequency signal to her base."

According to several prominent Muslims, that signal was
squarely aimed at voters who were uneasy about Islam. "We had
a government in Quebec led by Pauline Marois which was openly
hostile to Muslims and wanted to strip them of their rights,"
says Haroon Siddiqui. Alia Hogben also suggests the Charter of
Quebec Values was primarily aimed at Muslims: "Very, very anti-
Muslim, and that was all there was to it. There was nothing else
to it. Jews had been wearing their kippahs for years and years and
nobody objected. Catholics had been wearing crosses, large ones,
around their necks. Nobody objected. And as soon as it's about
Muslims and Muslim women's clothes or something, it comes
down on you like a ton of bricks."

Despite some polls showing a majority of Quebeckers supporting the Charter of Quebec Values when the next election was
held in 2014, the PQ was defeated. Hogben and many others read

that as evidence that when push came to shove, the majority of Quebeckers were not ready to support such exclusionary policies. The reasoning behind that conclusion is that it is one thing to casually express support to a pollster or click "Yes" on a media website, but another thing altogether to stand in a voting booth and actually vote for something. "I'm glad it got defeated. It gave me more hope in the sanity of the majority of Québécois," Hogben says.

Omar Alghabra agreed. "When the general public could come to terms with what that would mean to an individual perhaps having to choose between their faith or their job, people realized that it is not a fair thing to do," he says. It's a reasonable—and encouraging—assessment. However, it is worth noting that the PQ's slide in the polls coincided with their announcement that controversial businessman Pierre Karl Péladeau had been nominated as a candidate. Péladeau's forceful demands for another referendum on Quebec separatism brought that age-old question to the forefront of the debate once again. Since many elections in Quebec have been decided on that issue, it is equally fair to suggest that the PQ government fell not because Quebeckers didn't want the Charter of Quebec Values, but because they didn't want a third referendum.

* * *

An analysis by American philosopher and former Harvard professor Martha Nussbaum refutes the arguments in favour of niqab bans in general. In her view, the argument that the niqab represents the domination of women is unfair, as there are numerous legal examples of women being dominated in mainstream Western culture. The argument that women are being coerced is unfounded as there is no evidence of more spousal abuse in households in which women wear a niqab than in other households. The argument that a face covering is unhealthy can be dismissed because high heels, for example, are permitted. Finally, the idea that there is some inherent obligation to show one's face in public can be refuted by the fact that, during winter, many Canadians walk around with no more than the barest sliver of our faces visible.

So what's the problem? It might be a fear of terrorism. Terrorism is a legitimate threat (although Canadians are more likely to die from car crashes, cancer, obesity, drowning in their own bathtubs or being struck by lightning than from terrorism). But to equate terrorism with women in niqabs is unfair, as most people would acknowledge. Indeed, focus groups have shown that Canadians' discomfort with niqabs actually has more to do with values than security. Ultimately, the issue is more about our comfort level with basic religious and cultural plurality.

Surely the question of whether or not to wear a niqab is a personal one. Alia Hogben notes that no one in the CCMW wears a niqab, and that, in their view, wearing one is not required by Islam. However, as the Supreme Court has ruled, an individual's sincere religious belief is of greater weight than what religious authorities say, and some women do wear niqabs as a matter of religious conviction. "I don't agree with it, but it doesn't mean that I wouldn't defend the right of any woman to wear it, to dress as she so pleases," Hogben said. "People wearing the niqab or the 'burkini' to go swimming, well, what does it matter whether some women wear bikinis, and some women go naked, and some women cover themselves up, as long as they're safe in the water? Why all the big fuss? It's only because it's Muslims."

Despite the question being a personal one, Canadians seem to have a lot of opinions about whether niqabs are compatible with Canadian values. Recognizing Canadians' preoccupation with values, in 2011, Conservative immigration minister Jason Kenney banned women from wearing niqabs during citizenship ceremonies. Over the next four years, two women were denied citizenship because they refused to comply with the ban. It is impossible to know how many women simply chose not to apply. "To segregate one group of Canadians or allow them to hide their faces, to hide their identity from us precisely when they are joining our community, is contrary to Canada's proud commitment to openness and to social cohesion," Kenney said.

The idea that women in niqabs might be hiding their identity during citizenship ceremonies is patently false. Identities are verified multiple times before the actual ceremony takes place. Face coverings are removed in private in the presence of officials. Applicants must show a variety of documents, including proof of language proficiency, education records, passports and travel documents, two official photos in which full facial features are visible, and two more pieces of personal identification, at least one of which must have a photo. The RCMP and CSIS run background checks. If there are any doubts, officials can also ask for fingerprints. Despite Kenney's statement that the ban was meant to prevent women from hiding their identity, some felt it was really just pandering to Islamophobia.

One of the two women whose citizenship was denied, Zunera Ishaq, launched a court challenge. Before a judge, the government abandoned the argument that an applicant's identity needed to be verified and argued that officials needed to see the applicant's mouth moving when reciting the Oath of Citizenship. The judge rejected that argument and overturned the ban, noting that such a requirement would prevent mute people or monks who'd taken a vow of silence from becoming Canadian. A week later, on February 12, 2015, Stephen Harper's Conservative government announced it would appeal the decision, once again turning to the same rhetoric about women in niqabs hiding their identity. "I believe, and I think most Canadians believe, that it is offensive that someone would hide their identity at the very moment where they are committing to join the Canadian family," Harper said.

It was an election year.

*　*　*

In 2002, Stephen Harper took over the leadership of Canada's primary conservative party, the floundering Canadian Alliance, from the gaffe-prone Stockwell Day. It seemed unlikely he would be moving into the prime minister's residence at 24 Sussex anytime soon. Harper was stiff and decidedly unhip. The Liberal leader, Paul Martin, had a reputation as a sound fiscal manager. Many expected he would reinvigorate a party that had tired of Jean Chrétien's controlling leadership style. But Harper was not to be underestimated. Said to be a skilled chess player, Harper orchestrated a merger with the Progressive Conservative Party, eliminating his chief rivals for right-leaning voters. When the Liberals were rocked by the sponsorship scandal, in which taxpayer dollars were funnelled to Liberal-connected firms in Quebec in exchange for little or no work, Harper took full advantage, hammering the Liberals on their apparent corruption.

What followed were three successive minority governments (one Martin's and two Harper's) which were squabbling, fractious and accomplished little. In 2011, Harper was able to capitalize on voter frustration with an ineffective parliament to win his long-coveted majority government. Four years later, the man once mocked for the ill-fitting leather vest he wore to the Calgary Stampede when he was leader of the opposition had emerged as one of the most formidable and polarizing forces in recent Canadian political history.

Harper's bid for re-election in 2015 raised major questions about the sort of county Canadians wanted. Supporters tended to see Harper as a steady hand at the wheel who was cutting taxes and getting things done for the conservative movement. Critics contended he had demonstrated inaction on the climate crisis, governed parliament with unprecedented control and failed to safeguard the electoral system. (Following years of allegations, two Conservative officials were eventually sent to prison for election-related crimes.) But it wasn't immediately clear to voters that either of the other major national parties were ready to take the reins. The Liberals had replaced their deeply unpopular leader, Michael Ignatieff, with Justin Trudeau, the fresh-faced, two-term MP and son of the former prime minister Pierre Trudeau. He had panache but little experience.

The NDP, on the other hand, had decades of baggage as the perennial third or fourth party, seemingly destined to eternity on the opposition benches. But they had achieved a breakthrough under their late leader Jack Layton, who had vaulted them to Official Opposition status. Their new leader Thomas Mulcair, Quebec's former Minister of the Environment, had undeniable credibility. The three leaders presented drastically different visions for the country. With all three major national parties in a virtual tie in public opinion polls, for perhaps the first time ever, it was anyone's guess who would win the election.

But that wasn't the story everyone was talking about.

As Andrew Coyne put it in the *National Post*, "Whatever else the election of 2015 will be remembered for, it will be remembered as the election in which thousands of votes—the fate of parties, perhaps—turned on the question of whether a handful of religiously-observant women should be required to uncover their faces to take the oath of citizenship." Responding to Jason Kenney's statement that the judge who overturned the ban on wearing niqabs during citizenship ceremonies had acted contrary to Canadian values of "openness and the equality of men and women," Coyne wrote, "It would be one thing if the women who insist on their right to wear the niqab at the citizenship ceremony, to the point of going to court to defend it, were in fact being forced to wear it. But there is no evidence of this: quite the contrary. Far from meek and submissive, they give every sign of being quite obstreperously independent, rock-ribbed individualists, willing to assert their rights even in the face of a hostile majority. We talk a lot about Canadian values in this debate. I am inclined to think that, in their own way, it is the niqabistes who best embody those values. In their ornery unwillingness to bend to others' sensitivities, in their insistence on going their own way on a matter of principle, those women are in the finest Canadian tradition of hellraising."

But it appeared Stephen Harper's team had hit on a winning strategy. A government-commissioned poll found that 82 percent of Canadians supported the ban. The Conservatives highlighted the ban in their fundraising literature. Despite their defeat in the courts, they promised to pass a bill enshrining the ban in law within the first hundred days of their new government if re-elected. This promise kept people like the NCCM's Amira Elghawaby at the forefront of the debate throughout the 2015 campaign. "I would joke with media producers, CBC or CTV or wherever I happened to be, that I should just bring a sleeping bag and camp out in the newsroom waiting for Mr. Harper to talk about the niqab again," she recalls. "Because he really made it into a central issue, which was really ludicrous."

It was classic wedge politics. The Charter of Quebec Values hadn't managed to get the PQ re-elected in Quebec, but Harper had reason to believe the math would work out differently for the federal Conservatives. The thinking seems to have been this: if the NDP and Liberals supported the ban, they'd likely alienate many of their core supporters, who were generally against the ban. These core supporters are the ones who send donations, put up signs, knock on doors, and most reliably show up on election day. Alienating them would cost a lot. However, if they came out against the ban, they'd be espousing a broadly unpopular position, which would hurt their chances of growing their voter base. "Harper understood and embraced the fact that anxieties about a changing Canada and a changing world were not confined to Quebec, and that a market for this kind of politics exists through large swaths of English Canada. Harper took a classic 'Quebec file' scalpel and fashioned it into a base-rallying, elite-denying broadaxe to be wielded across the country," wrote John Duffy in *Maclean's*.

And so, the battle lines were drawn. On the one hand were the Conservative Party and the resurgent Bloc Québécois who also favoured the ban; one of the Bloc's campaign ads actually featured an ominous drop of black oil morphing into a woman in a niqab. On the other side of the wedge were the other two major national parties, Thomas Mulcair's NDP and Justin Trudeau's Liberals. Trudeau was particularly passionate in his denunciations of the ban and the motives behind it. "These are troubling times. Across Canada, and especially in my home province, Canadians are being encouraged by their government to be fearful of one another," he said. "For me, this is both unconscionable and a real threat to Canadian liberty. For me, it is basic truth that prime ministers of liberal democracies ought not to be in the business of telling women what they can and cannot wear on their head during public ceremonies.... What's even worse than what they're saying is what they really mean. We all know what is going on here. It is nothing less than an attempt to play on people's fears and foster prejudice, directly toward the Muslim faith."

Further public remarks from Conservatives only strengthened the link being made between the niqab and either terrorism or the oppression of women. Asked about the ban on niqabs in citizenship ceremonies, Chris Alexander, the Conservative MP who had by then replaced Kenney as Minister of Citizenship and Immigration, unambiguously drew the link to terrorism. "The overwhelming majority of Canadians want that rule to continue to apply. We've done a lot in the past year to strengthen the value of Canadian citizenship. People take pride in that. They don't want their co-citizens to be terrorists. They don't want people to become citizens who haven't respected the rules," he said. The implication was quite clear: preventing women from wearing niqabs during citizenship ceremonies was linked to preventing terrorists from becoming citizens. Asked a similar question during Question Period in the House, the prime minister was even more explicit in his response. "Why would Canadians, contrary to our own values, embrace a practice at that time that is not transparent, that is not open, and, frankly, is rooted in a culture that is anti-women?" said Harper.

That statement is worth parsing. Generally, statements of government policy are submitted to a rigorous and lengthy approval process. They're pored over by policy analysts, directors general, deputy ministers and political aides, in both official languages. Question Period is different. Under the glare of TV lights, amid a din of over three hundred raucous MPs, ministers are expected to instantly come up with succinct responses to questions they haven't been given in advance. Certainly they have binders of prepared talking points, but it's easy to get flustered. In that high-pressure environment, did Harper misspeak? Did he mean to say that the practice was anti-women? Some would consider that objectionable enough, but it's a far cry from saying that the culture is anti-women. Or, straying from prepared statements, did Harper say what he really thought?

Either way, it provoked a response. Nadia Kidwai, an active member of the Muslim community in Winnipeg, was interviewed by the CBC. "When I was at Oxford University, a lot of my friends wore the face veil, and these were Oxford graduates who were thinking, intellectual, smart women who went on to work," she said. "[Harper's comment] was shocking because it was so blatant, and then it wasn't shocking because he's been inferring this anti-Muslim, anti-Islamic mindset for years. But you just don't think it gets as blatant as it did," she continued. Zunera Ishaq's lawyer, Lorne Waldman, made the same interpretation. "They're playing to Islamophobia. When you put together the terrorism issue and the niqab issue, it really appeals to a base, crass fear that people have," he said.

The issue of women wearing niqabs during citizenship ceremonies was the main topic during the French-language televised leaders' debate. Harper even addressed it in his closing remarks. Throughout the campaign trail in Quebec, Bloc leader Gilles Duceppe hounded Mulcair about his position against the ban. At a press conference, standing right beside Mulcair, Montreal mayor Denis Coderre did the same thing. The NDP, which had been

58

leading in the polls at various points in the race, began to see its support plummet. NDP staffers started filling empty chairs at rallies. Campaign signs were vandalized.

NDP staffer Jennifer Pedersen describes the impact on incumbent Quebec NDP MP Hélène Laverdière's campaign: "I cleaned dozens of signs where a niqab had been drawn on her face with a Sharpie. Dozens more had the word 'niqab' written on her forehead... Several campaign staff carried around bottles of acetone and paper towels to clean the graffiti off the signs. Every morning and evening I cleaned a dozen or so signs on the way to, and from, the campaign office. This started when the niqab issue became a story in the press and continued for weeks.... We heard a lot of racist words directed at Muslims." The ugliness started to take an emotional toll on Laverdière's team. The campaign manager decided to shut the campaign down for a day to give volunteers twenty-four hours away from the tension, an unheard-of move in a winnable riding where every vote counts. Fellow incumbent NDP MP Pierre Dionne Labelle did the same thing.

In general, the media called out the distraction for what it was, while simultaneously devoting pages of coverage to the topic. "As Canadian politicians bickered on the evening news, 1,074 Aboriginal children and 6,265 Aboriginal women were sexually assaulted.... But sure, let's talk about the niqab instead," read *Maclean's*. A *Globe and Mail* editorial condemned the obsession emphatically: "The day a government imposes 'normal' cultural values is the day Canada's basic freedoms go down the drain. We cannot become a country that selectively bans religious practices that have no demonstrably harmful consequences for others. Canada, Mr. Harper's semantics notwithstanding, is not a 'family' governed by a parental authority that lays down a dress code. This country is more free than that. And it faces real issues in this election, such as the economy, that should not be overshadowed by an ugly distraction."

The clear positions of the parties and the prominence of the question during the campaign often made it seem like the election had become a referendum on the niqab. If identity issues began as a distraction, they arguably became the campaign itself. "When the head of the Islamic Supreme Council of Canada, Calgary imam Syed Soharwardy—a man who has worked closely with the RCMP to combat Islamist radicalism and who has been threatened by the Islamic State of Iraq and Syria (ISIS)—says he believes Harper has actively targeted Muslims for political gain, you have to stop and listen," wrote journalist Evan Solomon in *Maclean's*. "These comments cannot be ignored. It's one thing to have genuine policy disagreements. Good, we need that. It's another to have serious people believing their ethnic group is being targeted for political gain."

After the niqab issue, the most notable example of identity-based political warfare during the 2015 campaign occurred when Chris Alexander, Minister of Citizenship and Immigration, and Kellie Leitch, Minister for the Status of Women, announced plans to create an RCMP tip line for Canadians to report on each other for what they called "barbaric cultural practices." Defending their plan, Leitch said, "These practices have no place in Canadian society." She went on to make a partisan attack: "By contrast, Justin Trudeau and Thomas Mulcair are more worried about political correctness than tackling these difficult issues that impact women." The proposal was derided as a snitch line that would be more at home in the former East Germany than in Canada. It was also unnecessary; Canadians could already report crimes to the police. As well, the "barbaric cultural practices" were left undefined, effectively inviting citizens to express any and all of their prejudices. While the overall context of the announcement during the 2015 campaign made it clear enough who might be targeted, Alexander made it clearer still by linking it to the niqab debate. "We need to stand up for our values," he said. "We need to do that in citizenship ceremonies. We need to do that to protect women and girls from forced marriage and other barbaric practices." Announced during the election, the tip line never became operational.

Lest undue criticism be directed to the Conservative government, several other points need to be considered. During the election, as the civil war in Syria raged with a devastating human cost, Harper promised to double the number of Syrian and Iraqi refugees Canada was willing to take in, although the promised numbers were still less than those the NDP and Liberals were proposing. When the photo of the body of a three-year-old Syrian boy who had drowned trying to reach Canada went viral, Harper was visibly shaken. "Yesterday, Laureen [Harper] and I saw on the Internet, the picture of this young boy, Alan, dead on the beach. Look, I think, our reaction to that, you know the first thing that crossed our mind was remembering our son Ben at that age, running around like that," he said, choking up. It was shortly after that that the Conservatives announced Canada would be taking in more refugees. There are also rumours in Conservative circles that Harper didn't know that an announcement was going to be made about a "barbaric cultural practices" tip line, and that he was privately furious when it happened. It is also said that Harper warned the Conservatives in caucus that it was dangerous to take on identity issues in an election. Furthermore, questionable comments weren't limited to the Conservative campaign. One NDP candidate, contrary to his party's position, supported the ban on niqabs during citizenship ceremonies. He even went so far as to support the drastic measure of opening up the constitution in order to get it done. A Liberal candidate, meanwhile, was dropped after comments she'd made on social media came to light in which she remarked, "Santa has to be white!!! You can't have a brown guy with a beard sneaking into your house in the middle of the night! You'd be calling the bomb squad!" Nevertheless, Harper's was the only national party accused of running a campaign with an anti-Muslim tinge. He had opportunities to correct the impression, but he didn't.

In an interview with Harper, the CBC's Rosemary Barton asked him whether some Conservative policies might be encouraging anti-Muslim sentiment. Hate crimes directed against Muslims had skyrocketed that year, up 60 percent from the previous year. In Ottawa, Staff Sergeant David Zackrias had made a public appeal for calm. In response to Barton's question, rather than take the opportunity to denounce Islamophobia, Harper pivoted to his government's policies on crime. "Priorities going forward in this parliament are additional measures in the areas of drunk driving, 'life means life,' and [ensuring] people who commit certain heinous acts actually serve a life sentence for their crimes," he said. Barton pressed further, giving him another chance to make it clear that the Conservative Party condemned Islamophobia. "Look, I don't think you can use that kind of thing to discredit legitimate political debate. Violence against women is unacceptable, which is why our government has brought forward laws to crack down on violence," he responded.

Stephen Harper lost the 2015 election, and Justin Trudeau's Liberals were elected with a majority government. With identity issues having taken such a central role in the campaign, one might see the results as a repudiation of Harper's views on issues like the niqab ban and a vindication of Trudeau's, but the reality is probably more complicated. Polls showed that the ban was popular cross the country. Both Mulcair and Trudeau had opposed the ban, but it was the future prime minister's words that were stronger and more passionate. One might suppose he would have taken a political hit for that, yet for some reason, it seemed to be Mulcair who paid the price. In August, Mulcair was the most popular leader in Quebec. By October, with the election just weeks away, the NDP had fallen seventeen points in the province. "The emergence of the niqab as a point of debate is perhaps the most obvious factor in the NDP's slide. Mulcair's opposition to the government's attempt to ban the veil during citizenship ceremonies has coincided with a significant drop in support for the NDP in Quebec, where support for a ban is strongest," wrote Aaron Wherry in *Maclean's*.

There were broad consequences to the niqab debate, but not just for the NDP. For a number of years, an "Anything But Conservative" movement had been brewing, as NDP and Liberal voters saw a greater commonality with each other than with Harper's Conservatives. While the niqab ban may have been generally popular, other issues had left many voters with a deep distaste for Harper. After four years of a Harper majority, many pledged that they would vote strategically to support whichever party had the greatest chance of defeating him. In the months approaching the campaign and through much of the campaign itself, with the NDP and Liberals often neck-and-neck, it was unclear which party had that chance. But when the NDP's Quebec numbers fell dramatically, their national numbers took a corresponding hit. Once they did, Trudeau looked like the man to beat Harper, and the anti-Harper vote coalesced around him.

If Mulcair was punished in Quebec for his stance on the niqab, why wasn't Trudeau? "The fact that we would take those positions is baked into people's expectations of the Liberal Party. But in Quebec, it wasn't baked into people's expectations of the NDP," veteran Liberal advisor David Serle explained to *Maclean's*. While Mulcair's stance was no surprise to most Canadians who followed the NDP, Quebeckers were less familiar with the party. In fact, before Jack Layton had led the NDP to a massive showing in Quebec just four years earlier, the NDP had been a virtual non-entity there. When faced with the NDP's opposition to the niqab ban, many NDP voters in Quebec, it turned out, decided they couldn't get behind that.

The Conservatives still garnered nearly 32 percent of the vote, not even eight percent less than in the previous election, when they'd won a majority government. As is common in a first-past-the-post electoral system like Canada's, a dramatic swing from one majority government to another did not necessarily mean there had been a massive shift among voters. What the results of the 2015 campaign say about Canadians is a matter of debate. Even when one issue dominates the airwaves, usually more than one issue determines how most people cast their votes. At the very least, though, some politicians appear to have thought there were votes to be gained by targeting Muslims, and a sizeable number of Canadians liked what they heard. In the years after September 11, 2001, a troubling public discourse about Muslims was echoed in the language of some Canadian politicians. For Canadians who had seen a race, culture or religion singled out before, the rhetoric was disturbing.

The Veneer of Justice: Muslims and the National Security Apparatus

IN 1885 PARLIAMENT passed the *Chinese Immigration Act*, which specified in law that Chinese immigrants had to pay a fifty-dollar levy—then a serious financial hardship—in order to come to Canada. It was a racist law designed to restrict Chinese immigration, and it is seen today as a terrible injustice. Apart from the *Indian Act*, which many feel is an unjust and outmoded vestige of colonialism, Canadian legislation no longer treats people differently according to their race or religion.

The modern legislative response to security concerns, therefore, doesn't explicitly target a race or religion the way the *Chinese Immigration Act* once did. However, key pieces of legislation do treat non-citizens and foreign-born citizens differently from how they treat Canadian-born citizens, even if they commit, or are suspected of committing the same crime. There's also a broad legal definition of terrorism that tends toward profiling, and an alarming lack of oversight monitoring the conduct of law enforcement agents. Given the vulnerability of Muslim communities in the post-9/11 environment, the security regime must be carefully examined.

When the first plane hit the World Trade Center on September 11, House of Commons security personnel hurried through Centre Block, informing everyone of what had happened. Most staff stayed put and continued to work. Soon after the second plane hit, staff were told the building was being evacuated. As staff streamed off Parliament Hill and bomb detectors were dispatched onto it, many felt a genuine fear that they might be the next victims.

Erroneous media reports circulating in the US that some of the hijackers had entered the US through Canada didn't help the sense of panic. Five days after the attacks, Liberal Minister of Foreign Affairs John Manley stated in a television interview, "We have to make every effort to satisfy the United States as to the level of our border security....We have simply too much at stake economically." When US President George W. Bush made a speech thanking various countries for their support and did not include Canada, it was taken as an implicit demand that Canada do more.

The Liberals immediately provided the RCMP with an additional $59 million, the Communications Security Establishment with an additional $37 million, and CSIS with an additional $10 million. Billions more would be provided to security agencies in the next budget. But the centerpiece of their response was Bill C-36, the *Anti-terrorism Act*.

The definition of terrorism contained in the bill was broad. It covered acts, or attempted or threatened acts, committed both inside and outside of Canada. It defined its motives (political, religious or ideological) and its results (intentionally caused death or risk to the health and safety of the public). One didn't have to be an actual terrorist for the law to apply: anyone considered to be facilitating terrorism could be charged, too. In some respects, the definitions were reasonable, but as legislation, it lacked nuance. After analyzing the bill, Svend Robinson, the veteran NDP MP, lawyer and expert in human rights law, concluded that the definition was so all-encompassing that, had the bill been law in the eighties, Canadians helping Nelson Mandela and the African National Congress in their fight against apartheid in South Africa could have been charged under the Act.

The discretion that law enforcement was given to identify and fight that broadly defined terrorism was wide. Among the provisions of the bill was a preventative detention clause. It would allow police to arrest without a warrant someone they suspected of planning a terror attack and hold them for up to seventy-two hours without charge, and then to keep them under house arrest for up to a year—all without a trial. Another clause would allow judges to undertake special investigative hearings in which witnesses who might know something about an attack would be stripped of the right to remain silent, arguably one of the most fundamental rights in criminal law.

Following several scandals in the seventies, the RCMP had lost their responsibilities for national security, and CSIS had been created instead. Nevertheless, Bill C-36 gave the RCMP new powers. (The Commission for Public Complaints Against the RCMP, on the other hand, was not. "I couldn't pry a sheet of paper loose from the RCMP," complained then-head of the Commission, Shirley Heafy.) The RCMP weren't the only ones to see their powers beefed up. The Communications Security Establishment was given the power to spy on Canadian citizens when communicating outside the country. In response Privacy Commissioner George Radwanski warned that the government was giving itself the authority to amass "a Big Brother file on every Canadian."

According to University of Toronto law professor Kent Roach, the bill was unnecessary. The existing Criminal Code would have offered the tools needed to prosecute the September 11 terrorists, had they planned their attack in Canada. Probably the biggest problem with the legislation, though, was that by defining terrorism by its motives, it would become necessary for police to investigate political and religious beliefs. Inevitably, this would open the door to prejudicial profiling.

During the Justice Committee's study of the bill, a number of key witnesses raised concerns that holes in the rushed legislation would allow racial profiling, specifically the targeting of Muslim communities. "It's a bad bill. Muslim Canadians, Arab Canadians and those who are similar in appearance or name to those known to be Muslim and Arabs, will be the most targeted group in this country, and we should not allow this to happen," testified Mohamed Elmasry, national president of the Canadian Islamic Congress.

The Congress lawyer, Rocco Galati, concurred. "This bill is, in my humble submission, obscene in the net it casts. You might as well have deleted the constitution from our landscape. The bill is so overbroad, it catches socio-economic and political offences," he said. "The Muslim and Arab communities are going to bear the brunt of this injustice." While some witnesses made comparisons to the internment of Japanese Canadians during World War II, Galati acknowledged that parliamentarians intended to do no such thing to Muslims. However, he also explained that the point was not what parliamentarians intended by drafting the legislation, but what law enforcement might be able to do with it. He noted that there had already been some eight hundred illegal detentions of Muslims and Arabs since September 11, even without the provisions of the bill. The last thing that was needed was more discretionary power. "If it were you parliamentarians who were going to enforce the law, I wouldn't be here today," Galati continued. "You have a naive view of law enforcement agencies and what they will do with the legislation once they have it. I spent my teen years being beaten up by the Toronto police because of a perceived Mafia threat, on College Street in Toronto under loitering and World War II laws. That's where I come from in bringing this to the table. You say we're fighting a shadowy enemy. I agree. Terrorism is serious. That shadow is going to take a real human face in this country, and it's going to be Arab and Muslim."

Other witnesses on the panel that day recalled the harassment by csis during the Gulf War and saw history about to repeat itself. "In a climate of anxiety and fear, in a climate of war, where there is a targeting of a community as the enemy, we don't trust that this suspicion will not be exercised against Arabs and Muslims," said Amina Sherazee of the Canadian Arab Federation. As witness after witness identified the same criticisms of the legislation, the members of the committee might have started to lose interest.

"I know that the level of sugar in the blood is going down and down, and the caffeine effect of the morning is not really holding, but let me share with you a couple of points," Mohamed Elmasry added. "You have in your hands the future of Muslim Canadians in this country. You have in your hands the civil liberty of all Canadians in this country. This is not an ordinary committee of members of parliament getting together in order to have hearing after hearing. Sometimes it's boring. I've been on committees in my career for a long time. This is a special one, and you have to have a special attitude."

The committee passed the bill anyway and sent it back to the House for further debate, but some Liberals were starting to get uncomfortable with their own government's legislation. Liberal MP John McKay called the bill "a deal with the devil." Hungarian-born fellow Liberal Andrew Telegdi also criticized it, saying "Being one who lived under a communist dictatorship, I know what human rights and civil liberties mean." Led by Svend Robinson, the NDP continued hammering the bill. The Bloc Québécois had supported it in the past, but were now backtracking. Under increasing pressure, the Liberal cabinet resorted to procedural tactics to curtail further debate and force the bill through. Less than three weeks later, the Senate passed it without amendment.

* * *

The *Immigration and Refugee Protection Act* allows the government to use what's called a "security certificate" to detain or deport a foreign national or permanent resident (but not a Canadian citizen) for national security reasons. An earlier form of this law had been on the books since 1978, and until September 11, it was generally used for quick deportations. The Liberal government already had changes to the process in the works prior to September 11, but these changes did not become law until after the attacks, while debate on the *Anti-terrorism Act* was still underway.

Under the new process, the Minister of Citizenship and Immigration and the Solicitor General could co-sign an order to subject a non-citizen to a security certificate. A Federal Court judge (previously the Security Intelligence Review Committee) then reviewed the evidence to determine whether it was reasonable. The judge's decision was final, and no appeal was allowed. (The previous process whereby the accused's counsel could cross-examine CSIS agents was revoked.) Neither the detainee nor his or her lawyers could be present at the hearing, and they didn't have to be shown the evidence of why the accused was being detained under the security certificate (where previously, some access to evidence had been allowed).

Once the security certificate process was in the hands of Federal Court judges instead of the Security Intelligence Review Committee, its flaws became more widely known. "We hate it. We hate hearing only one party. We hate having to decide what, if any, sensitive material can or should be conveyed to the other party," said Federal Court Justice James Hugessen. He explained how serious a flaw it was that allowed CSIS to present evidence to judges without sharing it with the accused or their lawyers. Without cross-examination, judges were more likely to take the evidence at face value. "When it is only given to us by one party, we are not well-suited to test the materials that are put before us," said Hugessen. He added that he sometimes felt like a fig leaf, providing the veneer of justice to cover up an unfair system. Some called the process Canada's version of Guantanamo Bay, the hated US military prison in Cuba where detainees were left to languish without trial for years.

Taking evidence presented by CSIS as incontrovertible fact is problematic. There is no reason to doubt that, at various times in their organization's history, CSIS agents have done difficult, heroic work. Part of the nature of their work is that they may never get public credit for what they do and the plots they foil to keep Canadians safe. However, CSIS can make mistakes. Lawyer Paul Copeland once represented an Armenian client accused of making a bomb. Because the lawyer was able to see the evidence, he was able to prove that it was just a readily available consumer product meant to start a car.

"The quality of [CSIS] work is sometimes unbelievably shoddy," Copeland told the *Ottawa Citizen*. CSIS doesn't have to follow the same rules as police do; they have greater powers to destroy evidence, for example. Some have also argued that CSIS has a track record of building a case to support a pre-conceived bias. "There could be one hundred pieces of evidence that contradict one piece of evidence, but they will go with that one piece if it supports their argument," Jean-Luc Marchessault, a former CSIS counterterrorism agent for much of the nineties once testified in court. It's just one former agent's assessment, but if true, the revelation is a bombshell that confirms the suspicions of the organization's harshest critics.

In 2007, the Supreme Court ruled unanimously that the way people were being detained through the security certificate process was unconstitutional. "Before the state can detain people for significant periods of time, it must accord them a fair judicial process," stated Chief Justice Beverley McLachlan. The remedy the government (by then Stephen Harper's Conservatives) developed was to provide the detainees with "special advocates" who would have access to the evidence against them and be present at the hearings. The special advocates would all be lawyers, of course, but being represented by a special advocate would be nothing like being represented by a lawyer in the normal sense. The accused wouldn't be able to choose their special advocate; the government would choose for them. They wouldn't have attorney-client privilege, meaning the special advocate could be compelled to report on what the accused had told them in confidence. Finally, if the special advocate simply wanted to consult with the accused, the Crown would need to be informed in advance of what would be discussed.

The special advocate system was modelled after a similar system in the United Kingdom, but it was hardly a model worth emulating. Of the fifteen special advocates in the UK, eleven eventually either resigned, or publicly stated that it was impossible to provide justice for the detainees under that system. When the system was imported to Canada, many Canadian lawyers were dismayed. "The structure is just nonsensical, and I suppose people who are in this business, and are following this, would think, 'Why would I apply for a job that Mickey Mouse should be doing?'" lawyer Ronald Poulton told *Lawyers Weekly*. "There is no one in the defence bar, on the criminal or immigration side, who could hold their head up after being in a job like that." It was a justifiable remark, but eventually it became clear that a better, fairer system for the detainees simply wasn't on offer. In the end, several of the lawyers who had taken on security-certificate detainees as clients ended their attorney-client relationships in order to become special advocates instead, believing that the system, bad as it was, was nevertheless the detainees' best available option.

After the special advocate process concludes, a judge rules on whether the security certificate was "reasonable." If yes, the decision must then be made whether or not to deport the detainee. The answer depends on how likely the detainee is to be tortured or killed once brought back to their country of origin. That possibility is highly likely because many of the countries of origin in question implicitly trust Canada. If we indicate we believe someone's guilty, security forces in those countries will automatically presume guilt as well, and proceed according to their laws and customs, which may include torture or execution. The question of whether or not to deport is therefore much weightier than in a typical deportation case. "I regard this case to be as serious as a capital punishment case," Paul Copeland said in reference to one of his clients. Conservative public safety minister Stockwell Day was less concerned about detainees who didn't think the system was fair. "At any time they can leave, walk out, and return to their country of origin," he said. It's hard to read that statement without picturing a shrug.

Worse, the threshold for deportation is shockingly low. This is a country in which the Canadian Food Inspection Agency will recall tofu for undeclared nut content. Health Canada will recall children's jackets if the drawstrings are at risk of catching on playground equipment. The Toronto Blue Jays offer nut-free seating areas at Jays games. Canadians are nothing if not cautious. Yet under the security certificate system, as the *Ottawa Citizen* has reported, if the risk that a detainee will be tortured when returned to their country of origin is only moderate, the deportation will probably happen. Incredibly, even if the risk of torture is more substantial, the detainee is still sometimes deported.

The more common practice so far, however, when the risk of torture is substantial, has been to leave the accused in detention in Canada indefinitely. Here again, the question of threshold _ eeds to be addressed. Recall that the judge is not finding an accused guilty of being a security threat; he or she is only finding that the accusation is "reasonable." The legal standard, therefore, required for de facto indefinite detention of a non-citizen—that an accusation simply be "reasonable"—is a far cry from the right of Canadian citizens to be considered innocent until proven guilty beyond a reasonable doubt. "They don't even have to have a 50 percent likelihood that you are in fact a terrorist," says Barbara Jackman, an esteemed lawyer who has worked on these cases for years. "You could go, 'On balance, it's more likely than not that this guy is not a terrorist, but it's possible. Maybe he is.' Then, they can go on less. They can go on a 20 percent chance." Ultimately, the process that non-citizens are subjected to offers fundamentally fewer rights than those afforded to citizens. Accusation is being treated far too much like proven guilt. Presumption of innocence before the courts should be a fundamental human right, whether one is a citizen or not.

There was a telling moment during parliamentary consideration of the bill adopting the special advocate system. At first, MPS on the committee studying the bill didn't want to hear from Adil

Charkaoui or Mohamed Harkat, two men detained under security certificates. The Supreme Court had set a deadline for the new rules to be in place, and MPs felt there wasn't enough time to hear from the detainees and still take an adequate Christmas vacation. "We break in mid-December and don't come back until the end of January... We could sit in January, but I'll be in New Zealand," one MP told the *Toronto Star*. "I haven't had a holiday since 2004," said another.

Following pressure from human rights advocates working with Charkaoui and Harkat, the committee backed down and agreed to hear from the two men. Evidently some committee members felt they were doing the men a great favour. During questioning Conservative MP Gord Brown took a moment to express how impressively liberal the committee was being by allowing people accused, but not proven guilty, of a crime the right to speak: "I'd first like to say it is probably quite extraordinary for people who are subject to security certificates or their equivalent in other countries to have an opportunity to have a say in a government committee on how the government may be changing legislation. I think that's a real testament to the Canadian system."

As a legal tool, the security certificate process is a sledgehammer, and one with the potential to cause incredible chaos in human lives. Unsurprisingly, many of those lives have been Muslim. Consider the case of Mohamed Harkat. In 1995 he arrived in Canada from Algeria as a refugee using a fake Saudi passport. On December 10, 2002—International Human Rights Day—as the Ottawa resident and Petro-Canada employee was on his way to work, he saw a group of plainclothes agents running toward him. At first, he assumed they were chasing someone else. Even when they arrested him, he assumed a mistake had been made and they were looking for another Harkat.

Among the allegations CSIS has made are that Harkat was acquainted with prominent members of al-Qaeda, and that while in Pakistan, he ran either a mujahedeen camp or a guesthouse for travelling mujahedeen. A report CSIS made public is vague, asserting that he "assisted" extremists in Canada and "engaged in terrorism by supporting terrorist activity."

Judging the case against Harkat is inherently difficult because of the secrecy of the security certificate process. Most of the evidence CSIS says they have has not been made public. It is not the purpose of this chapter to judge the case against him, other than to restate that, like any other citizen or non-citizen in the country, he ought to have the right to a presumption of innocence. And, there are enough hints to suggest that the picture painted by the government is incomplete. A chief piece of evidence that has been made public is that Abu Zubaydah, once thought to be one of Osama bin Laden's top lieutenants, identified a man matching Harkat's description while in US custody.

However, it has since been reported that Zubaydah, who had been shot in the groin and thigh and was being denied medical care, was also being waterboarded, beaten and subjected to extremely loud noises and bright lights, all of which severely undermines the reliability of what he might have said. Conveniently, the CIA has also destroyed the tapes of his interrogations. Worse still, it was later determined by American officials that, far from being a top bin Laden operative, Zubaydah's alleged connections with al-Qaeda had been greatly exaggerated. Another problematic element of the government's case is that an inform-ant against Harkat failed a polygraph test. Furthermore, one of the CSIS agents monitoring Harkat ended up being fired for a romantic relationship she had with another person of interest she was monitoring, a lack of professionalism that casts doubt on the quality of intelligence she may have provided about anyone she was investigating.

Harkat's wife Sophie never doubted him. After his arrest, she took a month's leave from work, trying to do whatever she could to help. She tried to return to work later but found she was so consumed by the case that she couldn't manage it. She became a full-time activist. Years started to slip by. "It is hard for me to describe the pain, suffering and anger I have been living [with] the past two years in a few lines. I remain positive that the truth will come out in the future and that we will be reunited one day! This nightmare has been hard," Sophie wrote for the website socialist. ca. She looked ahead to his release, a day she firmly believed would come. "Every day will be a new day for both. I am looking forward to his laugh, his hugs and kisses, his smile, his smell, his presence," she wrote. "I am looking forward to having him back... I miss him terribly, and miss everything about him. You don't realize how important someone is until they are taken away suddenly."

In 2005, after years in detention, a Federal Court judge finally ruled that the security certificate was reasonable. Sophie was with her husband in the Ottawa-Carleton Detention Centre when he heard the news. She watched him as he banged his head over and over on the glass partition between them repeating, "Oh my God."

Although deportation would remain on the table, because of the uncertain risk of torture, Harkat would stay in jail in Canada for the time being. Sophie began to suffer from high blood pressure, migraines and sleeplessness. In thirty-one months, Sophie and her husband were only able to touch each other twice. Despite Sophie's enduring faith, Harkat had to contend with a seemingly unalterable perception that because a judge had ruled that the security certificate was reasonable, he was a guilty man.

He began to suffer from depression and post-traumatic stress, the origin of which was likely his first year of incarceration. For the first two weeks, he hadn't been allowed a toothbrush. For the first two months, he wasn't allowed a Koran. One guard refused to call him by his name, calling him only "Terrorist." Most of that first year of incarceration was spent in solitary confinement in a three-by-two-metre cell.

Research shows that solitary confinement has serious psychological consequences. According to an article in the *Journal of the American Academy of Psychiatry and the Law*, solitary confinement can result in depression, cognitive disturbances, perceptive distortions, paranoia and even psychosis. In fact, solitary confinement has been shown to be "as clinically distressing as physical torture." Even the most psychologically stable inmates are at risk of permanent harm from prolonged isolation. It's what eventually led the BC Supreme Court to rule that indefinite solitary confinement is unconstitutional in 2018.

A psychiatric evaluation showed prison was exacting a terrible toll on Harkat. "I believe that Mr. Harkat's mental health is liable to worsen the longer he stays incarcerated," stated Dr. Colin Cameron. "In particular, his vivid nightmares of facing torture in Algeria have started only since his incarceration... [He] even experiences body sensations as if his fingernails are being pulled out or his skin is being scraped off... If anything, he may have a tendency to under-report the severity of his symptoms and difficulties. The severity of Mr. Harkat's depression is a cause of concern for me, and I believe that it should be treated." Cameron also evaluated the risk to the community of releasing Harkat and found it negligible.

In an attempt to secure bail, supporters, led by Sophie, raised about thirty-five thousand dollars in cash. Contributions came from author Naomi Klein, former NDP leaders Ed Broadbent and Alexa McDonough, and Alexandre Trudeau, the son of Pierre and brother of Justin, the past and future prime ministers. In a bail hearing, though, government lawyers asked how much of the money had come from Muslims. The fact that government lawyers were comfortable asking such an irrelevant question is appalling. Worse though, is that neither this support nor Dr. Cameron's troubling diagnosis ultimately helped Harkat's cause. Bail was denied. In 2006 he was transferred to a new maximum-security, purpose-built facility for security certificate detainees on the grounds of Millhaven Institution in Kingston. "We've built a special jail for Muslims," Salam Elmenyawi of the Muslim Council of Montreal stated at a rally.

Later in 2006, Harkat was finally released on bail with what have been called the most restrictive bail conditions in Canadian history. He was forced to wear a GPS device at all times. His phones were tapped and his mail was intercepted. He was forbidden from using a computer or cell phone. He wasn't allowed to speak Arabic for fear he might start plotting in a language his guards didn't understand. He was only allowed to leave his house for four-hour outings three times a week, accompanied by armed agents. These outings needed to be approved forty-eight hours in advance by the Canadian Border Services Agency, who were involved because of the ever-present possibility of deportation.

He was required at all times to be in the company of either his wife or his mother-in-law. Fortunately, he had a very understanding mother-in-law. Because of this stipulation, the couple lived in the basement of Sophie's mother's south Ottawa home. One of the outings he requested was to attend his own fortieth birthday party. The government determined it would be a political gathering and denied it. To honour him in his absence, attendees put an empty chair in the middle of the room and decorated it with balloons.

After the Supreme Court quashed the security certificate legislation and the government redrafted it to include the new special advocate process, Harkat was issued a new security certificate. It had the wrong name on it. Sophie was appalled. "Mistake number one! Wrong guy? Wrong allegations? Imagine what goes on in the back. Imagine what kind of evidence is presented in secret," she wrote to activists.

In the end, bail did little to reduce the stress. At any time, the government could order deportation, which Harkat was convinced would mean torture and death in Algeria. Eventually the relationship between Harkat's mother-in-law and her live-in partner began to break down. "You can't have human beings immersed in this situation and not expect it," said Matt Webber, one of Harkat's lawyers. Due to the tension between the mother-in-law and her partner, the Harkats put a lock on the basement door, which was a breach of his bail conditions. Harkat was arrested while in the shower and briefly taken back to prison.

In March 2009, Harkat's bail conditions were eased: he could stay home alone, have up to five weekly outings, use public washrooms without supervision, attend political rallies, and speak with his imam or reporters. Later that year the Canadian Border Services Agency launched a six-hour raid on the house. They found Sophie's keys for the computer room hidden in her underwear drawer. (She was forced to keep the room locked because Mohamed wasn't allowed to use the computer while on bail.) She asked what she was supposed to do when she took a shower, which is what she was doing when agents burst into their home. She was told she should have kept the keys on a string around her neck. "Since the raid at our house, I haven't been the same person. It's been totally life-changing. My husband wears a bracelet around his ankle, but I felt like I've been wearing a bracelet around my neck the whole time," she said.

Harkat's bail conditions were further loosened in September 2009. The next year a judge ruled that Harkat's second, revised security certificate, which initially had the wrong name on it, was reasonable, too. The judge even reflected on the Harkats' nine-year marriage, characterizing it as a marriage of convenience. "My husband and I married for all the right reasons. I don't care what the court document says. I don't care what you think," Sophie said afterwards.

More than sixteen years after his arrest, Mohamed Harkat has not been deported or tried under criminal law for his alleged crimes. The government has failed to prove any case against him, but he is still denied the presumption of innocence. While in jail, he was interviewed by Peter Mansbridge, the voice of Canada himself. Despite his sterling reputation for journalistic ethics, Mansbridge was remarkably aggressive in the interview. Later he wrote an op-ed about the ethics of interviewing convicted serial rapist and murderer Paul Bernardo; in the article, he referred to the "somewhat similar" question of interviewing Harkat, a man only accused of a crime.

Mohammad Mahjoub, another man subjected to a security certificate, voluntarily returned to jail because of the strain his humiliating bail conditions were causing his family. Barbara Jackman, who has been one of Harkat's lawyers, blamed the judicial sledgehammer approach on a fear of Muslims. "That's the real root of the Harkat case: Islamophobia," she told the *Toronto Star*. Sophie has watched her friends carry on with their lives, reach milestones, have children. "I blame the certificate for costing us a family. I absolutely blame the certificate for that," Sophie told Journalists for Human Rights. "I was meant to be a mom. At least one. At least one."

* * *

Until 1947, Canadians were British citizens by law. In 1977 Canadians were permitted to become dual citizens, without restriction. In 2014 Stephen Harper's Conservative government passed Bill C-24. They named it the *Strengthening Canadian Citizenship Act*, but that was a misnomer. To anyone who read the bill, it didn't strengthen citizenship at all, but constituted a transparent weakening of the citizenship of dual citizens and created a two-tiered citizenship structure in Canada. The law allowed the government the discretion to revoke the Canadian citizenship of any dual citizen convicted of terrorist offences. No one would object to convicted terrorists being punished, and punished severely, but the new law raised serious questions about fairness. In contrast to dual citizens, there was absolutely nothing other Canadian citizens could do, no crime too evil or heinous, which could result in losing their citizenship. That status has always been considered not a privilege to be granted for good behaviour, but, once obtained, a fundamental, inalienable right.

"Bill C-24 gives the government the kind of sweeping power that is common in dictatorships, not in a democracy built upon the rule of law, where all citizens are equal. The changes to the *Citizenship Act* erode those basic principles, creating a two-tier citizenship that dilutes what it means to be Canadian," read an editorial in *The Globe and Mail*.

In analyzing this policy, it's important to bear in mind who Canada's dual citizens are. At the time the bill was passed, there were 863,000 dual citizens in Canada, nearly all either immigrants, children of immigrants or grandchildren of immigrants. Many were dual citizens by default. Since Canada doesn't restrict dual nationalities, if an immigrant leaves a country that permits dual citizenship with Canada, they would have to actively renounce their other citizenship once they became a Canadian citizen to avoid becoming a dual citizen. Disproportionately, those impacted by the new law would be recent immigrants and their descendants. They would not be "old-stock" Canadians, a term Stephen Harper once used in a televised leaders' debate when discussing refugees.

Terrorism is a repugnant crime, but the solution is not to make Canadian citizenship conditional for one group of citizens and not for another. A member of an immigrant community already faces a lifetime of moments in which mainstream society tells them they do not belong, and no matter how many Timbits they eat or hockey games they watch, they never will, their children never will, and their children's children never will. In a way, Bill C-24 turned that prejudice into law: their citizenship would never be worth the same as the citizenship of an old-stock Canadian. "I think it's wrong. I have a strong feeling it makes the citizens, the new immigrants, feel they're not as important as older citizens," Erfan Attar, a new Canadian from Iran, told *Maclean's*.

Muslims weren't specifically singled out by the new law, but it fit well into the popular narrative that did single them out. Notably, in defending the law, immigration minister Chris Alexander mentioned as justification the "ever-evolving threat of jihadi terrorism." The citizenship of recent immigrants and their descendants had been devalued, even though the law would only be applied if they committed a crime they would never dream of committing. Unfortunately, of the 863,000 dual citizens in Canada, one did.

* * *

On October 22, 2014, Michael Zehaf-Bibeau, a Canadian of French-Canadian and Libyan descent with a history of drug and mental health problems, shot and killed Corporal Nathan Cirillo, a ceremonial guard at the Tomb of the Unknown Solider. He then made his way to Parliament Hill, shooting a guard as he forced his way into Centre Block. He died in a gunfight, just steps from where MPs were holding their weekly caucus meetings. In moments, MPs went from being in charge of everything on the Hill, with a flock of staff at their disposal, to hiding behind overturned tables or trying to fashion flag poles into makeshift spears. The most powerful man in the country, Stephen Harper, was reduced to hiding in a closet in accordance with his security training. The previous year, Daesh had released a statement threatening that Canadians shouldn't feel secure "even in your bedrooms." At the time it was largely interpreted as an empty, even laughable, threat. In response on social media, Conservative MP Michelle Rempel uploaded a photo of herself snuggled in bed with the caption, "Secure Bedroom Selfie." On October 22, 2014, that confident sense of security vanished in seconds. In the hours after the Parliament Hill attack, when it was unclear whether there had been only one shooter or if others were still at large, Rempel tweeted, "mom im ok im in hiding."

The next day when MPs and staff returned to work, furniture was still strewn throughout the hallways and near doors. The limestone walls of the Hall of Honour were still scarred by bullets. There was a tenderness in the air that isn't usually present in the hyper-partisan atmosphere. People who saw each other every day but didn't necessarily acknowledge each other, now shared a smile or a kind word, each glad the other was okay.

But there was not only tenderness in the days that followed, there was also anger and fear. Not long after the attack, it became known that Zehaf-Bibeau was a convert to Islam. It was in this highly charged atmosphere that the Conservative government introduced Bill C-51, an update of the previous Liberal government's anti-terror legislation. "The Harper government has pushed variations of these laws unsuccessfully for years. But it was the Ottawa attacks, followed quickly by [other terror attacks] in Paris, that created a window of political opportunity prior to federal elections to throw together the package. The measures are the most sweeping change of Canada's national security laws since the 2001 terror attacks on the United States," stated Ronald Deibert, a director at the Munk School of Global Affairs at the University of Toronto. The bill might have been a calculated measure timed to take advantage of a shocked and frightened public, or it might have been an overreaction borne of genuine fear on the part of lawmakers. That fear could lead them to adopt hasty, emotion-based legislation. Law professors Kent Roach and Craig Forcese thought as much. "The fearful and politicized context in which C-51 was introduced and debated is not conducive to clear thinking or recognition of its long-term and unintended implications," they wrote. What was clearer, though, was who it would target. Roach and Forcese warned that Muslims would pay a disproportionate price for the new laws.

Bill C-51 allowed judges to grant law enforcement the power to violate the Charter of Rights and Freedoms after a secret hearing with only the judge and a government lawyer present. The definition of terrorism was further broadened to include undefined "promotion" of terrorism, not just "facilitation." Attacks against property or essential services, not just against human life, would now be considered terrorism. Hate speech like the promotion of terrorism and attacks against property or essential services were already illegal, but the police who would have investigated those crimes had the constitutional right to a certain independence from the government. CSIS doesn't. By allowing these same crimes to be classified as terrorism, and therefore under the purview of CSIS and not the police, the government would have a much bigger say in how investigations proceeded and against whom Roach and Forcese argued.

The bill dramatically increased security agencies' ability to collect data on Canadians and share that data with foreign agencies. Instead of looking for a needle in a haystack, the government would "collect haystacks," according to Lisa M. Austin, an assistant professor of law at the University of Toronto. In her view, Bill C-51 "authorizes a 'collect it all' philosophy with respect to all personal information held by the government... It goes well beyond the concern that a person or group will be wrongly subjected to increased surveillance. Big Data thrives on bulk collection, and bulk collection is non-targeted, suspicion-less collection. For example, if you want to analyse who is at risk of joining ISIL, it is relevant to examine data on all people who have not joined ISIL."

Again, the government strengthened the agencies' powers but didn't correspondingly strengthen the bodies that would monitor them. The Communications Security Establishment, with the largest operational budget of all intelligence agencies in Canada, was monitored through an annual review by a single retired judge with eleven staff. The judge was empowered only to monitor a selection of their activities and only to ensure those activities were consistent with the Department of Justice's interpretation of the law. Such a review process was utterly toothless. Unsurprisingly, at the time that Bill C-51 was introduced, they had never produced a single finding of non-compliance.

"The language of Bill C-51 is so broad it will almost certainly cast a chill over members of our community," warned executive director of the NCCM Ihsaan Gardee in a meeting of the House of Commons committee studying the bill. Many Muslims in Canada had fled authoritarian regimes where people could be punished harshly for voicing their opinions, he explained. Regardless of what their opinions were, many would likely keep quiet in fear of the new laws. Unfortunately, in national security terms, this could produce the opposite of what was intended. Open communication is essential. De-radicalization requires engaging with at-risk individuals and vigorously debating ideas. "Rather than debating opposing views and risking being associated with tainted individuals, those who could be on the vanguard of de-radicalization will be scared into silence," Gardee said.

In a telling moment, following Gardee's remarks, Conservative MP Diane Ablonczy began attacking the credibility of the NCCM saying that the NCCM's American counterpart had been supportive of Hamas, the Palestinian organization regarded by some Western countries as a terrorist organization. "Mr. Gardee, I'd like to start with you because I think Canadians are hoping that moderate Muslims—and the majority of Muslims in Canada are moderate Muslims—will join and raise their voices against jihadism, jihadi terrorism, because, as you rightly say, that is a real threat here in Canada... I think it's fair to give you an opportunity to address these troubling allegations because in order to work together, there needs to be satisfaction that this can't be a half-hearted battle against terrorism. Where do you stand in light of these allegations?"

By saying that Canadians are "hoping" moderate Muslims will raise their voices against jihadi terrorism, Ablonczy was clearly implying that they hadn't yet. It is a frustration among Muslim communities that no matter how many vigils they hold and no matter how many times they denounce terrorism—terrorism that is abhorrent to their faith and which has killed Muslims worldwide—they are told that Canadians are waiting to hear where they stand. The obstinate ethos behind Ablonczy's question is the same as the one behind Bill C-24 that created two classes of Canadian citizenship: no matter what Muslims say, some Canadians just aren't ready to trust them. Gardee refused to play that game. "The NCCM is not going to submit to a litmus test of loyalty used against Canadian Muslims and their institutions which underlies such offensive questions. We are here today to answer questions about Bill C-51 and the real concerns of Canadians, including Canadian Muslims, about the impact of this far-reaching legislation. McCarthyesque-type questions protected by parliamentary privilege are unbecoming of this committee," he responded.

The broad definition of terrorism leaves gaping holes open to serious abuse. For any identifiable group to be under fire, all it would take would be a few bad apples in law enforcement, or societal or structural biases against that group. It would be worse if there were both.

Names like Mohamed: How We're Unfairly Applying the Law

PROMINENT MUSLIMS AND legal experts warned that the new security regime would have enormous potential for abuse, and that Muslim communities in particular would be at risk of an unfair application of the law. After seeing the security regime created by Bills C-36 and C-51 in operation, many of those critics maintain the belief that Muslims have indeed been unfairly targeted. Lawyer Barbara Jackman compares the present environment to the notorious McCarthy Era in the US when Senator Joseph McCarthy led a witch hunt to root out the communists he believed were hiding under every bed in the nation. "Every Hollywood actor was perceived to be a communist. It's that mentality against Muslims now," she said.

When Alia Hogben of the CCMW was asked for her views on whether Muslims have been unfairly targeted, she was stunned and almost incredulous at the question. "Yes! And I don't think it's a perception. I think it's a reality. Far more Muslims than any other group. Which other group would you think would have been targeted?" she asked rhetorically. Liberal MP Omar Alghabra has heard the same thing from the Muslim communities he's talked to. "There's no doubt in my mind that the Muslim community feels targeted," he said. Many Muslims describe an intense scrutiny that has only grown since 9/11. They describe feeling as though they are under a microscope. For those who are visibly Muslim (or more broadly, for anyone whose skin colour or style of dress leads people to assume they are Muslim), those feelings are even stronger.

Even if it were only a perception that Muslims were being sin-gled out, the mere fact that such a perception existed would be a problem. Multicultural harmony and national unity depend on all segments of society maintaining the faith that they will be treated fairly. If they don't have that faith, law enforcement needs to work toward earning it. Staff Sergeant David Zackrias cites one positive response to the concern: the training now provided to the Ottawa Police Service to help officers overcome implicit biases. Other jurisdictions are taking similar steps. Unfortunately, despite these efforts, there is ample evidence that it's not just a perception, and that Muslims are indeed being singled out for unfair treatment by a variety of security agencies.

The unbearable security certificate process inflicted upon Mohamed Harkat—the process that allows CSIS to arrest non-cit-izens and detain them indefinitely without trial if a judge deems the certificate is "reasonable"—has been used repeatedly against Muslim men. Critics warned that the security certificate system had flaws that left it open for abuse and that in its application, innocent Muslims would likely be targeted. While Harkat's case is still open (Harkat having thus far failed to prove himself innocent beyond a reasonable doubt as the process requires), there are sev-eral other Muslim men who were subjected to the security certifi-cate process who were eventually cleared and released. This raises the question of why they were targeted in the first place.

Hassan Almrei was detained on a security certificate in 2001. At first kept in solitary confinement, he was allowed only five minutes of fresh air per day in an outdoor pen. He began several hunger strikes. It took a special court order for guards to allow him shoes. Supporters sent him books to help him pass the time. Ironically, or perhaps all-too-appropriately, George Orwell's *1984* and Franz Kafka's *The Trial* were confiscated. It took until 2009 for his security certificate to be ruled unreasonable and struck down.

Mahmoud Jaballah, a father of six, was also detained on a sec-urity certificate in 2001. For years, he was unable to embrace his wife and children. His son said he wanted to join his dad in jail so they could play together. In 2016 a judge finally ruled the security certificate was unreasonable. On rabble.ca, journalist Matthew Behrens described how suspicions about Jaballah's religion and ethnicity transformed banal "evidence" against into a sinister portrait of a dangerous man. "In one instance, a CSIS lawyer argued that Jaballah was a terrorist communications relay expert because when he came to Canada, he not only wasted no time in setting up a Bell phone account, but also carried a cell phone with him while his wife was pregnant, 'procured' a fax machine (because Arab Muslims don't simply purchase, they 'procure,' usually with eerie music playing in the background), and started learning to surf the Internet. Readers with such skills: beware, you may be next," Behrens wrote.

Adil Charkaoui, a father of three, was detained on a security certificate in 2003. Two years later he was released with bail conditions stricter than Karla Homolka's. While on bail, he was able to testify in front of a House of Commons committee studying the security certificate process. He passionately illustrated the impossible situation biases had put him in. "According to CSIS, if I integrate myself in Quebec society, I am a sleeper cell. If I don't integrate myself, I am preparing an attack. If I open a business to earn a living, it's to finance illegal activities. If I don't work, then I must be receiving money from hidden sources. Whatever I do, I am guilty," he told them. In 2009 his security certificate was dropped, too.

An access to information request filed in 2013 revealed that in an internal RCMP review about how the security certificate process was unfolding, then-Assistant RCMP Commissioner for National Security Bob Paulson was bluntly critical. He admitted that there wasn't enough evidence against the men being held under security certificates to warrant prosecution. "If we had the threshold belief that we could take criminal action, we would do so," he stated. "As it is being applied now the [security certificate system] is completely off the rails."

Another worthwhile example of prejudicial application of the law was Project Thread, a widely publicized 2003 joint operation between the RCMP and the Department of Citizenship and Immigration. It took seven months to complete and cost over a million dollars. At first, it was heralded as a breakthrough success. Media trumpeted how Canadian investigators had uncovered a possible Canadian al-Qaeda sleeper cell. Two dozen men were taken into custody and kept for several months in a high-security Toronto prison. Interrogators spent hours demanding they reveal the whereabouts of Osama bin Laden.

It turned out the supposed sleeper cell was actually an immigration scam, totally unrelated to terrorist activity. In brief, a bogus business college was granting students documents for money. Of the approximately four hundred individuals who had been involved, only twenty-four men and some of their associates had been targeted for investigation. "I guess we want to know why they only arrested the Muhammads," said one of the men, Muhammad Wali Siddiqui.

The RCMP had to admit they hadn't caught any terrorists. "There is absolutely no evidence to suggest that there is any terrorist threat anywhere in this country related to this investigation," confirmed RCMP Commissioner Giuliano Zaccardelli as Project Thread unwound. Nevertheless, the men had overstayed their visas and were deported. Because of the accusation of links to terrorism, several of the men sent back to Pakistan were interrogated once they got home. The stigma of the accusation, from a respected country like Canada, had the potential to change their lives. Later, some of the men reported decreased job and marriage opportunities and even death threats. An access to information request revealed that the RCMP considered Project Thread to have been "an embarrassment to the Government of Canada," but they never publicly admitted fault.

A more mundane but common example of an unfair application of the law happens every day at the border. Airports and border crossings have become particularly stressful for Muslims, especially for those wearing head or face coverings. They report constant delays and secondary searches while others who don't appear to be Muslim or Arab stream through. Even children have been subjected to the searches. Alia Hogben tells of how Canadian officials have repeatedly conducted special searches on a five-year-old child with a Muslim name, separating him from his parents. In her view, the consequences on the boy are obvious. "And then to say that that child would not grow up and feel discriminated against in Canada?" she asks.

Laya Behbahani, a university lecturer who has been in Canada since age thirteen, described being stopped at the border and interrogated by the Canadian border guard. Having ascertained that she was Canadian, the guard then asked, "How Canadian do you really feel?" The inquisition continued with questions about her religious beliefs. These questions are illegal, and they are not questions non-Muslims ever have to answer at the border. "As Canadian as you feel, when individuals acting in the capacity of the government do things like this, it sends a very loud message that, 'No, you're not one of us,'" Behbahani said.

There have even been suggestions that police, in an effort to get their man, may deliberately take advantage of public hysteria about Muslims and terrorism. In January 2016, a British man with a rare vision impairment came to Canada to get treatment at the Wellspring Clinic for Holistic Medicine in Vancouver. He also wanted to visit a friend, Mohammed Sharaz. At the CF Pacific Centre mall downtown, the two men and Sharaz's son, who is also visually impaired, were spotted taking photographs of mall entrances and exits. That might seem strange, but because of their rare visual impairment, they had to take photos to be able to see the way other people do. As Dr. Weidong Yu of the Wellspring Clinic for Holistic Medicine later explained, they took pictures of everything because they could see things in pictures more clearly than they could by looking at them directly. Entrances and exits just happened to be some of the things they photographed as they found their way around the mall. In a mall frequented by selfie-loving teenagers, it was not the first time that photos had been taken there. This time, mall security phoned the police and an internal bulletin went out to put police on the lookout for three Middle Eastern men.

It was bad enough that police were looking for suspects to charge with "taking photos while being Middle Eastern" but then someone leaked it to the press. Once public, an unjust but comparatively mundane matter of racial profiling had the potential to create mass hysteria. It isn't clear who leaked it, but it does seem clear that the police didn't take steps to prevent the leak. Although the Vancouver Police Department later stated the information was never meant to become public, the journalist who broke the story said that, to be prudent, he had checked in with the police department before running it. According to him, they confirmed the story and didn't ask him not to run it. Had they asked him not to run it, perhaps for fear of hampering an ongoing investigation with unneeded public hysteria, he wouldn't have run it. But no such suggestion was made and the story ran. It wound up being national news, but fortunately the potential mass hysteria never materialized. The men were quickly located, they cooperated, and the investigation concluded that they were completely innocent. Still, the men felt they had to remain inside for the rest of their trip concerned about the potential for vigilantism the press coverage might have provoked.

Part of the reason law enforcement seems to target Muslim communities with an unfair application of the law might be that police are fundamentally disconnected from those communities. That disconnection sometimes results in fishing expeditions. There have been allegations of csis agents going to mosques and offering cash for information. This is problematic police work. Sometimes people who really need the money take it, whether or not they really know anything, resulting in bad intelligence and baseless investigations that can destroy innocent lives. When this kind of thing happens, everyone starts to look guilty. A secret CSIS brief listed growing a beard and adopting traditional dress as warning signs of radicalization. They weren't talking about hipsters.

It might be argued that profiling is justified because while most Muslims in Canada are nonviolent, Muslims are still responsible for a higher number of incidents of violent extremism than any other group in Canada. But that's simply not true. White supremacists hold that title. According to statistics compiled by the Canadian Incident Database (a publicly funded research initiative supported by several Canadian universities), a strong majority—64 percent—of violent extremist attacks carried out in Canada since 2001 have been perpetrated by white supremacists. Pre-9/11 statistics tell a similar story. In other words, it's not even close. In fact, white supremacists have been responsible for more attacks than every other group combined. The number of hate crimes they commit continues to rise.

The far-right hate groups who count those perpetrators as their members are growing. A *Globe and Mail* investigation in 2019 detailed how they use aliases and covert means to communicate over the Internet such as by disguising their chat rooms as video game sites. They are working to infiltrate political parties, both to recruit potential members and to support candidates they believe will support them. Many own illegal weapons and conduct training exercises. They are found in trusted professions including in the educational sector. Frighteningly, a number have even been identified as current and former members of the Canadian Forces.

Surely the dangerous people behind such a significant threat to public safety deserve serious attention from law enforcement, involving prevention, prosecution and de-radicalization. For some reason, when they are caught perpetrating hate crimes, these criminals are dismissed as lone wolves, and aren't treated as part and parcel of a broader security threat the way Muslims are. We continue to waste time being afraid of the wrong things. Incredibly, in 2014 CSIS publicly claimed that far-right hate groups weren't a major security threat, despite the statistics proving otherwise. Although CSIS has since begun to pay closer attention, as of 2019 there are still no far-right groups on Canada's terror watch list. "It's a very strange juxtaposition. You're dealing with two qualitatively similar phenomena that are treated completely differently," James Ellis of the Canadian Network for Research on Terrorism, Security and Society told *The Globe and Mail*. Alia Hogben's incredulity at the question of who has been treated unfairly in the application of the law makes sense. If this isn't unfair, then what is?

* * *

Muslims are not the only group who report being unjustifiably harassed by law enforcement. It is often the experience of Indigenous peoples, black Canadians and others. They can be unfairly subjected to the fullest weight of Canadian law upon the flimsiest evidence, or sometimes, it seems, upon none at all. However, when Muslims actually do appear to have committed or planned acts of terrorism, the reaction from law enforcement, politicians, the media and the public is very different from their reaction when non-Muslims are charged with the same crimes. When the terrorist or attempted terrorist is Muslim, a firestorm of hysteria ensues that dominates the national conversation, way beyond the scale of the actual threat.

In 2006, eighteen Muslims were arrested for a terror plot to attack Parliament Hill and behead Stephen Harper. Their plot was repugnant, but the group's actual capacity to achieve their goal was extremely limited. They were being watched all the time by Mubin Shaikh, an RCMP mole and community leader who'd been paid a large sum of money to report on them. Another RCMP mole helped them get the ammonium nitrate fertilizer they needed for the bomb they were planning to make. They didn't manage to obtain most of the other materials they would need. Shaikh helped organize their preparatory boot camp, a paintball and camping trip, which he later described as a "potty-training exercise." They were in poor shape and regularly left the camp dressed in their battle fatigues to go to Tim Hortons. The degree of involvement from the RCMP in shaping and equipping the plot caused the defence team to raise questions of entrapment. The judge didn't agree, but there was certainly a degree of proactivity on the part of the police that hasn't always been present; for example, in investigations into missing and murdered Indigenous women.

Naturally, anyone plotting to behead Stephen Harper would grab a few headlines, but the trial of the so-called "Toronto 18" was a circus. "From sharpshooters on the roof of the Brampton Court House to frenzied reporters running after women in face veils, the staging of the trial was a bizarre mixture of militarism and carnival. This spectacle militated against any presumption of innocence for those charged," wrote Jasmin Zine in *Omar Khadr, Oh Canada*. The Ontario Human Rights Commission reported a rise in hate incidents targeting Muslims after the arrests were made public. Media referred to the Canadian suspects with the phrases "Canadian-born," "brown-skinned" and "home-grown threat." Referring to Canadians as "Canadian-born" implies that they are not real Canadians, that their Canadianness deserves some sort of asterisk. Not only was their status as genuine Canadians questioned, the variety of ethnicities they represented was conflated as well.

To some, what was really important was to highlight their religion. In *The Globe and Mail*, Christie Blatchford complained that police referred to the accused as coming from a variety of backgrounds. They did come from a variety of backgrounds, but for Blatchford, they were all the same. "The accused men are mostly young and mostly bearded in the Taliban fashion. They have first names like Mohamed, middle names like Mohamed and last names like Mohamed. Some of their female relatives at the Brampton courthouse who were there in their support wore black head-to-toe burkas... which is not a getup I have ever seen on anyone but Muslim women," she wrote. Blatchford pays the bills with aggressive, right-wing commentary, but the bullying tone of this editorial went beyond the pale.

In the end, charges were dropped for several of the participants in the terror plot. For those found guilty, sentences ranged from two-and-a-half years in prison for a youth involved in the plot to seven years to life for the ringleaders. Of course they deserved to be punished. Why is the response from authorities, media and the public so different, though, when the accused terrorist is not a Muslim?

By contrast, nobody called Michael Sandham "Canadian-born" or a "home-grown threat." He was a police officer turned gang member who was charged with the murders of eight people. His crimes occurred around the same time that the eighteen men were clumsily traipsing through the woods in battle fatigues. No one referred to "light-skinned, Canadian-born" Randall Shepherd or "Asian-American" Lindsay Souvannarath when they were arrested in 2015 for a plot to murder civilians at a Halifax shopping mall. Their planned crime was as odious as the planned attack on Harper. Shepherd, Souvannarath and a third suspect, James Gamble, who killed himself before he could be arrested, had planned to shoot and kill as many people as possible in the mall on Valentine's Day. They even intended to use Molotov cocktails to maximize the death toll. In general, the response from politicians, media and police couldn't have been more different from their response to the disrupted Toronto 18 plot. "The attack does not appear to have been culturally motivated, therefore not linked to terrorism," stated Conservative justice minister Peter MacKay, who also referred to the trio as "murderous misfits." MacKay's interest in whether the plot was "culturally" motivated is curious. Recall that the definition of terrorism focuses on religious, political or ideological motives, not cultural ones. One wonders what culture MacKay might have believed motivates terrorism. In the *Toronto Star*, Thomas Walkom noted the seemingly arbitrary determination that the case didn't constitute terrorism. "Had police found Islamic State propaganda on their computers, Souvannarath and Shepherd almost certainly would have been charged with terrorism. But social media sites said to belong to the suspects show an interest only in Nazis and violence. That, it seems, is insufficiently ideological to merit a terror charge," he wrote. Why committing violence inspired by Daesh counts as ideological, while violence inspired by Adolf Hitler just makes you a murderous misfit, is anyone's guess.

At first the RCMP didn't publicly name Shepherd and Souvannarath, the two surviving suspects, to deprive them of the fame and notoriety the police believed they craved. The *National Post* decried the police's decision as an unfair dehumanizing of the defendants. Naming them would help them maintain the public's presumption of their innocence and protect their rights, reasoned the paper. "People without names or faces are easier to throw into a cell forever and forget about," wrote Joseph Brean. Ironically, the paper was not famous for such passionate defense of the rights of prisoners in Guantanamo Bay.

There was no circus this time. The story quickly faded from the news. Two months after the arrests, *Maclean's* published a feature called "Six Stories in Canada We're Watching." Those stories included one about Prime Minister Harper attending the Summit of the Americas in Panama, and another about whether it was safe to take medication after the best-before date. The Halifax plot wasn't one of them. Instead, a reference to Shepherd and Souvannarath appearing in court was placed under the header "Also in the News Today," above a note that the Royal Bank was holding its annual general meeting in Toronto. No laws were changed as a result of the plot. No Christian churches were vandalized. The names Shepherd and Souvannarath have never been uttered in the House of Commons.

There are other examples of a stark contrast in the way we react to Muslims and non-Muslims when they commit similar crimes.

Consider the October 22, 2014 attack on Parliament Hill. Michael Zehaf-Bibeau was a misfit. He was a crack user. He once tried to rob a McDonald's with a pointed stick. He likely suffered from a mental illness. Before his attack in Ottawa, he had reached out to his mother for the first time in five years. She offered him a place to stay, but he wound up in a homeless shelter instead. He might have become attracted to violent extremism and committed a terrible crime, but in some ways, Zehaf-Bibeau was a man society failed. When he shot and killed a ceremonial guard and stormed Centre Block, he was hit by thirty-one bullets within seven seconds of entering the building. Then his corpse was handcuffed.

The government responded with Bill C-51, anti-terror legislation so sweeping that Green Party leader Elizabeth May called it the most dangerous thing she'd seen in a democracy. Parliamentary security was revamped and RCMP officers began to carry submachine guns on the Hill. The story dominated front pages. Mosques in Ontario and Alberta were vandalized. For Stephen Harper, it was his moment to emulate Winston Churchill's famous resolve: "We will not be intimidated. Canada will never be intimidated. In fact, this will lead us to strengthen our resolve and redouble our efforts and those of our national security agencies to take all necessary steps to identify and counter threats and keep Canada safe here at home, just as it will lead us to strengthen our resolve and redouble our efforts to work with our allies around the world and fight against the terrorist organizations who brutalize those in other countries with the hope of bringing their savagery to our shores. They will have no safe haven," Harper intoned.

Contrast that reaction with what happened in Moncton just four months before Zehaf-Bibeau's attack. Twenty-four-year-old Justin Bourque armed himself heavily and went hunting for police officers. His social media profile revealed an extreme ideologue: he was a libertarian who believed the Canadian government was an oppressive force that needed to be violently resisted. "Don't worry, I'm not out to kill civilians. I'm after government officials," one witness reported hearing Bourque say. It was meant to be a direct attack on our institutions and way of life. Bourque killed three RCMP officers and wounded two others. He would be sentenced to life in prison without the chance of parole for seventy-five years, but in general the response from Canadian society was markedly different from what happened after the Ottawa attacks. Harper's brief statement of condolences after the murders of the RCMP officers made no mention of terrorism.

When deadly Daesh attacks occurred in Paris in 2015, the University of Toronto Press published a compilation of essays by leading academics called *After the Paris Attacks: Responses in Canada, Europe, and around the Globe.* In it, University of Toronto law professor Mohammed Fadel pointed out that the university hadn't put together a book called "After Breivik" in response to the murders committed by terrorist and Nazi-sympathizer Anders Breivik in his war against Islam in Europe. In comparison to the non-stop coverage of the Paris attacks, Breivik's case barely made a ripple in Canada. This hypocrisy isn't uniquely Canadian; rather, it seems a constant in the Western world. Stephen J. Toope, director of the Munk School of Global Affairs at the University of Toronto, noted the inconsistency in the global response to terrorism. "Why was this attack not linked to attacks on immigrants in Europe, prompting soul-searching over a new era of right-wing violence? Or as journalist Mark Steel argued in the *Independent*, why were there no calls for Christian clerics to denounce violence, or to apologize for Breivik's actions, yet a different set of expectations seems to be in place when Muslims commit terrorist acts?"

* * *

The perception that Muslims are being singled out by Canada's security agencies is supported by compelling evidence. Unequal, hypocritical treatment exists in the public realm, too. By treating all Muslims as potential suspects and then broadcasting their

Muslimness in a wild overreaction when a legitimate Muslim suspect is arrested, we are tainting all with the crimes of a few. No one deserves this. Muslims in Canada deserve to feel what non-Muslim Canadians feel when they hear of a vicious crime or a foiled plot committed by someone who looks like them: abhorred by the crime but knowing that the crime reflects upon the perpetrator alone. Any other thought process should never have to occur.

O Canada: Breaking the Law

OUR CURRENT SECURITY laws leave ample opportunities for abuse, and the application of those laws has disproportionately targeted Muslims. Perhaps worst of all, several shocking episodes demonstrate why some Muslims in Canada fear they can't even count on the rule of law itself. For example, there is a process in the US known as "extraordinary rendition." It may be most familiar to Canadians as the plot of a Hollywood movie, but it is very real. Former CIA agent Robert Baer explained the process to the *Guardian*: "We pick up a suspect, or we arrange for one of our partner countries to do it. Then the suspect is placed on civilian transport to a third country where, let's make no bones about it, they use torture. If you want a good interrogation, you send someone to Jordan. If you want them to be killed, you send them to Egypt or Syria," he said. In Canada, extraordinary rendition is illegal. There should be no question of it ever happening to any Canadian. That doesn't mean it hasn't.

The idea of torture conjures images of medieval torments like the rack or the iron maiden. Many modern tortures are less exotic, though no less insidious. Waterboarding, for example, requires only three things: a bucket of water, a cloth and a victim. The different ways that mankind has invented to cause pain are unlimited. The Convention against Torture and Other Cruel, Inhuman or Degrading Treatment or Punishment (commonly known as the United Nations Convention against Torture), which Canada has signed, defines torture as any severe mental or physical pain inflicted at the instigation of a public official to get information or a confession. It's a deliberately broad definition meant to cover even the most creative torturers. In other words, if something seems like torture, it probably is.

Jean Amery, a Second World War torture survivor, has written that being tortured by the Gestapo changed his view of mankind forever and stole from him his trust in the world. "Torture has taught him that a person can be transformed thoroughly into flesh," wrote Kim Echlin in *Omar Khadr, Oh Canada*. None of Amery's personal attributes—his skills or even his intrinsic value as a human being—were recognized by his torturers. The psychological effects may have been the worst. Unlike physical wounds, the psychological wounds from torture don't heal with time. Decades later, Amery never stopped feeling that, in present tense, he was still dangling above the ground with dislocated arms, helpless before his tormentors.

Apart from the fundamental inhumanity of torture, there's another reason it's a horrendous practice. Despite what US President Donald Trump has insinuated, torture doesn't work. Innocent or guilty, when someone is tortured, they will say anything. Eventually, they will say whatever the interrogator wants them to. The result is bad intelligence. "What torture has proven is exactly what experienced interrogators have said all along: first, when tortured, detainees will give only the minimum amount of information necessary to stop the pain. No interrogator should ever be hoping to extract the least amount of information. Second, under coercion, detainees give misleading information that wastes time and resources—a false nickname, for example," wrote Matthew Alexander in *Foreign Policy Review*. Furthermore, once an interrogation crosses the line and becomes torture, the interrogator can't go back, even if it becomes clear the target doesn't have any relevant information. To protect their own reputation, the interrogator then needs a confession, and any confession will do. "Otherwise," wrote author David Keen, "you are left torturing an innocent person."

As signatories to the UN convention, Canada is not only forbidden from committing torture, but also from causing it to happen, either directly or indirectly. We can't ask someone else to do it for us; we can't pretend we don't know someone else is doing it for us; and we can't just wag our finger when we find out someone's been doing it for us but accept the intelligence they provide anyway. Crucially, according to the convention, Canada is bound to take steps to actively prevent torture from happening. It's a responsibility we have seen Canada take extremely seriously to protect Canadian citizens, particularly those detained in countries with questionable human rights records. It is just one of the reasons Canadian citizenship is so cherished: Canada will go to bat for you.

However, some Muslim Canadians have concluded there is a difference between what Canadian citizenship legally entitles them to and what it might offer in reality.

Is that a fair assessment? In the real world, does citizenship entitle some Canadians to more rights than others? Although the UN convention compels signatory governments to act, it doesn't provide rules detailing what exactly the government must do to help a citizen detained abroad and at risk of mistreatment. No Canadian laws define what to do either. That's fair enough; each situation is unique. It means the only way to evaluate accusations of bias is to look at past practice.

A high-profile 2008 case offers a good example of Canada's standard practice. Brenda Martin, a Canadian working illegally in Mexico and alleged to be part of a money-laundering scheme, was arrested by Mexican police and sentenced to five years in jail. The prime minister of Canada phoned the president of Mexico. The foreign affairs minister met with his Mexican counterpart. The secretary of state for multiculturalism flew to Mexico to meet with Martin in prison. Nine days after her conviction in Mexico, she was on a chartered jet back to Canada. Nine days after that, she was on full parole. It's what many Canadians firmly believe their government would do for them if they were caught in an unfortunate situation abroad. However, as a pattern of cases involving

Canadian Muslim men shows, not every Canadian can count on such support.

In examining these cases, two issues are at play. Firstly, Canadian law-enforcement agencies have shared false evidence with foreign-security agencies, seemingly knowing it could result in the torture of Canadian citizens. Secondly, once the government knew or should have known that Canadians were being tortured, they either dragged their heels in seeking repatriation or assisted with the interrogations, thereby becoming complicit in the torture. Both are violations of Canada's responsibilities under the UN convention. Kerry Pither's *Dark Days: The Story of Four Canadians Tortured in the Name of Fighting Terror* is an outstanding chronicle of four of these cases. It is worth considering their stories in the context of an unchecked security regime operating in an environment of public hysteria and political scapegoating.

On September 22, 2001, suspecting that what had happened on 9/11 was about to repeat, overworked CSIS agents shared mountains of files with the RCMP and asked for their help. Two days later RCMP officers launched what they called Project O Canada. They were ill-prepared for the task. It had been nearly twenty years since the RCMP had been in charge of national security. In 1970, Canadians were shaken to the core by the October Crisis, in which members of the Front de libération du Québec kidnapped and murdered Quebec politician Pierre Laporte. In response, the RCMP determined that they had to do whatever it would take to prevent something like that from happening again. Apparently there were a lot of lines they were willing to cross: break-ins, theft, forgery, mail opening, and once even burning down a barn. By the end of the decade, these allegations had become an embarrassment, and Pierre Trudeau's Liberal government established CSIS to take over the RCMP's national security responsibilities.

As a result, the RCMP officers tasked with helping CSIS in 2001 had little to no experience in national security investigations. With Project O Canada, once again the RCMP seemed willing to do whatever it took. When they crossed lines this time, there were devastating consequences for real human lives. "Security officials engaged in their own game of 'six degrees of separation,' zealously connecting real and imaginary dots, and ensnaring anyone who fit the preconceived profile of an al-Qaeda wannabe. Acknowledging lack of evidence to convict any of their suspects, they went on to 'disrupt and diffuse' the so-called threat by means that at times circumvented the law," wrote Sheema Khan in *The Globe and Mail.*

An early target of Project O Canada was Ahmad El-Maati. Once a mujahid fighting the Soviets in Afghanistan, he became a Canadian citizen in 1986. In the summer of 2001, he was working as a long-haul truck driver making a cross-border delivery to the US. Since his regular truck was being repaired, he had to use an alternate. Left in the truck with someone else's reading glasses as an old map of Ottawa meant for deliveries. It was an outdated map that included the Atomic Energy of Canada building and virus-control labs that no longer existed. He also had an airline boarding pass with him from a recent trip to see family in Syria. Apparently, that was enough to make the American border guards suspicious. El-Maati was detained by an armed guard and photographed against a wall holding a numbered plate to his chest. After eight hours of interrogations and insults, he was allowed through. He was told they'd be keeping an eye on him and that future crossings wouldn't be any easier. Distressed, El-Maati described the incident to his supervisor, who gave him a letter he could use if detained upon future crossings. Eventually the stress he felt every time he approached the border grew too much, and he quit to take a job making only local deliveries.

He should have been allowed to leave that distressing incident behind him, but hours after the 9/11 attacks, CSIS agents knocked on his apartment door. They asked again about the map of Ottawa. After El-Maati said he wanted a lawyer, the agents made a not-so-subtle allusion to extraordinary rendition. "You know that we are called Mukhabarat," one agent allegedly said, referring to the

Syrian intelligence agency. "You know how the Mukhabarat in Canada deals with citizens, and you know how the Mukhabarat deals with their citizens over there." The implication was that if CSIS didn't get what they wanted from El-Maati, perhaps Syrian intelligence would be given the opportunity to try, and they wouldn't be as gentle.

From then on, El-Maati was subjected to constant surveillance. Meanwhile, the map story made it into the news. On October 15, 2001 the *National Post* ran a story with the alarming headline "Terrorists Eye Nuclear Plants, Expert Says: 'Ample Evidence': Kuwaiti Man Had Sensitive Documents on N-plant, Virus Lab." The article began, "Terrorists are clearly gathering information for their next move..." It was a fearful time. That very morning, the Liberals introduced Bill C-36, their anti-terror legislation, in the House of Commons.

In November, El-Maati travelled to Syria to get married. It should have been a happy occasion, but the veiled threat allegedly made by CSIS came true. Upon arriving in Damascus, El-Maati was escorted outside the airport and shoved in a car with a hood thrown over his head. He was taken to a small cell barely taller and wider than him and only seven feet deep. It smelled of human waste. "Your name is number five now," a guard said.

For the next months, El-Maati would be subjected to brutal torture. He would be stripped and whipped with a metal cable. When he passed out from the pain, his captors would dump ice water on him to revive him. Many of the questions he was asked indicated his Syrian interrogators had intimate knowledge of his Canadian activities. "We need to hear something new," the interrogators said. "You can invent something." Eventually they drafted a confession for him, which he wasn't allowed to read. He refused to sign it. They burned cigarettes on his shins and told him his eyes would be next.

Later an official inquiry concluded it was most likely that the RCMP had provided information on El-Maati to the US, who had in turn provided it to Syria, leading to El-Maati's detention. No one had forced El-Maati to go to Syria; however, Canadian authorities should have known that information shared with the US might end up in Syrian hands, and that this could put El-Maati in danger. The implicit threat made by CSIS agents about the Mukhabarat seems to indicate that they knew it all too well. But even if no one working for the Canadian government said anything about the Mukhabarat to El-Maati, they should have known there could be consequences for sharing information with the US. The American practice of torture-by-proxy has long been suspected.

In 2002, El-Maati was transferred from Syria to Egypt. The US State Department has identified Egypt as a country that uses torture. El-Maati was blindfolded at all times, even in his cell. His hands were handcuffed behind him for all but ten minutes a day when they would be cuffed in front so he could relieve himself and eat. Sometimes it took so long to get his arms moving again that he wouldn't have time to do what he needed to do before he was returned to his cell, his hands cuffed behind his back again. "If I lay on my stomach, I couldn't breathe. If I lay on my side, it hurt my shoulders, and I couldn't lie on my back because the hand-cuffs were eating my hands, which were bleeding and infected. So I couldn't sleep, which is what broke me down to pieces," he told Kerry Pither. Eventually, they even electrocuted him. Any Canadian in that situation would wonder what their country was doing to get them out. One of the guards told him that Canada was feeding them questions.

On July 18, 2002, RCMP National Security Investigations Branch Superintendent Wayne Pilgrim sent a memo to Commissioner Giuliano Zaccardelli noting that El-Maati may have been subject to "extreme treatment" in Egypt. There is no evidence on the public record of what action, if any, the RCMP took next. The Department of Foreign Affairs requested consular access and asked that the RCMP be allowed access as well. "We didn't know any of the background at this point. We didn't know that the RCMP were the ones that were probably instrumental in making sure that the poor bugger ended up in this situation," former Foreign Affairs diplomat Gar Pardy told Pither. In August, nine months after El-Maati's arrest, consular access was granted. He told embassy staff he had been tortured, and they appeared to be surprised. They asked if he'd be willing to speak with Canadian intelligence agents, and he said he would, but only in Canada.

Allegations of the torture of a Canadian in a country known for human rights abuses should have caused concern at the highest levels of the Canadian government. The day after the meeting with the embassy staff, though, the government's focus didn't seem to be on helping El-Maati. Instead, the team investigating him held a meeting described as "a proactive measure to discuss media lines." CSIS and Foreign Affairs told El-Maati's family in Canada not to talk to the press. Meanwhile, an anonymous source in the government got El-Maati's name into the public domain, but he was cast as a suspected al-Qaeda terrorist.

It was a dirty trick for the government to play, but a common one. Naturally, journalists and political operatives have relationships with each other. They are often on a first-name basis, and sometimes they even hang out socially. Leaks play an important, if sometimes sordid, role in how politics is done. Sometimes information is leaked by accident. Sometimes damaging information is leaked by a disgruntled employee or a virtuous whistleblower. Sometimes information will be strategically leaked to earn goodwill and more favourable coverage from a journalist. Anonymous or secret information might be leaked because it's tougher for a journalist to corroborate. Officially no one's talking. But if the journalist takes the bait and reports it, even with caveats, the perception is out there. In El-Maati's case, it would be much more difficult to generate sympathy for him if the family decided to go public since there would already be a perception of El-Maati as a terrorist. It could be overcome, but first impressions are powerful and El-Maati would have to be on the defensive.

In Canada, law enforcement harassed El-Maati's family, including asking them questions about how religious they were. In Egypt, despite the attention from consular officials, El-Maati remained in prison and the torture continued. One day, while shocking El-Maati in the genitals with an electric rod, the interrogators asked him about his will. This may be the clearest indication that Canada was still cooperating with his detention; the RCMP had only found the will while raiding El-Maati's father's house while El-Maati was already in captivity.

On January 14, 2004, more than two years after he had been arrested, he was released. Intimidated by Syrian intelligence, his intended spouse Rola had voided their marriage agreement. He returned to Canada alone. He needed seven surgeries so he could walk properly, and even so, walking for anything longer than a block requires a rest. His left leg goes numb if he stands for more than five minutes. He is plagued by post-traumatic stress and still feels as if he is being followed. One wonders what might have happened had he used a different truck on that fateful day in 2001. "The future he'd imagined for himself back then—a simple life with Rola, children and steady work—bears no resemblance to the shattered existence he struggles through today," wrote Pither.

Information was shared without regard to how it might be used, security agencies and consular officials did not appear to be working together, and anonymous leaks to the press were used to spread suspicion. Worse, it wasn't just a one-off miscarriage of justice, a tragic story of one man who fell through the cracks. It was more like a playbook. The pattern established in El-Maati's case would, with variations, be repeated with other Muslim men.

To assist Project O Canada, regional teams were developed. In Ottawa, a subdivision of the project called Project A-O Canada investigated Abdullah Almalki, an electrical engineer the RCMP suspected of selling computer equipment that, through intermediaries, wound up in the hands of terrorists. (Eventually journalists, and not the RCMP, would discover that one of the intermediaries receiving products from Almalki was the Pakistani military, which was also the recipient of American aid money to fight terrorism. If Almalki was a terrorist on that basis, so was the US government.) Like Project O Canada, Project A-O Canada was managed by staff who had little to no training or experience in national security investigations. The RCMP put Michel Cabana in charge and instructed him to share any and all necessary information with the FBI or CIA. At the time getting evidence that could be used in a court of law wasn't the focus. "Right now, the priority is not to accumulate the information in an admissible format; the priority is to make sure that nothing blows up," Cabana would later recall of the thinking at the time. That kind of approach makes great TV, but the rule of law requires a little more discipline. It's the rule of law that protects us from miscarriages of justice, but it did not protect Almalki.

Like El-Maati, Almalki and his family were placed under surveillance. Almalki told Kerry Pither that the surveillance was so obvious it seemed as if the security agents wanted to be seen. Tired of the harassment, the family decided to take a break from Canada and visit Almalki's wife's family in Malaysia. Almalki expected delays at the border, so to make it easier on his family he travelled separately. There were no delays. In retrospect, he wondered if what the agents had wanted all along was for Almalki to leave the country.

After he left, his family and friends in Canada were questioned at length. They were told security agencies had a chart of al-Qaeda leadership showing Almalki's name at the top. They didn't believe it but felt they had no choice but to answer the intrusive questions. "We were all scared. There was this new terrorism bill where you could be taken away for no reason. I mean, when I went down and was interviewed [by law enforcement], my lawyer said, 'If it wasn't for this bill, I wouldn't even let him talk to you guys,'" Youssef Almalki, Abdullah's brother, told Kerry Pither.

What Almalki's family and friends experienced was Bill C-36 in action. Recall that the Liberals' legislative response to the 9/11 attacks had not only broadened what might be considered facilitating terrorism but had also enhanced security agencies' powers to arrest and detain suspects without warrants or charges. Previously, Almalki's family might have been able to accuse their interrogators of harassment; now they had to cooperate or risk being put in jail. Lawyer Rocco Galati and other experts had cautioned MPs debating the bill that they were naïve to think that law enforcement wouldn't use their new powers to target Muslims, but the warning was ignored. It was precisely this scenario Galati and others had envisioned.

Meanwhile Almalki left Malaysia to visit his ailing grandmother in Damascus. When he arrived at the airport in Syria, he was immediately taken to prison, and the interrogations began. After his first answer, he was slapped. "Abdullah's whole world shifted at that moment. For the first time in his adult life, he had no control. His skills, his confidence, his upbringing couldn't help him now. There was no negotiating with these people. This was a totally different world," wrote Pither. Like El-Maati, he was beaten and whipped with metal cables. They made him run on the spot periodically to keep the blood flowing through his numbing body to make sure he'd keep feeling the pain.

Certain questions relied upon information that could only have come from Canada, such as the corporate names Almalki had applied to register through Industry Canada. One interrogator told him directly that they were keeping him in custody at Canada's behest. On June 21, 2002, there was a meeting at RCMP headquarters to discuss Almalki. Corporal Rick Flewelling's notes suggested the RCMP took great interest in Almalki's ongoing interrogation. "We may have to take and be satisfied with the prevention side of the mandate and hope additional information can be gleaned with respect to his plan, other plans we are not aware of, other individuals or groups, etc.," he wrote. What Flewelling meant by "the prevention side of the mandate" was his organization's mission to stop terrorist attacks from happening, whether or not they had any evidence that would be admissible in a court of law. In other words, the mandate to arrest credible suspects with evidence that would be enough to convict them in a Canadian court, would not be fulfilled. In the meantime, they might get some intelligence out of Syria—no matter what Syria had to do to get it.

On July 4, 2002, the RCMP's liaison officer for the Middle East, Steve Covey, met with Syrian intelligence to discuss Almalki. Canada's Ambassador to Syria, Franco Pillarella, set up the meeting but he didn't advise the branch of Foreign Affairs meant to help Canadians detained abroad. As a result, only law enforcement attended from the Canadian side, so there was no one present to intercede on Almalki's behalf. It was the first of several questionable decisions Pillarella would make. After the meeting, Covey returned to Canada and told Cabana that in his view, Almalki would never be released.

Foreign security agencies can't just snatch up Canadians without charges and keep them forever. But on September 10, 2002, Cabana sent a fax to a colleague which read, "We would request that you approach your Syrian contact to see if they will grant us access to conduct our own interview of this individual. The Syrians have been most cooperative with our earlier requests and we are hoping that our requests will be met with favourable review. In the alternative, we are contemplating providing the Syrian officials with questions for ALMALKI... I propose that the Syrians be approached and advised that we would like to extend an invitation for their investigators to come to Canada and meet with our team to share information of common interest." Clearly, the two security agencies—Syrian and Canadian—were fully cooperating.

Simultaneously, though, there was an active effort to rescue Almalki from the barbaric conditions in which he was being held. The bureaucracy wasn't getting it done, so Almalki's family got a few Canadian MPs involved, and they put on the pressure. This can be a smart tactic. Backbench MPs, whether from the opposition or the government, are more unfettered than cabinet ministers in terms of what they can say, where they can look, and how hard they can push. They don't have to temper their actions because of broader geo-political concerns the way a head of state, for example, might have to. Because of their confidence that no one would harm an MP from a rich and powerful country like Canada, backbenchers are hard to intimidate, even in rougher parts of the world. They can threaten to disrupt diplomatic relationships and trade. This can make them powerful advocates.

For Syrian officials, dealing with the Canadian MPs must have been a frustrating experience. "First you tell us to detain people. Then you criticize us for detaining them and ask us to release them. Then, when we release them, we get criticized for mistreating them," Syrian President Bashar al-Assad reportedly once privately told a delegation of visiting Canadian parliamentarians. Perhaps to save face, Syrian officials gave Almalki a trial and acquitted him. After nearly two years in prison, Almalki was released, but was told by Syrian officials that he had to remain in Syria for a year. Curiously, he was also told that he had defaulted on his compulsory military service, and he was given two days to resolve the issue. Liberal MP Dan McTeague, who'd been a key figure in pressuring Syria to release him, sent word to Almalki that he should to go straight to the Canadian Embassy and stay there. When he got there, he was told that McTeague had no authority over the embassy. When the embassy closed at the end of the day, he'd have to leave. He called their bluff and waited in the reception area. They weren't bluffing. When the embassy closed, he was shown the door. He spent the night at a friend's. The next morning, his friend had a thought: what if, by giving him two days to resolve the issue of his military service, the judge was subtly giving Almalki the opportunity to leave the country?

He tried it and it worked. He got through the border easily and was finally reunited with his wife and children. Unfortunately, he brought his psychological wounds with him. "He had a lot of nightmares. He talked in his sleep, and almost every night the pillow and sheet covers were wet from his sweat. I used to put a dry towel on them. While sleeping he made strange sounds and used to get up in his sleep and look at the door or point to it," his wife, Khuzaimah, told Kerry Pither. To Pither, Almalki recalled how as a child he learned about work by watching his dad and uncle, and lamented that his children were learning very different things from what he was modelling. "My kids do not have this. Now they're learning what? They're learning about torture. They're learning about a father who is broken."

* * *

The Charter of Rights and Freedoms protects Canadians from guilt by association, or at least it's supposed to. One fall day in 2001, months before his arrest, Abdullah Almalki went to lunch with a casual acquaintance he'd known since high school. At the time he didn't know he was a person of interest to Project A-O Canada and was being followed. The man he met was Maher Arar. The punishment Arar would endure for meeting Almalki that day will likely stay with him for the rest of his life.

Arar lived in Ottawa and worked as a telecommunications engineer. Born in Syria, he'd been in Canada since 1987. After meeting Almalki for lunch, Arar became a person of interest to Project A-O Canada, too. After a few weeks of investigating Arar and his wife, Monia Mazigh, the RCMP didn't find any evidence linking the couple to terror, but they asked Canadian and American customs officials to look out for them anyway, saying they were suspected of al-Qaeda links. Officials attempted to question Arar but backed off when he, reasonably enough, said he wanted a lawyer present.

Meanwhile, at Bagram Air Base, a US military installation in Afghanistan, a crucial piece of "evidence" against Arar emerged. Following a firefight between US soldiers and suspected al-Qaeda militants, US soldiers brought a badly injured fifteen-year-old boy they'd captured to the base for interrogation. The boy's name was Omar Khadr, a Canadian citizen and son of an alleged al-Qaeda financier. Expecting Khadr to be a treasure trove of intelligence, the US kept him behind bars in brutal conditions. His story is detailed in the next chapter, but there is one small, sinister intersection with Arar's story, an unfortunate coincidence which, like his lunch with Almalki, would seal Arar's fate.

In Bagram with no lawyers present, US military interrogators went to work on Khadr. Although he was injured and a minor, he was subjected to dozens of interrogations, put in stress positions which would aggravate his injuries and even threatened with dogs. Eventually interrogators showed him a photo of Arar. At first Khadr said he didn't recognize him. After further interrogation, he said he might have seen Arar in Afghanistan. Surveillance records would later prove Arar hadn't been in Afghanistan at the time in question, but the Americans felt they had the evidence they needed. Khadr went back to his cell, and the interrogators passed on what they'd learned to investigators back home.

In June 2002, Arar and his family visited Mazigh's father in Tunisia. Arar had to return to work so he left Tunisia earlier than the others. On a stopover in New York City, he was pulled aside. There is no doubt that Canadian officials were involved in what happened next. The RCMP knew he was going to be questioned by the Americans because the FBI had told them. The FBI asked if Project A-O Canada had any questions they wanted asked, and the RCMP faxed some over. They also provided a package of information with no caveats about how it could be used or who else could see it. In the package, they claimed Arar had refused to be interviewed (he had agreed, but he had insisted upon his right to have a lawyer present); they suggested he had fled the country after refusing to be interviewed (he had left Canada five months later); and they claimed he'd been in Washington, DC on September 11, 2001 (he was in San Diego on a business trip). "The problem was they acted on stereotyping," lawyer Barbara Jackman says. "They sent off information without knowing whether it was true or not, based on assumptions or presumptions [about] the Muslim community."

In New York, Arar was questioned, forced to sign something without reading it and given an injection without being told what it was. On the sixth day of questioning, he was finally allowed a phone call. On the eighth day, a Canadian consular official visited and told him that because he was a Canadian, they were confident he wouldn't be deported to Syria. That was likely of some comfort. Meanwhile the CIA got in contact with Project A-O Canada. Once again, the RCMP dutifully handed over their files to the CIA, just as they had to the FBI. (For the first time, though, they admitted that they had not yet proven a link between Arar and al-Qaeda. This time they also asked that the information not be acted upon without their consent).

Unlike the FBI, the CIA's area of focus is outside the US. Their sudden involvement in the case should have been a red flag to the RCMP that Arar would soon be on the move. On the tenth day of Arar's detention, an FBI agent called Project A-O Canada's Corporal Rick Flewelling. The agent explained that the FBI didn't have the evidence they needed to charge Arar with anything and asked if the RCMP could charge him if he was returned to Canada. Flewelling said no. The agent then asked if Canada could legally deny Arar entry. Again, Flewelling said no. Reading between the lines, unless the US was willing to let Arar go, the Americans were left with one option: extraordinary rendition.

Canadian consular officials might have believed Arar would be returned to Canada. Flewelling later said the idea that the US might deport Arar to Syria never occurred to him, and he'd never even heard of extraordinary rendition. Not everyone on the Canadian side was so naive. Some knew full well what has about to happen. On October 10, CSIS deputy director Jack Hooper wrote a memo stating, "I think the US would like to get Arar to Jordan where they can have their way with him." That is damning evidence, proving that some Canadian officials were pretty sure what would happen to Arar, and those who didn't know, should or could have known. We must assume the RCMP didn't know they were working with faulty intelligence. We must assume they genuinely believed that Arar was somehow linked to terrorism. Clearly, though, the risk of sharing information with the US was that it could be used to violate Arar's human rights. "They should never have sent the information," says Jackman when it was so obvious that it could put Arar at risk. "I think they either knew, or they didn't care, which is the same thing."

Arar was indeed deported from the US to Jordan, driven across the border to Syria and thrown in a cell. The next day he was whipped with a metal cable. They hadn't even begun asking him questions. When they did, he agreed to everything, just to stop the torture. But it didn't stop.

Back in Canada, Monia Mazigh managed to get high-level attention for her husband's case. But what followed was a pattern of various Canadian officials seemingly working at cross-purposes. foreign affairs minister Bill Graham was furious, not only with the Americans, but also with Canadian officials who couldn't seem to give a straight answer about their involvement. Asked today, he recalls getting more information by sharing a whiskey with American Ambassador Paul Cellucci than by asking Canadian security agencies. At the same time, CSIS was also holding meetings about Arar. They determined that he probably wasn't being tortured in Syria because if he had been, more damning evidence would have come out of the interrogations. That attitude betrays what CSIS believed about torture: that it would work.

On October 22, 2002, Canada negotiated consular access. Arar was cleaned, shaved and warned by guards not to talk about what was happening in the prison. At the meeting, the Canadian consular official told Arar that dual citizens needed to be careful when travelling and referred him to a Department of Foreign Affairs publication with tips for dual citizens. This wasn't very helpful, but at least it didn't make anything worse. On the other hand, Canadian Ambassador Franco Pillarella handed Syrian intelligence a list of questions the RCMP wanted answered.

On Parliament Hill, Stephen Harper's Canadian Alliance took Arar's guilt for granted and used him as a political football. MP Diane Ablonczy recast what were simply allegations against Arar as cold, hard facts. "Mr. Speaker, it is time the Liberals told the truth: that their system of screening and security checks is pathetic. Arar was given dual Syrian and Canadian citizenship by the government. It did not pick up on his terrorist links, and the US had to clue it in. How is it that the US could uncover this man's background so quickly when the government's screening system failed to find his al-Qaeda links?" she asked. Harper accused Graham of taking part in "high-level consultations to defend a suspected terrorist," as though there was something dishonourable about providing suspects with a defense. In response, the Liberals could have vigorously defended Arar's right to be considered innocent until proven guilty, but they did not. Instead, they went into damage control to bury a perception that they were soft on security matters. "Mr. Speaker, if honourable members on the opposite side would listen, I want to make it very clear that we are on top of our game in terms of international security. The RCMP and CSIS are very much on top of their game in ensuring that we are protecting Canadian citizens against terrorism," insisted Solicitor General Wayne Easter, the minister responsible for the RCMP.

In April 2003 Liberal MPs Marlene Catterall and Sarkis Assadourian presented Syrian intelligence with a letter from Bill Graham stating that the Canadian government wouldn't impede Arar's return to Canada. This decidedly weak language was the strongest the government was prepared to use. Nevertheless, Arar's supporters hoped the weight of a letter from a minister of the Crown would get Arar freed. They had hoped to get Solicitor General Wayne Easter to sign Graham's letter, too. However,

Canada still wasn't speaking with one voice. Easter refused to sign. The battle between bureaucrats continued. On June 24, Jim Gould, deputy director of Foreign Affairs' little-known intelligence section, wrote a memo stating, "csis has made it clear to the Department that they would prefer to have [Arar] remain in Syria, rather than return to Canada. csis officials do not seem to understand that, guilty or innocent, Maher Arar has the right to consular assistance from the Department and that in the circumstances in which he presently finds himself, the best outcome might be his return to Canada." Franco Pillarella, meanwhile, kept insisting that Arar wasn't being tortured. He wrote in an email that a planned meeting with Syrian intelligence would, "help us rebut the recent charges of torture." A later inquiry would note that Pillarella seemed more interested in disproving allegations of torture than protecting Arar.

Bill Graham finally threatened Syrian officials that bilateral relations and Canadian investment in Syria would be jeopardized unless Arar was released. Despite mixed messages from Canada, that threat to Syrian financial interests might have made the difference. On October 5, 2003, Arar was released. More than two hundred journalists greeted him at the Montreal airport.

The House of Commons Standing Committee on Foreign Affairs called Wayne Easter to testify, hoping to get to the bottom of what had gone wrong. The members of the committee, including heavy hitters like former Progressive Conservative prime minister Joe Clark and human rights advocate and NDP MP Svend Robinson, hammered Easter with questions about how actions by Canadian officials might have contributed to what happened. Easter dodged them all, refusing to divulge operational details. In general, his cagey testimony did little to assure anyone that Canadian officials had all acted in good faith.

Finally safe at home, Arar would have liked to focus on putting his life back together, but that wasn't allowed to happen. In an attempt to deflect criticism of the security agencies, someone in the government made a number of anonymous leaks to the media, downplaying the allegations of torture and repeating insinuations that Arar was linked to al-Qaeda. Several newspapers carried stories claiming Arar had trained at an al-Qaeda camp in Afghanistan. They suggested that if the evidence of Arar's guilt was made known to the public, "there would be hair standing on end."

The smear campaign kept Arar in the public eye, still under a cloud of suspicion. It seemed that his release was not enough to allow him the presumption of innocence. To confirm his innocence, and to refocus the debate on the wrongdoing by Canadian officials, Monia Mazigh, Kerry Pither and others convinced the government to conduct a public inquiry. Justice Dennis O'Connor's report was released in 2006, and it was a bombshell. "Mr. Arar has asked that I 'clear his name'... I am able to say categorically that there is no evidence to indicate Mr. Arar has committed any offence or that his activities constitute a threat to the security of Canada," confirmed the report. O'Connor concluded that it was very likely that the extraordinary rendition had taken place based on information provided by Canada. Furthermore, he warned of a "pattern of investigative practices... that point to systemic problems that go beyond Mr. Arar's case."

There was plenty of embarrassment to go around. During the inquiry, Franco Pillarella testified that, as ambassador to Syria, he "didn't have any indication" that Syria was committing verifiable human rights abuses. The comment drew ridicule, including from a former ambassador who confirmed that Syria's human rights record was well known in the Department of Foreign Affairs. After the report was released, RCMP Commissioner Giuliano Zaccardelli publicly apologized. Although no one in the RCMP would be disciplined, Zaccardelli acknowledged that some of those responsible for the errors had undergone retraining. When the National Security and Public Safety committee later studied the affair, his questionable testimony about what he knew and when, led to his resignation.

Arar was compensated by the federal government, and although the ordeal had taken place under the Liberals' watch, Conservative Prime Minister Stephen Harper issued a formal apology on behalf of the Canadian government. Harper also complained personally to US President George W. Bush, while Canada lodged a formal protest. Years later, the RCMP also issued a Canada-wide warrant and Interpol notice for the arrest of one of Arar's torturers, whose whereabouts were unknown but who was likely still in Syria.

When Arar's story became known, Canadian security agencies should have been put on notice immediately. They had conducted a baseless investigation, shared information with foreign partners without regard for the consequences, cooperated with the brutal Syrian interrogation, and tried to stymie high-level Canadian attempts to bring him home. Once all this became public knowledge, strong measures should have been taken to ensure that what happened to Arar never happened to anyone else. But it did.

* * *

In 1991, Muayyed Nureddin defected from the Iraqi army and escaped to Canada. Like many Muslim men, he eventually fell under the suspicion of Canadian authorities. He was questioned but not arrested. However, on a business trip to Syria in 2003, he was detained at the Syrian border and taken to prison. There, he was interrogated by the same man who had interrogated Ahmad El-Maati, Abdullah Almalki and Maher Arar. He was beaten with cables on the soles of his feet for so long that his feet seemed to glow a fluorescent white. Then he was made to jog on the spot. The ordeal unfolded in just as disgusting a manner as it had for the three Canadian men who'd come before him. After a few days, he was suddenly released to Canadian embassy staff.

Again, it appears that various Canadian officials were working at cross purposes. The sudden and rapid end to Nureddin's brutal captivity suggests that someone in Canada put pressure on Syria to release him, possibly either the Department of Foreign Affairs or someone at the political level, however there is also evidence that Canadian law enforcement had again, directly or indirectly, contributed to his detention in the first place. Amnesty International expressed their concerns to the Canadian government that CSIS had been involved. "The similarity of the questioning Mr. Nureddin faced in Canada and in Syria points in that direction, as does the fact that Canadian consular officials reportedly learned of Mr. Nureddin's release from CSIS sources," wrote Amnesty Secretary General Irene Khan.

While acknowledging the difficulty in proving, beyond a reasonable doubt, the criminal actions of any specific Canadians involved in extraordinary rendition, Barbara Jackman feels that if ever a successful prosecution of Canadian officials could have happened, it could have happened in Nureddin's case. "Arar was back in Canada. They knew Arar had been tortured, and with Muayyed, they still sent the information," she said. In other cases, before Arar's story became so widely known, officials might have more plausibly claimed ignorance. That was not possible in Nureddin's case. "They can't deny they knew what the consequences would be," says Jackman. Yet no one was ever charged.

After the evidence uncovered by the Arar inquiry, the government allowed an inquiry into what had happened to El-Maati, Almalki and Nureddin. Justice Frank Iacobucci found that, in all three cases, Canadian officials had acted improperly. However, limited by a narrow mandate, the report contained no recommendations and some of the evidence was initially censored. No individual was held to account. After examining the report, the opposition majority on the Public Safety and National Security committee concluded there was enough evidence to recommend an apology and compensation to all three men, but the Conservatives refused. Almost a decade later, Justin Trudeau's Liberal government formally apologized and agreed to a financial settlement for the men.

* * *

Another occasion in which Canada failed a man in similar circumstances is the bizarre story of Abousfian Abdelrazik. In 2003, he went to Sudan to visit his mother. Sudanese officials told him he was suspected of being a member of al-Qaeda. He was detained and kept in a cold cell for eleven months, sometimes beaten with a rubber hose or made to stand at attention for hours at a time. Eventually, he was given a letter from the Sudanese government clearing him of connections to al-Qaeda and was released. He booked a flight back to Canada with Lufthansa, but the company cancelled his ticket, apparently following a request by CSIS. Sudanese intelligence told him they wanted to speak with him again. Canadian consular officials encouraged him to speak with the Sudanese, promising to follow up to make sure he was okay. This was tragically bad advice. He was detained and tortured again for another nine months. An investigation by the Security Intelligence Review Committee found that Canada, yet again, had shared inaccurate and exaggerated evidence with the security services of a foreign government. Worse, in this case, CSIS agents had travelled to Khartoum North Common Prison (commonly known as Kober) in Sudan and interrogated Abdelrazik themselves, despite the fact that Canadian consular officials weren't allowed access. In 2006, he was released; however he was designated a terrorist by the US State Department. Later the UN, CSIS and the RCMP acknowledged that they had no evidence against Abdelrazik, but Canada refused to grant him an emergency passport so he could come home (his passport having expired during his detention). He went to the Canadian embassy to plead his case. He would end up in the embassy foyer for the next fourteen months.

Documents later obtained from the federal government showed that despite CSIS and the RCMP having admitted they did not have evidence against Abdelrazik, Canada was more concerned with what the Americans thought. "Senior government of Canada officials should be mindful of the potential reaction of our US counterparts to Abdelrazik's return to Canada as he is on the US no-fly list," read one document.

In 2008, the Federal Court ruled that the government had violated his constitutional rights by refusing to provide an emergency passport and ordered him returned home. Once home, he found that his assets were frozen, and it became a crime to provide him with financial assistance. As a result, he was denied child assistance benefits for his children. In 2011, the UN removed his designation as a terrorist. Abdelrazik's assessment of his treatment by Canada was blunt: "The Canadian government has a racist mind. It is because I am black and Muslim."

In *The Globe and Mail*, Sheema Khan warned that these cases sent a clear message to Canadian Muslims: "Our security agencies will cooperate with the worst of the worst if we, or the Americans, have suspicions about you. Your Canadian citizenship means nothing, and your government will let you languish in a hellhole if need be."

These high-profile cases, however horrific, didn't force the government to wash their hands of extraordinary rendition. In 2010 the Conservative minister of public safety, Vic Toews, issued an order to CSIS allowing them to, in exceptional circumstances, "share the most complete information available at the time with relevant authorities, including information based on intelligence provided by foreign agencies that may have been derived from the use of torture or mistreatment." Toews expected to be kept informed of the use of the directive "as appropriate." Despite its unreliability and obvious inhumanity, Canada and its allies would be able to share evidence gleaned by torture. In effect, they would be creating a market for it. In July 2011, Toews issued a further directive to CSIS codifying their right to release information to foreign governments even when there is a substantial risk of torture occurring as a result. In his eyes, it would appear these interrogations were sure to save human lives, and if interrogators needed to torture detainees to make that happen, the trade-off was worth it. It's like in *24* when Kiefer Sutherland has to rough up some terrorists to make them talk. It's okay, because Kiefer's the good guy.

The Head of the Spear: How Everything Went Wrong for Omar Khadr

THIS BOOK HAS charted incidents of harsh or questionable treatment of Muslims by the media, the government and the Canadian public at large. It has analyzed how Muslims in Canada have been victims of an unfair application of the law, and how at times they have been failed by the rule of law itself. While there are many examples, there is one particularly famous case involving both Liberal and Conservative governments in which each of these issues intersects. It is the story of Omar Khadr, the Canadian Muslim notorious for being the last Western citizen held in the US military base at Guantanamo Bay, Cuba. Competing political activists have portrayed him as a demonic poster child for the evils of extremism, or a tragic symbol of the injustices of the War on Terrorism.

Omar Khadr was born on September 19, 1986 at Centenary Hospital in Toronto. Before Omar was born, his parents, Maha Elsamnah and Ahmed Khadr, had moved their growing family several times between Canada and the east. Before the end of the fall, with newborn Omar in tow, the family moved back to Peshawar, Pakistan, where Ahmed worked with a relief organization. Around this time Ahmed befriended Ayman al-Zawahiri, the man who would one day succeed Osama bin Laden as leader of al-Qaeda. The family bounced back and forth between Canada and Pakistan throughout Omar's childhood. "Omar, like all the Khadr children, was comfortable in both worlds," wrote Michelle Shepherd in the superb *Guantanamo's Child: The Untold Story of Omar Khadr.*

In 1992, Ahmed visited a refugee camp in Afghanistan and stepped on a land mine. Badly injured, he returned to Canada and spent a month at Toronto's Sunnybrook Health Sciences Centre. "People who knew the father say he was committed to creating a puritanical Islamic state in Afghanistan. And when a landmine crippled his arm and leg in the early nineties, he attempted to turn his sons into instruments of his unfulfilled dream," suggested the CBC's Nazim Baksh. In 1994, he sent Omar's older, pre-teen brothers to an al-Qaeda training camp in Afghanistan, entwining his family's destiny with that of al-Qaeda and Osama bin Laden.

On November 19, 1995, terrorists set off a bomb at the Egyptian Embassy in Islamabad, Pakistan. Three separate extremist groups claimed responsibility. Ahmed was suspected of involvement and arrested by Pakistani authorities. For weeks, he was held without charge and subjected to aggressive questioning and threats. In protest of his mistreatment, he began a hunger strike. Because Ahmed was a Canadian citizen, media took notice and sympathetic coverage appeared on the front pages of Canadian newspapers. When Prime Minister Jean Chrétien passed through Pakistan on a trade mission, he met with Pakistani Prime Minister Benazir Bhutto and raised Ahmed's case, demanding her word that Ahmed would get a fair trial. Privately, some Canadian security officials felt that Chrétien had been duped into sticking up for a Canadian they saw as unworthy of his rights. They called it the "Khadr effect." The next time a member of the Khadr family needed help, they would remember Ahmed.

Ahmed was eventually released. The family continued to alternate between Canada and Pakistan, and then moved to Kabul, Afghanistan. They visited Osama bin Laden's camp outside of Jalalabad regularly. The camp reminded the kids of a *Star Wars* movie set. Ahmed tried to justify the atrocity of 9/11 to his family as his second son, Abdurahman, recounted to Michelle Shepherd: "One of the famous explanations of September 11 is these people [the victims] pay taxes, the taxes go to the government, the government puts it into the army, the army gives it to the Israelis, and they kill Muslims. You know, that long chain of explanation." After 9/11, when the bombs started dropping and Kabul fell, the family fled the city. The older children were armed. "The order was if anyone stopped, if anyone stopped the car, you shoot. If anyone asked us to stop, you shoot. You don't think, you shoot," Zaynab, the eldest daughter, told Shepherd. "So you're sitting there going, 'I can do it, I can do it. I hope I don't have to do it. I can do it. I hope I don't have to do it.'"

In that terrifying atmosphere, Ahmed and Maha discussed sending Maha and the youngest children back to Canada. However, they remained so committed to their cause that, despite the danger, they elected not to. Ahmed and his older sons would disappear for weeks at a time leaving Omar, by then fifteen, with his mother and sisters. After a while, Abu Laith al-Libi, an al-Qaeda associate, started asking Ahmed about Omar, too. Likely pleased at the interest being shown in another of his sons, Ahmed sent Omar to join al-Libi and his men. It was then that Omar became a child soldier. Al-Libi knew how to suck people in. "He was one of those cool characters. He knew a lot about Dubai. He knew about cameras. He knew about planes, laptops and stuff that's cool," Abdurahman explained to Shepherd. At first, al-Libi just asked Omar to translate. Then he was made to watch US military bases and report on any movement. Finally, he participated in building an improvised explosive device. It was classic indoctrination by a smooth operator: pick an impressionable youth in an unstable environment, lure them in by making yourself relatable, and start small—assigning tasks until orders are unthinkingly obeyed.

* * *

In July 2002, long before democratic elections would be held in Afghanistan, most of the country was a hotly contested battleground between the Taliban, various warlords and American and

Canadian forces and their allies. On July 27, the US National Security Agency detected a suspicious satellite phone being used. It belonged to al-Libi's men. Dispatched to the scene were members of Utah's 19th Special Forces and 82nd Airborne Division, a few Afghan soldiers and several members of Delta Force, an elite counter-terrorism unit of the US Army. "They do not serve warrants and they do not make arrests… their job is to kill people we want killed," one former Delta Force soldier told the *New York Times*.

Two of the Afghan soldiers approached the house where the satellite phone had been used and were shot dead by the men inside. A firefight began, and several US soldiers were hit. They called for air support, and after four hours of bombardment, the place was largely reduced to rubble. Everything went quiet. The soldiers approached the remains of the building, weapons drawn. One last grenade was lobbed their way. They didn't have time to get out of the way, much less see who had thrown it. The Delta Force soldier it killed was twenty-eight-year-old Sergeant First Class Christopher Speer.

Moments after the grenade was thrown, the soldiers saw that one of al-Libi's men had survived. They shot him in the head. They saw another survivor leaning up against some brush with his back to them. They shot him twice. They approached him as he lay in the dust with his eyes closed. He had two gaping holes in his chest, big enough that you could almost see his inner workings. He was still breathing. It was Omar.

* * *

Following the firefight, Omar was brought to Bagram Air Base for interrogation. Bagram was a nasty place. Detainees were kept in wire cages that could hold up to a dozen at a time. Talking was not allowed. Sometimes detainees were made to stand, naked and hooded with their arms outstretched while loud music blared at them. (Several of the American military interrogators at Bagram would later be transferred to Abu Ghraib prison in Iraq, where their sadistic mistreatment of detainees would be captured in photographs that would shock the world.) Five days after Omar's capture, the White House issued a directive narrowing the definition of torture. It would now include only activities that caused death, organ failure or the permanent impairment of a significant body function. That left a lot of room to be creative. Omar was there for three months.

"We were all so angry. Everyone was. You're talking less than a year after September 11. The mindset of the average American soldier over there was hatred. We hated them," recalled Damien Corsetti, one of the interrogators at Bagram. Omar's interrogations began when he was still on a stretcher. During the three months he was there, he was interrogated over forty times. He was put in stress positions that were especially painful due to his injuries, and he was threatened with vicious dogs. "Several times, the soldiers tied my hands above my head to the doorframe or chained them to the ceiling and made me stand like that for hours at a time. Because of my injuries, particularly the bullet wounds in my chest and shoulders, my hands could not be raised all the way above my head, but they would pull them up as high as they thought they could go, and then tie them there… Sometimes they would shine extremely bright lights right up against my face, and my eyes would tear and tear and tear. These lights caused me great pain, particularly since both my eyes were badly injured, and had shrapnel in them," Omar would later swear in an affidavit. His chief interrogator was Sergeant Joshua Claus, later sentenced to five months in prison after a wrongly accused detainee was beaten to death at Bagram.

Following the interrogations at Bagram, Omar was brought to the American military base in Guantanamo Bay. A few days later came a new commander: Major General Geoffrey Miller, who had orders to get tougher with detainees and get them talking. He, too, would later graduate to Abu Ghraib. In Guantanamo

Bay, detainees were subjected to severe beatings, stress positions, extreme temperatures and extreme noise. Sexual humiliation of Muslims also became part of the repertoire. In *Inside the Wire*, military translator Erik Saar describes how a female interrogator discretely covered her hand in red ink, and then in front of a detainee, reached into her pants and then smeared her hands onto the detainee's face, making him believe he was being covered with her menstrual blood. It was more than Saar could take. "I hated myself when I walked out of that room, even though I was pretty sure we were talking to a piece of shit in there. I felt as if I had lost something. We lost something. We lost the high road. We cashed in our principles in the hope of obtaining a piece of information. And it didn't even fucking work," he wrote.

This would be Omar Khadr's new home for the next ten years.

* * *

Analyzing the case against Omar is inherently challenging. It may never be known who threw the final grenade that killed Sergeant Speer. As noted, two people had survived the aerial bombardment. Omar had been hit in the face with shrapnel and was probably nearly blind by the time the grenade was thrown. Photos released in 2009 show Omar's body half buried in dirt after the bombings. A soldier who was present has testified that he accidentally stepped on Omar because he didn't see him under all the rubble, testimony which seems to contradict other soldiers' accounts of finding Omar sitting with his back to them. An even more troubling inconsistency would eventually come to light. In the army's initial field report of what happened, Speer's killer was reported as "killed," indicating that the soldiers believed it was the survivor they had subsequently shot in the head who had thrown the grenade that killed Speer. At some point, the official record was altered to read that Speer's killer had been "engaged," allowing it to be plausible that it could have been Omar.

War is murkier business than the police procedurals we see on TV where crime-scene investigators can conclusively prove guilt with a single hair or a thread of microfiber within a forty-five-minute episode. Some have argued that on the battlefield, the burden of proof is different. A policy report written by the Conservative Party of Canada read, "Many witnesses are dead, there's no forensic detective squad to document the scene, and most of the surviving witnesses are serving overseas at the time of trial. For all these reasons, military commissions throughout history have not applied the same evidentiary standards we demand of a civilian criminal trial. If they were required to do so, it would be virtually impossible to ever try detainees." But according to Barbara Jackman, that's not true. Based on the evidence, there's reasonable doubt as to whether Omar threw the grenade. Whether Speer's death had been on a battlefield or in a back alley, the burden of proof against Omar hadn't been met. "If you're going to make your case, you should have to prove your case," Jackman says.

Leaving aside whether Omar threw the grenade, the case against him had a lot of holes. To begin with, it is worth questioning whether throwing the grenade was even a crime. Of course there are rules in war; it is a crime to use civilians as human shields or to kill a surrendered combatant, for example. Even if Omar did throw the grenade, he hadn't killed a civilian or a prisoner of war. The grenade had killed an armed, uniformed soldier. Under normal rules of war, that's not illegal. However, under the US *Military Commissions Act*, passed after Omar was already in custody and retroactively applied to him, any resistance to the invasion of Afghanistan was a war crime. Rather than fighting enemy soldiers, who would be protected by the Geneva Conventions, the US now classified its enemies as "unlawful enemy combatants." In other words, anyone who fought against them was a war criminal. This was a definition that wasn't even applied to the Nazis. In the compelling essay compilation *Omar Khadr, Oh Canada*, Audrey Macklin wrote, "While it may seem intuitively appealing to criminalize membership in al-Qaeda or the Taliban, the problem with calling it a war crime is that the laws of war are about regulating armed conflict between adversaries, not about making participation in armed conflict unlawful per se. Yet, once it labelled him an 'alien unlawful enemy combatant,' the *Military Commissions Act* made it illegal for Omar Khadr to do anything other than surrender or die."

Most crucially of all, even if it is accepted that Omar threw the grenade, and even if it is accepted that such an act was or should have been illegal, Omar was fifteen years old at the time. In Canada, fifteen-year-olds are not deemed mature enough to drink, drive, vote or pay taxes. If they commit a crime, they are subject to the *Young Offenders Act*, an acknowledgement of their reduced capacity to take full, adult responsibility for their actions. In the eyes of the UN, too, a fifteen-year-old is a child, subject to the Convention on the Rights of the Child, which Canada has signed. According to the Convention, "No child shall be deprived of his or her liberty unlawfully or arbitrarily. The arrest, detention or imprisonment of a child shall be in conformity with the law and shall be used only as a measure of last resort for the shortest appropriate period of time."

Omar was a child soldier, a designation supported by Human Rights Watch and the UN High Commission for Human Rights. Former general Romeo Dallaire, possibly Canada's most trusted expert on child soldiers, said that Omar "by every definition" was a child soldier. It was not only Omar's age that defined him as a child soldier, it was also the fact that he was likely coerced into participating in the conflict. "It seems quite certain that Ahmed Khadr, as a senior member and financier for al-Qaeda, brought his children into the world of militancy and fed them an ideology of hate. He recruited his children to take part in the Afghan conflict," noted W. Andy Knight and John McCoy in their contribution to *Omar Khadr, Oh Canada*. "One is left to wonder why Omar's case has not been viewed as a case of illegal recruitment of a child into a non-state and irregular military organization."

His status as a child soldier should have entitled him to rehabilitation, not detention. In other conflicts that featured child soldiers, such as those in Rwanda, Sierra Leone and Yugoslavia, no combatant Omar's age was charged with a crime. The US and her allies should already have been on the lookout for child soldiers in Afghanistan, since the UN had reported that children as young as eleven were being used by the Taliban. One would not expect Omar's arrest to be acceptable to Canada, a nation that prides itself on being active in the fight against the use of child soldiers and protective of the rights of children globally.

Even if we believe that Omar threw the grenade, we accept that throwing it was illegal, and we forget that he was a child soldier, he was still entitled to basic rights while in detention: the right not to be tortured, and the right to a fair trial in a reasonable time, for example. However, both of these rights were violated. Canadian officials should have known he might be tortured while in US custody. It's a tough accusation to make against Canada's closest ally, but Canada has not been blind to evidence of US torture in other cases. At one point, a Foreign Affairs document actually listed the US as a known torturer, before Foreign Affairs removed the listing and apologized. Omar's right to a fair trial in a reasonable time was ignored, as year after year passed, and Omar still hadn't been tried. In Canada this a right guaranteed by the Charter. When tested in another case, the Supreme Court determined that a two-year delay was a violation of that Charter right, resulting in a stay of the prosecution. In other words, two years was unconstitutional. By Charter standards, once Omar approached that threshold of time, his rights had been violated.

Omar's Canadian citizenship should have spurred Canadian officials to do whatever it took to ensure his rights were respected. Canada has a long history of going to bat when a Canadian citizen is detained and mistreated, although as noted, this has not always been the case for Muslim men. In this case, a child was being detained on suspect evidence by a country with a suspect human rights record, with no signs of release or a fair trial on the horizon. It is fair to acknowledge that the US is a military and economic behemoth with clout human rights abusers like Egypt or Syria don't have. Canada wasn't exactly holding all the cards. Yet every other Western nation with a citizen held in Guantanamo Bay managed to negotiate their release until only Omar was left.

What did Canada do? Following Omar's capture and imprisonment at Bagram Air Base, Canada made the following requests to the US: that consular access be granted, that Omar's age be taken into consideration, that he not be sent to Guantanamo Bay and that he not be executed. The US refused to guarantee any of these meek requests.

Omar's story was quickly in the news. Amnesty International launched an investigation. On Parliament Hill, Svend Robinson raised it in Question Period, demanding to know what the Liberals were doing to ensure Omar's rights were respected. Anticipating that the media would ask questions about his age, Foreign Affairs initially drafted talking points that used the term "child soldier." A Foreign Affairs lawyer, however, sent a note warning colleagues to "claw back" on public statements acknowledging that Omar was a minor. At the time, the relationship between Canada and the US was more delicate than usual; many were concerned that American dissatisfaction with Canada's obedience in the war on terror would hurt Canada's economy. Asked by reporters about Omar's case, Canadian Alliance leader Stephen Harper had little to say about Omar, but he warned that "Canada cannot be seen as being an insecure country in the eyes of its major trading partners."

Later Bill Graham, who was minister of foreign affairs at the time, would regret that Canada had not been more aggressive on Omar's behalf. Speaking in the documentary *You Don't Like the Truth: Four Days Inside Guantanamo*, he stated: "What we knew then was, here is a young man; he has been accused of killing an American soldier; we have been told 'He's in American custody, he's being properly treated under Red Cross rules.' This is by our best ally, a defender of freedom around the world with an impeccable reputation. And we accepted it. And I said that in the House of Commons time and time again, and I believed it when I said it. With historical hindsight, I now know that things were different. So would I have acted differently then, if I knew? Of course."

*   *   *

What Canada did was dispatch CSIS to Guantanamo Bay to interrogate Omar. To make life easier for CSIS, the Americans decided to soften him up first. For three weeks, he was subjected to what was called the "frequent flier program," a form of sleep deprivation determined to be torture by the US Center for Constitutional Rights. CSIS was informed that Omar had undergone the frequent flier program, but agents went ahead with the interrogation anyway.

The interrogation was taped. CSIS erased some of the recording but not all. It has since been released. The interrogation began with an agent offering him a Big Mac.

> AGENT: So I guess we're the first Canadians you've seen in a while?

> OMAR KHADR: Canadians?

> AGENT: Yeah.

> OMAR KHADR: Finally!

"He was so excited, so hopeful, even in his body language, when he hears about Canadians. And I think Omar is probably under the impression that these are people from the diplomatic corps of Canada, and they're there to find out about his situation and to help him," said psychiatrist Dr. Raul Berdichevsky upon viewing the released tape in *You Don't Like the Truth: Four Days Inside Guantanamo.*

On the second day of the interrogation, Omar took off his shirt to show the Canadians the extent of his injuries. He tried to let them know that he'd been coerced into giving false information to his American interrogators. "Everything I said to the Americans was not right. I just said that because they tortured me very badly in Bagram. So I had to say what I said," he told the Canadians.

OMAR KHADR: I can't move my arms and all of these—is this healthy? I can't move my arm. I requested medical over a long time. They don't do anything about it.

AGENT: No, they look like they're healing well to me. I'm not a doctor, but I think you're getting good medical care.

OMAR KHADR [crying]: No, I'm not. You're not here.

The Canadians accused him of lying and left the room. Omar broke down, tearing at his hair and crying for his mother. The next day the interrogation continued. To no avail, Omar tried to explain why and how he'd been placed with Abu Laith al-Libi's men. For CSIS the pressure was on to get something they could use.

OMAR KHADR: What was my mistake, being in the house where they shot the American?

AGENT: Exactly, being in the house was your first mistake.

OMAR KHADR: What's my mistake? My father put me in this house with all those people.

AGENT: Your father put you in this house. Well, all I know is that every day you get up in the morning, and there's a young American who, every morning, doesn't get up. How do you think his family feels?

...

AGENT: Your best course of action—this is all I can recommend to you—is you have to start realizing that complaining, whining, denying what happened, is counterproductive.

...

AGENT: Is there anybody you know who might be in Canada, or from Canada, or on his way to Canada, who may be trying to hurt us?

OMAR KHADR: No.

AGENT: Because information like that, one piece of information like that, could go a long way to... helping you if we could bring something like that in to the Canadian government. That would get you a lot of goodwill.

The final day of interrogation produced more of the same. When it was over, Omar expressed his dismay that the Canadians had done nothing to help. "We can't do anything for you. Only you can help yourself. I'm telling you, if you ever get the chance to speak to somebody like myself again, then I would think about your future," one agent said before leaving.

In February 2003, Foreign Affairs stated publicly that officials had met with Omar and that he seemed in good health. No mention was made of CSIS or of the allegations of torture that Omar made. By participating in the Guantanamo Bay process, CSIS broke international law. "If one state is engaged in violations of international human rights provisions, and another state, even though it doesn't have effective custody in that case, is in any way participating in or complicit in it, they share responsibility under international law," noted Craig Mokhiber, deputy director of the UN Office of the High Commissioner for Human Rights in *Omar Khadr, Oh Canada.*

After the Canadians departed, Omar's paltry possessions, including his blanket and Koran, were confiscated by the guards. He was spat on. He was threatened with rape. He was left in an interrogation chamber for hours with his ankles and wrists bound to a bolt on the floor. When he inevitably urinated, the guards poured cleaning fluid on his chest and used him as a human mop to clean it up. He wasn't given fresh clothes for two days. In the fall, the Canadians came back, and CSIS interrogated him all over again.

In 2004, the US Supreme Court ruled that prisoners in Guantanamo Bay should have access to lawyers and the right to challenge their detentions. In response, the military established Combatant Status Review Tribunals to determine whether each prisoner was an enemy combatant. Hearsay evidence or evidence gleaned by torture was admissible; lawyers were not. Omar's military tribunal ruled that his continued detention was appropriate. Finally, in November 2004, Omar was allowed to speak to two American lawyers. For the first time since his detention, someone had come to advocate on his behalf, and they were not Canadians.

"He grew up before our eyes. He was really, really a kid when we saw him. He certainly passed through puberty. He grew taller, he broke out, and I think he got more tired and more cynical, hardened as time passed. It felt like he was in a darker place. I think the isolation just took an immense toll," lawyer Rick Wilson told Michelle Shepherd.

In 2005, amid reports of guards cranking up the radio during daily prayers and flushing a Koran down the toilet, detainees began a hunger strike, demanding to be treated according to the Geneva Conventions. Omar was one of them, and the guards didn't like it. Omar later swore in an affidavit, "I was very weak and could not stand. Guards would grab me by pressure points behind my ears, under my jaw and on my neck. On a scale of one to ten, I would say the pain was an eleven. They would often knee me repeatedly in the thighs." For Omar, the hunger strike ended on the tenth day, when he collapsed.

*   *   *

On November 7, 2005, not long after Khadr's nineteenth birthday, the Pentagon charged him with murder, attempted murder, conspiracy and aiding the enemy. The death penalty wouldn't be sought. The plan was to try him under a military commission before a military presiding officer (they weren't called judges). The military would pick his lawyer. Before the process had even begun, the military commission was a joke. Experts derided it as rigged to ensure convictions. "Even if you dress it up, a kangaroo is still a kangaroo," read the headline of an article about the process in the *Los Angeles Times*. A number of foreign countries denounced it. Through Foreign Affairs, Canada announced that the government was pleased the death penalty wasn't being sought. Early in the trial, with the support of his military-appointed lawyer, Khadr decided to boycott the proceedings. He had been advised it wasn't in his best interests to dignify the process with his participation.

In June 2006, the US Supreme Court ruled that the military commissions were unconstitutional. Khadr turned twenty and passed another year in Guantanamo Bay. After the Supreme Court ruling, the Americans rejigged the military commission process. In June 2007, Khadr was back before a revamped military commission and tried a second time. Once again, the process was farcical.

On the first day, the presiding officer (still a military officer, but now called a judge) ruled that the Pentagon had jurisdiction over "unlawful" enemy combatants, but that the Combatant Status Review Tribunal had determined only that Khadr was an enemy combatant, and had not specified whether he was "unlawful" or not. The charges were dismissed without prejudice, but the next month the ruling was overturned, and the charges were reinstated. "This is legal anarchy. Washington appears determined to rewrite the rules until it manages to secure a conviction," argued an editorial in the *Toronto Star*.

By fall the system was starting to crumble. After spending months defending the process, chief prosecutor Moe Davis resigned. "I think it's a disgrace to call it a military commission— it's a political commission," he said. He specifically criticized what was happening to Khadr. "We look like hypocrites for detaining a fifteen-year-old in indefinite confinement and subjecting him to this extraordinary process which we would not condone, I would hope, if it was a fifteen-year-old American being detained by another country," he said. Davis wasn't the only prosecutor disgusted by the process. Over time, seven prosecutors resigned from the Military Commissions.

In 2009, under newly elected President Barack Obama, the rules were changed again to include new rules about whether evidence gleaned by torture was admissible. Confusingly, such evidence was determined to be inadmissible; however, if a tortured detainee later gave the same evidence to a "clean team" of non-torturing interrogators, then the evidence would be admissible. This new process remained fatally flawed. The detainee, tortured once, would have every reason to fear being tortured again, so any evidence given from that point on would be suspect. As Moe Davis put it, "Once you ring the torture bell, can you ever un-ring it?"

In his third trial, in 2010, Khadr told the judge he'd again be boycotting the proceedings. A letter Khadr wrote to Dennis Edney and Nathan Whitling, Canadian lawyers by then assisting his American military lawyers, showed how Khadr felt at the time: "You always say that I have an obligation to show the world what is going on down here, and it seems that we've done everything, but the world doesn't get it, so it might work if the world sees the US sentencing a child to life in prison, it might show the world how unfair and sham this process is... justice and freedom have a very high cost and value... [but] I hate being the head of the spear."

* * *

As Khadr's captivity dragged on, he gradually became a household name in Canada and a deeply polarizing figure. In 2004, the CBC aired a documentary on the Khadr family entitled *The Khadrs*. In the documentary Khadr's brother Abdurahman admitted his family's strong links to al-Qaeda; his mother, Maha Elsamnah, disparaged Canada for its liberal attitudes toward homosexuality and drug use; and his sister Zaynab declared that the US "deserved" what happened to them on 9/11. None of this helped. Thousands of angry Canadians signed a petition to have the whole family deported. To some, it confirmed their worst suspicions about Muslim immigrants. "The interview was not only insulting to Canadians but profoundly detrimental to decent Muslims and other immigrants from the Middle East. I remember being horrified and dismayed, as if this madwoman held my fate in her hands. She gave Canadians the darkest possible window into the mentality of Middle Eastern immigrants in general, and shrouded Muslim women in particular," wrote Shadia B. Drury in *Omar Khadr, Oh Canada*.

University of Toronto law professor and Human Rights Watch co-counsel Audrey Macklin felt that despite justifiable anger about what some members of the Khadr family stood for, Canadians should have stepped up and demanded Khadr's rights be respected. Amnesty International and several NGOs fought for his release, but polls showed some 50 percent of Canadians were content to leave him languishing in Guantanamo Bay. For some reason, he didn't seem to count as a Canadian worth protecting. "Large swaths of the public seemed to regard the most basic human rights—the right to be free from torture, the right not to be detained indefinitely, the right to a fair trial—as privileges reserved for the popular," Macklin wrote in *Omar Khadr, Oh Canada*. In other words, according to many Canadians, if you or your associates hold certain reprehensible but not criminal views, or are accused but not necessarily convicted of certain crimes, you're not morally entitled to your rights, whatever the law says. "Demonstrating the illegality of the Guantanamo Bay regime was not difficult. What stymied me was that people knew it was illegal and did not care," continued Macklin.

That apathy had a tangible impact. Politically, there wasn't any desire to play hardball with the US to protect Khadr's rights. Foreign Affairs was finally permitted a few consular visits, but bureaucrats weren't able to do much. "What we will do is what we have done so far, which is, at the end of the day, the US will proceed as they see fit... We have sought assurances that he is not being ill-treated, and those assurances have been given by the US," stated Liberal public safety minister Anne McLellan in 2005.

In 2006, the Conservatives took office. No longer in power, the Liberals demanded that the new government take up Khadr's case more aggressively. The opposition-dominated House of Commons Standing Committee on Foreign Affairs and International Development produced a report calling for Khadr's transfer into Canadian custody. The Conservatives responded that they were merely continuing the policy of the previous Liberal government. They maintained their position that in Guantanamo Bay, Khadr was receiving due process. They supported the argument that "Canada's obligations to Omar Khadr are moral obligations at best, and leaving his fate in the hands of the United States should not linger negatively in the moral conscience of the nation." That cold analysis is heart-warming in comparison to what some others were saying. Conservative pundit Ezra Levant called Khadr the "Paul Bernardo of terror," and said he should have been executed on the spot. Levant, it must be said, has made a career of uttering outrageous statements, but he seemed to have a particular antipathy for Khadr. He has regularly ranted about him on Twitter and other media platforms, and published the 294-page diatribe *The Enemy Within: Terror, Lies, and the Whitewashing of Omar Khadr.*

Other countries seemed to be doing more to fight for Khadr's rights than Canada was. In the UK, the General Council of the Bar, the Law Society, the Criminal Bar Association, the Commonwealth Lawyers Association and Bar Human Rights Committee co-signed a letter condemning Canada's inaction. France's foreign minister personally asked US Secretary of State Hillary Clinton to review Khadr's case. The UN Special Representative for Children in Armed Conflict also filed a complaint with the US.

Instead of the Canadian government, a duo of Canadian lawyers made the most headway. First Dennis Edney and Nathan Whitling launched a court challenge to prevent further CSIS interrogations. The Federal Court of Canada agreed that CSIS had violated Khadr's Charter rights by interrogating him under such circumstances. "Conditions at Guantanamo Bay do not meet Charter standards," read the ruling. The judgement may read like an understatement, but in the legal world it was a stinging rebuke. There would be no more visits by CSIS agents to Guantanamo Bay after that. "It's disgraceful the Canadian government won't come to his rescue, but thank goodness the Canadian courts will," Edney said. Following that success, Edney and Whitling launched a case to have the results of the CSIS interrogation made public. That case went all the way to the Supreme Court, and they won there, too. Their most important battle, to bring Khadr home, remained.

On April 23, 2009, the Federal Court ruled that the Government of Canada was legally obliged to seek Khadr's repatriation.

According to the judgement, it was one of the government's responsibilities to its citizens: they had to at least try to get him back. The Conservatives appealed. The Federal Court of Appeal also ruled that Canada had to seek repatriation. Again, the government announced they would appeal, this time to the Supreme Court. In front of the justices, the government argued a broad range of points, including raising Canada's responsibility to fight terrorism. It was a curious legal argument since Canada's role in the fight against terrorism didn't preclude fighting to ensure Khadr's Charter rights were respected. "Overall, the Crown's submissions were so biased and lacking in understanding of the aspirational and mutually supportive character of international human rights law that it would have required at least a term at law school to correct some of its misconceptions," wrote legal historian Grace Li Xiu Woo in *Omar Khadr, Oh Canada*.

In its ruling in 2010, the Supreme Court was unequivocal: Khadr's Charter rights had been violated. "Canada actively participated in a process contrary to Canada's international human rights obligations and contributed to Mr. Khadr's ongoing detention," read the judgement. The government was ordered to do something to remedy that. The Supreme Court conceded, however, that the government had made one important point: the government was in charge of foreign affairs, not the courts. This was a human rights issue, but it was also a foreign affairs issue. The Federal Court of Appeal, the Supreme Court affirmed, had the authority to declare that Khadr's rights had been violated, but it didn't have the authority to determine which foreign affairs instrument the government should use to remedy the violation of his rights. In other words, the court couldn't tell the government that the only solution was to bring Khadr home. Judges couldn't usurp the Crown's prerogative to conduct foreign affairs as the government saw fit. Instead, the court would leave it up to the government to decide exactly how to remedy the violation of Khadr's rights. Days after the ruling, the government announced they would not seek repatriation.

While the Supreme Court had not ordered a specific remedy, doing nothing was not a legally valid option. Yet it didn't appear that the government was pursuing any remedy at all. Edney and Whitling filed for a judicial review of the government's inaction, and the Federal Court gave the government seven days to come up with a plan. The government appealed and were granted a pause in the seven-day deadline pending the results of the appeal, but the writing was on the wall. It was clear that, legally, remedying Khadr's rights without pursuing repatriation was going to be very difficult to do. Furthermore, Barack Obama's administration now wanted Khadr gone. Having a former child soldier in Guantanamo Bay was an international embarrassment for a president who had told the world he'd be closing the reviled prison.

Negotiations took place behind the scenes, and on October 25, 2010 Khadr pled guilty before the military commission. The military prosecutor asked the jury—seven military officers—to sentence him to twenty-five years. Given the circumstances, it was a shocking suggestion. He would be forty-nine years old when released, having spent most of his life locked up. The jury didn't sentence him to twenty-five years. They sentenced him to forty.

What the jury didn't know at the time was that as legal options to leave Khadr in Guantanamo Bay fizzled out, a deal had finally been arranged between Canada and the US and subsequently agreed to by Khadr himself. In return for pleading guilty to all charges, Khadr would serve no longer than eight further years, including one more year in Guantanamo Bay during which the US could continue to try to extract whatever intelligence they could from him. After that, the US would support a prisoner transfer to Canada, allowing Khadr to serve the remainder of his sentence in Canadian custody. Khadr was finally coming home. His last year in Guantanamo Bay passed by slowly. Khadr turned twenty-five. Former classmates graduated from university and got jobs. Maybe a few got married and had children. When the year was up, Khadr was still in Guantanamo Bay. Six more months passed. In March

2012, the *New York Times* reported that bureaucratic delays in Canada were the cause. Canada in turn blamed the US.

* * *

On September 29, 2012, more than ten years after his capture in Afghanistan, Khadr was released from Guantanamo Bay and into Canadian custody. The government classified him as an adult and remanded him to Millhaven Institution, a maximum-security prison where he received death threats. Not long after, he was transferred to Edmonton Institution where he was beaten by white supremacists within minutes of his arrival. Finally, he was transferred to Bowden Institution, a medium-security facility.

On April 24, 2015, at age twenty-eight, Khadr was granted bail, and a date was set for his release. The Conservative government pledged to stop it. "We are disappointed and will appeal this decision," stated public safety minister Steven Blaney. "Our government will continue to work to combat the international jihadi movement, which has declared war on Canada and her allies. Omar Ahmed Khadr pleaded guilty to heinous crimes, including the murder of American army medic Sergeant Christopher Speer. We have vigorously defended against any attempt to lessen his punishment for these crimes."

Demonstrating an extreme commitment to staying on message, Conservative MPs repeated Blaney's statement in the House of Commons and on social media like a mantra, usually word for word. They also added partisan jabs, accusing the Liberals and NDP of seeking financial compensation for Khadr, and presenting the Conservatives as the only party standing up for victims and protecting Canadians from terrorism. Recall that 2015 was an election year.

Blaney's statement is worth analyzing, particularly since it became a Conservative talking point. First, although Khadr had never been linked to any threat to Canada, he was characterized as an "international jihadi declaring war on Canada." Second, there was the curious inclusion of his middle name, Ahmed. He was already well known to the public as Omar Khadr. Some have suggested it was meant to associate him with his al-Qaeda-linked father, Ahmed Khadr—an attempt at guilt by association. Others have wondered if it was an attempt to accentuate his Muslim-ness. "Like with Barack [Obama]. Those who wanted to hate him always added Hussein as his middle name. I think it was deliberate," Alia Hogben says. "People already knew Omar Khadr very well, so they didn't need to add anything else to it."

Third, Christopher Speer was described as a medic, conjuring images of an unarmed stretcher-bearer with a red cross insignia on his shoulder. While Speer was a combat medic, he was also an armed Delta Force soldier. Finally, and most crucially, Khadr's guilty plea was taken at face value. There was no acknowledgement of the circumstances of his confession, which followed torture at Bagram Air Base and in Guantanamo Bay. "I must say, I'm one of the lawyers who encouraged him to say those things in order to get him out of there. I think he probably would have confessed to the Kennedy assassination, if that's what it would have taken to get him out of that place. And most of us, I think, would have done the same thing," Nathan Whitling said.

On May 7, Justice Myra Bielby refused the government's request for an emergency stay of the bail decision, and Khadr was released on bail. "Mr. Khadr, you are free to go," she said. Khadr emerged from the courthouse accompanied by his lawyers. He didn't speak to reporters, but Dennis Edney did. He began by thanking the judge for her decision and the prosecutor for his fairness. "As in each and every court we have been before over the last ten years throughout Canada, our judicial system is something to be incredibly proud of... Of course I am delighted. Incredibly delighted. It has taken too many years to get to this point. It is such an irony that I started this journey from the us Supreme Court to Guantanamo and back to the Federal Court system in Canada, and it takes an Alberta judge to release Omar Khadr." Asked why the government had gone to such lengths to keep Khadr behind bars, Edney was direct, unforgiving and provocative. "You would have to ask Mr. Harper. My view is very clear: Mr. Harper is a bigot. Mr. Harper doesn't like Muslims," he said.

The Conservative government stayed on message. "Mr. Speaker, we are in fact disappointed with today's decision and regret that a convicted terrorist has been allowed back into Canadian society without having served his full sentence. Omar Ahmed Khadr pleaded guilty to heinous crimes, including the murder of American army medic, Sergeant Christopher Speer, and he has admitted that his ideology has not changed. While the Liberal leader refused to rule out special compensation for this convicted terrorist and the NDP actively tries to force Canadian taxpayers to compensate him, we believe that the real victims of crime, not the perpetrators, are the ones who deserve compensation," stated Blaney's parliamentary secretary, Roxanne James, on the day of Khadr's release.

A few hours after his release, Khadr arrived at Edney's house where the court had ordered him to stay while on bail. Reporters greeted him on the driveway, and he said a few words. "I would like to thank the Canadian public for trusting me and giving me a chance. It might take some time, but I will prove to them that I am more than what they thought of me, and I'm—I'll prove to them that I'm a good person," he said. Asked what he wanted to do now, he said: "Everything, and nothing in particular. Everything."

He had a pronounced limp and shifted his weight regularly, but joy shone in his face. But at the end of the interview, before Khadr walked into a house for the first time in almost thirteen years, he accidentally bumped into a microphone. It was an innocent, unremarkable act, the kind that happens to most of us many times a day. But Khadr flinched and then froze. Despite his relief at being released, in that brief moment he looked like the child he'd been when he was first locked away, afraid to get in trouble.

* * *

While Khadr was incarcerated in Canada, authorities had refused to allow media to interview him. That impromptu press conference on Dennis Edney's driveway was Khadr's first chance to speak to the Canadian people, and his gentle demeanour that day helped redefine some people's attitudes about him. The *Calgary Sun's* Ian Robinson summed up his own reaction to what he saw: "This unrepentant redneck—whose attitude towards the 'War on Terror' can be helpfully summed up in this handy, seven-word phrase, 'Kill 'em all, let God sort them out'—has one thing to say after notorious war criminal Omar Khadr has been turned loose on the Canadian public. Welcome home, kid. And good luck."

Such a reaction was far from universal, however, and Khadr remained a polarizing figure. In 2017, Justin Trudeau's Liberal government agreed to provide Khadr with a $10.5 million settlement and an apology. "On behalf of the government of Canada, we wish to apologize to Mr. Khadr for any role Canadian officials may have played in relation to his ordeal abroad and any resulting harm," read a joint statement by public safety minister Ralph Goodale and foreign affairs minister Chrystia Freeland. To some, no amount of money could replace the years Khadr had lost, but that act of reconciliation inflamed the fury the vast majority of Canadians still felt about Khadr. An Angus Reid poll showed an overwhelming 71 percent of Canadians thought the government should have fought in court rather than agreeing to the settlement. Newly elected Conservative leader Andrew Scheer called it "disgusting." Tabitha Speer, Christopher Speer's widow, and Layne Morris, a US soldier injured in the firefight in which Khadr was captured, began a court battle to lay claim to the settlement money. Khadr's ordeal isn't truly over, and his name is likely to continue to inspire strong reactions from Canadians in the years ahead.

Is Dennis Edney's harsh accusation that Stephen Harper doesn't like Muslims defensible? As noted, Harper has hosted an event at 24 Sussex for Muslims during Ramadan. Harper appointed Rahim Jaffer, Canada's first Muslim MP, as chair of the Conservative caucus when he became prime minister in 2006. Khadr's captivity spanned Liberal and Conservative governments, preceding the involvement of Stephen Harper. No public figure in any party has implied that what happened to Khadr was appropriate because he was a Muslim. While the Conservative Party's track record on Islam has been criticized, their hard line on Khadr was also consistent with their views on justice issues in general. Maybe their vociferous opposition to his release had more to do with "tough-on-crime" image-making than with religion.

Leaving aside partisan blaming, Islamophobia does appear to have been a factor in the story. We know detainees faced Islamophobia at Guantanamo Bay where the Koran was reportedly mistreated and Islamic beliefs were ridiculed, and yet Liberal and Conservative Canadian governments left a Muslim citizen there. It's important to remember the context: Islamophobia has been stewing in the dark corners of the Internet where anonymous alt-right activists still rage against Khadr. There is a sizeable contingent of Islamophobic voters that some politicians have been only too happy to whip up into a frenzy. Canadian security forces have targeted Muslims before, and not all Muslims have been able to count on Canadian authorities to enforce the rule of law. Recall as well that when non-Muslim Canadian Brenda Martin was imprisoned in Mexico, Canada immediately went into diplomatic hyperdrive to get her out. In that context is it so difficult to believe that Islamophobia played some role in Khadr's ordeal?

The question can be put another way. If he had been a white Christian with an Anglo-Saxon name, would his government have been complicit in his years of captivity without a fair trial? Would they have ignored his age and the allegations of torture and conducted a relentless campaign to keep him behind bars? Would there have been intense public anger at attempts at restitution? Maybe. The spectre of terrorism provokes strong feelings. Asked to comment on whether they believe Islamophobia played a role in Omar Khadr's case, the prominent Muslims interviewed for this book typically responded with a long pause, and then a cautious, noncommittal answer. It's clear they have considered the question before but haven't come to a definitive answer. Many believe that the public's justifiable anger at terrorists would make a cool, level-headed analysis of the rule of law difficult, regardless of the skin colour or religious beliefs of the individual in question. Simultaneously, they acknowledge that Khadr's religion at a minimum made him an easier target and made it easier for people to believe he was a terrorist who got what he deserved. Popular conceptions of terrorism and Islam have become so linked that it's difficult to isolate the source of the public antipathy. It's not an easy question, and there is likely more than one fair answer, but one thing is certain: it's a fair question to ask.

A Canadian Is...: Where We Go from Here

THE 2015 ELECTION was something of a conundrum. Many of the policies touted by the Conservatives during the campaign, like the ban on niqabs during citizenship ceremonies, were popular with Canadians, but their government was defeated. The Liberals opposed those policies vociferously, perhaps even more than the NDP did, yet they won the election. The NDP vote, meanwhile, dropped. These counterintuitive results would not have been what the political minds on Stephen Harper's team predicted when planning their election strategy. As noted elsewhere in this book, strategic voting might explain the results. The NDP's position on the niqab ban hurt them in Quebec where taking such a position might have surprised Quebec voters. Many of them had voted NDP for the first time in 2011, and they were probably less familiar with the party's otherwise predictable positions on minority rights. That hit to the NDP numbers might have been just enough to inch the Liberals to the top of the polls. To strategic voters across the country, the Liberals then appeared to be the best-placed team to beat the Conservatives.

It's a reasonable analysis: a backfiring identity-issues ploy on the part of the Conservatives and strategic voting by progressives gave the Liberals their win. Identity issues were undoubtedly central in the campaign and could easily have shifted enough voters to produce that result. Still, there are many reasons Canadians vote the way they do. After a decade in power, most governments tend to look tired and ready for replacement. Stephen Harper, accused of an authoritarian management style, questionable electoral practices, a mismanaged economy and anti-environmental policies, looked long in the tooth. Justin Trudeau, by contrast, had a fresh, invigorating appeal. While Thomas Mulcair had developed a sterling reputation in parliament, Canadians had not chosen the NDP to govern in seventeen straight federal elections. The leader of the NDP always has a mountain to climb.

It's possible to read too much into the results of the election. Nevertheless, to the extent that the election was about identity issues, what can we learn about where Canadians stand? There are several important factors to consider. When shown the photo of three-year-old Syrian refugee Alan Kurdi, drowned during his family's attempt to reach Canada, Canadians reacted with genuine empathy. No one who saw that picture wondered about the boy's religious beliefs or imagined him as a future terrorist. When you see the photo, you desperately want to pick him up, warm his body, cover his eyes and comfort him, even in his lifelessness. You don't know how long he was on the beach, you just don't want to let him lie there for a second longer. In their ham-fisted, partisan way, each of the major political parties responded to that empathy by arguing that each had the most humane and generous plan to settle Syrians in Canada. Faced with that gut-wrenching image, religion didn't matter.

Ultimately, when the Conservatives tried to make the campaign about identity, they lost. According to defeated Conservative MP Paul Calandra, it was indeed this focus on identity issues that cost them the election. "A lot of first-generation Canadians said, 'Okay, we're not ready to endorse that,'" he said after it was all over.

Do those factors make a convincing case that social justice for Muslims is a vote-winner in Canada? It's still not easy to say. Many votes against Harper came from Muslims themselves. The percentage of Muslims who voted rose from the mid-forties to nearly 80 percent in 2015. "It's widely recognized that the Muslim vote was instrumental, or one of the instruments, in defeating the Harper Conservatives. Muslim people should rejoice in that they are recording their dissent in the most peaceful way, in the most democratic and most Canadian of ways," says Haroon Siddiqui. The Muslim vote is far too small to decide an election on its own, however. What about non-Muslim Canadians? There's an argument to be made that the virulent attacks against Muslims during the campaign caused non-Muslim Canadians to examine, maybe for the first time, the message being sent to Muslims in Canada. Politically incorrect comments are one thing. For some people, they're easy to utter privately when they think there will be no consequences. It's harder to stomach hearing that women are being physically attacked for what they're wearing. Most people in that circumstance would begin to question the views or language that could contribute to that kind of violence. "I think that led people to rethink whether they wanted to support a political party that was perpetuating policies based on fear, ignorance and division, and pandering to people that were holding these anti-immigrant, anti-Muslim views," says Amira Elghawaby.

While some policies that appeared to target Muslims were initially popular, many Canadians appear to have developed a new empathy toward those targeted. Individual Canadians might have been uncomfortable with certain visible expressions of the Islamic faith, but collectively that discomfort didn't translate into what political scientists call "tyranny of the majority"—the interests of the majority forced upon a minority. It explains why individual policies which appeared to target Muslims could be popular while an overall program of those policies could be unpopular. Most people who vote take their vote seriously, knowing their choice has real-world consequences. It's one thing to tell a pollster you don't support women wearing niqabs in citizenship ceremonies; it's another thing to use your vote to make it illegal. Canadians didn't want to go that far. "When you scratch beneath the surface, you realize that, while people may appear uncomfortable with certain practices because they're not accustomed to them, and they find them weird or different, if you ask them, when push comes to shove, 'Will you force somebody to abandon a deeply held belief?' they would say no," Liberal MP Omar Alghabra says.

Ultimately, several commentators do see the results of the 2015 election as proof that social justice for Muslims is a vote winner. "The more trouble Mr. Harper got into, the more he kept going back to the anti-Muslim antics," says Haroon Siddiqui. "But it completely backfired on him. It wasn't just the Muslims who defeated him, it was the people of Canada who defeated him."

It's worth noting that the Liberals beat the Conservatives by less than 8 percent of the vote. There wasn't necessarily a sea change in Canadians' attitudes. More important than how political scientists interpret the Liberal win was how Justin Trudeau interpreted it. He had just become the most powerful person in the country. In his first speech as prime minister-designate, moments after the CBC had projected his majority government, he made it perfectly clear:

> There are a thousand stories I could share with you about this remarkable campaign, but I want you to think about one in particular. Last week, I met a young mom in St. Catharines, Ontario. She practises the Muslim faith and was wearing a hijab. She made her way through the crowd and handed me her infant daughter, and as she leaned forward, she said something that I will never forget. She said she's voting for us because she wants to make sure that her little girl has the right to make her own choices in life, and that our government will protect those rights. To her, I say this: you and your fellow citizens have chosen a new government, a government that believes deeply in the diversity of our country. We know in our bones that Canada was built by people from all corners of the world, who worship every faith, who belong to every culture, who speak every language. We believe in our hearts that this country's unique diversity is a

blessing bestowed upon us by previous generations of Canadians, Canadians who stared down prejudice and fought discrimination in all its forms. We know that our enviable, inclusive society didn't happen by accident and won't continue without effort. I have always known this; Canadians know it, too. If not, I might have spoken earlier this evening and given a very different speech. Have faith in your fellow citizens, my friends. They are kind and generous. They are open-minded and optimistic. And they know, in their heart of hearts, that a Canadian is a Canadian is a Canadian.

The final words, "a Canadian is a Canadian is a Canadian," were delivered with a flourish, Trudeau's voice rising with a righteous thunder. The crowd of Liberal partisans cheered in approval. They believed that in electing Trudeau, Canadians had shown that they did not fear each other for their differences, and that the rights and freedoms cherished here applied to all, with no asterisk. The rhetorical tone set that night has continued since.

Policy reality, though, requires more careful scrutiny. Immediately after their election, the Liberals had to tackle one of the worst refugee crises the world has seen in a generation. The Syrian civil war, which began in 2011, has featured torture, rape, chemical weapons and the indiscriminate use of weapons in civilian areas. Millions of Syrians have fled. In 2013, the UN formally requested that its member countries accept them as refugees. In 2015, the Conservative government promised to accept only ten thousand. When adjudicating refugee claimants, the government specifically prioritized Syrians who were from religious minorities. In practical terms, that largely meant Christians.

To many Canadians, that was as far as we should go. "We need to proceed with caution. We should accept the vulnerable orphans, the abused, as well as the oppressed Christians, atheists, agnostics and gays," read a letter to the editor printed in *Maclean's*. The omission was obvious. In contrast, Trudeau had promised Canada would settle twenty-five thousand Syrian refugees by the end of the year, regardless of their religion. Before he'd been prime minister a month, extremists committed coordinated attacks in Paris that left 130 people dead and hundreds more wounded. Those terrifying incidents reverberated around the globe. Initially the culprits were believed to be refugees, although this was untrue. That false rumour led Canadians to worry that some of the Syrians fleeing to Canada to escape tyranny and death might be terrorists in disguise.

Like many fears, the fear is not very logical. As noted, white supremacists are a far more pressing threat. Refugees offered a safe haven would be less likely than anyone to repay it with the very violence they'd risked life and limb to escape. In general, over time immigrants become more committed Canadians than their old-stock neighbours. In response to the public pressure, though, Trudeau modified his original promise. He announced that now only ten thousand Syrian refugees would be allowed in before the end of the year, with the remaining fifteen thousand by February of the following year.

While the delay was short (although perhaps not short to a refugee in dire straits), the reasoning behind Trudeau's decision was troubling. "We realized that the most important thing is to be able to reassure Canadians that absolutely everything is being done to keep Canadians safe, and therefore ensure that these refugees are welcomed as new Canadians and not a cause for anxiety or division within the population," Trudeau stated. It almost seemed that, between the lines, the prime minister was acknowledging that he had to placate Canadians' prejudices, and that if he didn't, Canadians would greet the new arrivals with hostility.

It didn't exactly sound like the Canada he described in his victory speech. Rather than reassuring Canadians, the move legitimized the idea that refugees were a threat. Women, children, families and sexual minorities were prioritized under the Liberals—which meant that given the finite numbers being accepted, single males were generally excluded. Whatever the reasoning, to some this was evidence that the government saw single men as more likely to be terrorists than family men. It appeared to play into an increasingly familiar stereotype of Muslims: the women are oppressed, and the men are dangerous.

Despite their caution regarding Syrian refugees, the Liberals got to work rolling back controversial changes the Harper government had made. In the previous parliament, Trudeau had been scorned for voting in favour of Bill C-51, the national security bill critics had warned was dangerous and draconian. To ward off the criticism, Trudeau promised that if elected, the Liberals would amend it. A chief promise was to create an oversight committee that would be able to see classified information and scrutinize national security agencies. In 2016, they passed a bill creating the National Security and Intelligence Committee of Parliamentarians. For the first time, elected officials would have the power to review activities carried out by any department or agency relating to national security or intelligence, including ongoing operations. (The prime minister's office retained the right to censor their reports.) Critics had been calling for such a committee since CSIS was established in 1984. Later they passed a bill that went even further: it would limit certain CSIS powers, provide better definitions of terrorist activities and clarify in law that advocacy and protest did not undermine the security of Canada. The bill included a better review process when sharing intelligence between agencies, ensuring that proper records were kept and that the intelligence in question was also shared with a review agency. Shared intelligence would have to be accompanied by an analysis of its accuracy and the reliability of the way it was obtained.

In 2017, after some wrangling with the Senate, the Liberals passed a bill repealing the former Bill C-24, which had conferred a type of two-tiered citizenship upon Canadians. The new bill removed the government's power to revoke Canadian citizenship for national security reasons. The bill was intended to uphold Trudeau's assertion that a Canadian is a Canadian is a Canadian. ("A terrorist is a terrorist is a terrorist," remarked Conservative MP Bob Saroya in reference to the bill.)

Government lawyers were instructed to drop the Conservatives' attempt to have Omar Khadr's bail rescinded. "I'm surprised it took so long," said Khadr's lawyer, Dennis Edney. "It was about four months ago when they asked for an extension to consider their position. So I was surprised. But it's done. And I'm pleased about that." Khadr's bail conditions were further loosened: his ankle monitor was removed and he was allowed to speak languages other than English with his grandparents. On behalf of the Government of Canada, the Liberals apologized for the role Canadian officials had played in Khadr's ordeal and agreed to a settlement. The price they paid was more than financial. As previously noted, polls showed a strong majority of Canadians opposed the settlement. After the dollar figure was announced, comment sections of media websites were deluged with anti-Trudeau commentary. In March 2019, the court ruled that Khadr's sentence had expired, and that he was a free man.

Things have changed less for Mohamed Harkat. His ankle monitor has been removed, too, but he is still subject to a security certificate and under a deportation order. Any day he could be shipped off to Algeria and a horrifying fate. His wife, Sophie Harkat, told the *Toronto Star*, "We don't have kids because of this. We don't have good jobs because of this. We don't own a home. We don't have normal lives because of this. It's time for it to end." Harkat's lawyer, Barbara Jackman, was unequivocal in where she laid the blame. "That's the real root of the Harkat case: Islamophobia," she said. She has little faith that the Trudeau government will provide justice for Harkat. "You have to remember, the national security structure that we have in place in Canada was created by the Liberals. Harper's government fine-tuned and made it worse, but I don't think we can look to the Liberals to make it fair. They're not going to. It's just a kinder face," she says.

The jury may still be out on Justin Trudeau's performance, but progressives agree on one thing: the greatest challenge the Trudeau government has had to face has been the ascendance of Donald Trump to the office of President of the United States of America. Few saw it coming. Until election day itself, the billionaire businessman and reality TV star's campaign seemed ludicrously inept. He engaged in late-night bickering on Twitter with other celebrities. Media constantly caught him in outright lies. He made racist and sexist statements. An audiotape revealed that he boasted about sexually assaulting women. His shocking election so threatened to upend the established international order that many began to call German Chancellor Angela Merkel the "leader of the free world," a moniker previously reserved for the US president. This left Canada's inexperienced prime minister in a difficult position. Not ideologically sympathetic to Trump, Trudeau nevertheless had to recognize Canada's economic and military dependence on the US and on the mercurial president's goodwill.

And Trump had zeroed in on Muslims. During his campaign he'd advocated deporting all Syrian refugees, characterizing them as a 200,000-man army. He said he would "strongly consider" closing mosques and refused to rule out establishing a database of all Muslims in the US. One of his first acts as president was to institute a ban on entry to the US from seven countries, all with a Muslim majority. That was no coincidence. Rudy Giuliani, Trump's ally and the former mayor of New York City, revealed that Trump had privately referred to it as a "Muslim ban" and had asked Giuliani to help him "find the right way to do it legally." Perhaps fearing what Trump might do next, a number of refugee claimants in the US risked the perilous journey across the Manitoba border on foot in the dead of winter to seek asylum in Canada instead. At the time, one in four Canadians approved of Trump's ban. Despite the risk of alienating those voters and enraging a man it was said could be "provoked by a tweet," Trudeau was fearless. His response bore the hallmark of progressive values. "To those fleeing persecution, terror and war, Canadians will welcome you, regardless of your faith. Diversity is our strength," Trudeau tweeted, the day after Trump's ban was announced. The volunteer fire department in the border town of Emerson, Manitoba was given $30,000 in federal money to provide first aid to freezing asylum-seekers. When it was discovered that RCMP officers questioned asylum seekers crossing the border into Quebec about their religion, how often they practiced it, and their opinions about women's head coverings, public safety minister Ralph Goodale immediately ordered the practice terminated.

In this matter, it seemed Canada would chart its own policies. Trump's rhetoric had an impact, though. Suddenly conversations that would have been grossly politically incorrect the previous year had a place in the national discourse. As Trump's campaign ate up more and more airspace, a minor version of the so-called "birther" movement popped up in Canada. The birther movement was a campaign promoted by Trump questioning whether Barack Obama was born in the US, and therefore whether he was eligible to serve as president. The movement was widely seen as racist since no white president had been subjected to such baseless suspicion as the Hawaiian-born, first black president.

But in September 2016, *The Globe and Mail* started digging into Liberal MP Maryam Monsef's family history. She was a refugee, Canada's first Muslim cabinet minister and Canada's first Afghan-born MP. For some reason, certain journalists were skeptical about her background, and they did some extra research. Their questions uncovered an inconsistency that forced Monsef to have an uncomfortable conversation with her mother. "In recent days, my mother told me for the first time that my sisters and I were, in fact, born in Mashhad, Iran, approximately two hundred kilometres from the Afghan border," she told the CBC. She described how after her parents' wedding in Herat, Afghanistan, the town suffered incredible damage during the war with the Soviets. "No longer safe in their hometown, my parents decided not to take risks and went to Mashhad, Iran where they could be safe—with the hope of soon returning to the place their families called home for generations," she said.

She may not have been born in Afghanistan, but she was still an Afghan. "We were Afghan citizens as we were born to Afghan parents, and under Iranian law, we would not be considered Iranian citizens despite being born in that country," she explained. Demanding that her mother produce details about the scarring ordeal of fleeing the war simply to appease prying journalists wasn't easy. There was yelling and there were tears. "Some survivors believe healing comes from telling their story; others cannot fathom revisiting the past," Monsef said. "My mother never talked about the unspeakable pain that conflict and terror inflicted on her. This week, my sisters and I asked her to relive that pain."

Monsef was a refugee who'd become the youngest person sitting at Justin Trudeau's cabinet table. The details of her story might have been imprecise, but the fundamentals of it were true. Her exact birthplace was irrelevant, and the issue was unworthy of such over-eager, intrusive investigative journalism. Several prominent journalists saw it that way, too. "How would being born among Iran's viciously oppressed Afghan refugees at a time of pitiless barbarism somehow diminish the poignancy of the circumstances surrounding Monsef's childhood and her eventual flourishing on the Canadian federal scene, or make her any less Afghan, or any less a refugee, or any less deserving of sympathetic notice as a refugee success story?" wrote Terry Glavin in *Maclean's*.

But not everyone was satisfied. There was nasty anonymous commentary online. *The Globe and Mail* wouldn't drop the issue. "There is one gap in the plausibility of Ms. Monsef's story," read an editorial. "The implication in Ms. Monsef's story is that her mother was the sole keeper of this family secret. But it is clear that others knew or claimed to know otherwise, which is how Ms.

Monsef came to be asked about this matter in the first place…
Could it be that Ms. Monsef didn't know where she was born, but
others did? Maybe. But the story she has told so far is incomplete.
An MP and a member of cabinet has to be truthful about herself
with the Canadian public. Ms. Monsef especially needed to be
factual about her past when she was being vetted for a cabinet
position. The onus was on Ms. Monsef to come forward as early as
possible with any new information about her birthplace."

Words like "secret" and the implication that Monsef wasn't
being "truthful" or "factual" turned the banal issue of her birthplace into something sordid, and turned an inspiring figure into
another Muslim to fear. A tweet by Trudeau's top advisor, Ger-
ald Butts, summed it up: "*The Globe and Mail* endorses a home-
grown Canadian birther movement. Breathtaking… Canada's full
of people whose parents and grandparents were a little loose about
their birthplace. My gramma [sic] was at times Polish, Ukrainian…
Czech or Russian. My dad's family was the artfully termed 'Scotch-
Irish.' Funny how nobody asked them questions. Wonder why?"

Another notable incident of a Canadian politician being
harassed in the Trump era involved Jagmeet Singh, the turban-
wearing Sikh contending for the leadership of the NDP in 2017.
At a campaign event in Brampton, a woman named Jennifer
Bush stormed the stage waving her arms and jabbing her finger at
Singh, screaming accusations about Singh's alleged sharia agenda.
"When is your sharia going to end? We know you're about the
Muslim Brotherhood," she shouted. Captured on video, it was a
shocking display of anger and aggression that lasted for minutes
as Bush repeatedly inserted herself in front of Singh to continue
her tirade, inches from his face.

Singh responded by saying to the crowd, "We believe in love
and courage… We don't want to be intimidated by hate. We don't
want hatred to ruin a positive event… So let's show people how
to treat someone with love." Calmly he turned to the protester.
"We welcome you. We love you. We support you," he said. Later

some observers including prominent journalist Andrew Coyne wondered why Singh didn't tell her he wasn't Muslim. "While I'm proud of who I am, I purposely didn't go down that road because it suggests their hate would be okay if I was Muslim. We all know it's not. I didn't answer the question because my response to Islamophobia has never been 'I'm not Muslim.' It has always been and will be that 'hate is wrong,'" Singh responded.

Perhaps the best example of Trump's brand of politics at work in Canada was Ontario MP Kellie Leitch's campaign to become leader of the Conservative Party. Her high-profile candidacy featured a promise to screen immigrants for "anti-Canadian values." It was an echo of Trump's pledge to implement "extreme vetting" and "ideological tests" at the American border. She didn't offer any details about the questions immigration agents would ask or how the answers would be verified. More importantly, she didn't appear to have any plan for dealing with Canadians who already held whatever objectionable values she planned to screen for. Only immigrants, apparently, were the problem. The policy proposal generated a lot of publicity. "I suspect her message resonated with many Canadians who fear their way of life is being threatened and feel left out of decision-making in Canada," wrote renowned pollster Angus Reid for the CBC.

Leitch didn't have an exhaustive list of the values she considered "anti-Canadian," but she did say that "people who believe women are property, that they can be beaten, bought and sold, or believe that gays and lesbians should be stoned to death because of who they love don't share our Canadian values." Such beliefs are repulsive, of course, but it is offensive to presume they are held by immigrants. It's notable that, of the many examples she might have chosen as possible candidates for anti-Canadian values, Leitch chose negative stereotypes most commonly associated with Islam.

Some people felt Leitch was deliberately imitating Trump. She discouraged the comparisons when it looked as if Trump was going to lose, but when Trump won, Leitch sent out a fundraising note to her supporters proclaiming, "Our American cousins threw out the elites and elected Donald Trump as their next president. It's an exciting message and one that we need delivered in Canada as well." It was an unambiguous endorsement of Trump. "I don't know why she's doing this, whether she's deliberately anti-Muslim or she's realizing that won in the States and therefore might win here," says Alia Hogben.

Trump's election appears to have heralded a new era of racial, cultural and religious animosity in the US. Trudeau's election in Canada, on the other hand, did not end the devastating hate crimes directed at Muslims. Within a month of Trudeau's victorious declaration that a Canadian is a Canadian is a Canadian, a Montreal man posted a video of himself in a Joker mask threatening to kill one Arab per week. A Toronto woman on her way to pick up her kids from school—in broad daylight at three p.m.—was attacked from behind by two white men who pulled at her hijab, punched her in the face and stomach repeatedly, called her a terrorist and uttered that familiar motto of racists everywhere: that she should "go back where she came from." It was an ironic insult to be hurled by white men, themselves the descendants of immigrants, but it is the same insult that has been hurled at every minority group to immigrate to Canada. Fear of being attacked began to permeate the woman's community. At her mosque, women spoke of being afraid to jaywalk—afraid because no one wanted to give a driver an excuse to run them down. Later a University of Toronto student waiting for the bus was punched, spat on and told to remove his topi (also referred to as a *kufi*, or other terms, depending on the cultural background of the person), which is a skullcap worn by some Muslim men. "Islamophobia is real," the student told the CBC. "People are calling me, and they're scared," said Mohamed El Rashidy, a lawyer with the Canadian Arab Federation.

It got worse. In January 2016 in Vancouver, the Muslim Association of Canada organized a welcome event for Syrian refugees.

After the event, as attendees gathered outside to wait for the bus, a man cycled by and pepper-sprayed them. The dose was so strong that several children were knocked unconscious. Paramedics treated thirty people for exposure to pepper spray. "People are running and screaming, everyone's dashing inside. A bunch of kids were crying," recalled organizer Ammar Ramadan. "I feel like they came here to escape [persecution] and to escape all the struggles from the place they came from. And now, their first day back, they're going to experience something like this."

Justin Trudeau and Vancouver Mayor Gregor Robertson condemned the attack, but many other Canadians weren't as sympathetic. "Embarrassing as this was, I think this highlights the frustration some Canadians feel because of the inability to secure housing and a Doctor [sic], while people from other Countries [sic] just walk in and have everything given to them on a platter," read the single-most popular comment on the story on the CBC website. Such a comment reveals an unflattering portrait of Canadian insularity and entitlement. Among the immigrants here are refugees fleeing war zones, starvation and ethnic cleansing. To state that refugees are the ones getting everything on a platter is simply foolish. Still, the platter comment was at least more measured that the fifth-most popular comment on the website that "they should go back where they came from."

In Calgary, a high school was defaced with spray-painted messages like "Syrians are animals;" "Real Canadians hate Syrians;" "Burn all mosques;" "Syrians go home and take Trudeau" and "While Syrians feast in hotels, Canadians starve on the street, kill the traitor Trudeau." In Ottawa "ISIS Go Home" and "Die Bombers" was spray-painted on a Muslim elementary school overnight for children to see when they were dropped off the next morning. Local city councillor Mathieu Fleury's response was tepid: "I believe that everyone's entitled to their opinion. At the same time, we have to be respectful and again, you can share your opinion in different ways; you don't have to do it through graffiti." It sounded as though the biggest problem with what had happened was the unsightly paint on the walls. To dismiss hate incidents as merely disrespectful displays of opinion fails to recognize the gravity of the situation. It is the message itself that is the problem. After Jennifer Bush's verbal assault on Jagmeet Singh, some commentators focused on the newsworthy "rudeness" of her interruption, but didn't condemn its substance or lament how widespread it had become. After the Vancouver pepper spray attack, Trudeau stated the crime "didn't reflect the warm welcome Canadians have offered." He was probably correct that the creep with the pepper spray wasn't representative of average Canadians, but what about the Canadians behind keyboards who supported him?

Of course, the Charter of Rights and Freedoms provides Canadians with the inalienable right to be racist, if that is how they choose to exercise their freedom of speech. But no one has the right to be racist without consequence. Racism must be exposed, condemned and confronted with the full weight of social and political power, because when it is not, the infection grows and gets nasty. It's not something we can treat with a polite Canadian shrug and agree to disagree.

In June 2016, a pig's head was left on the doorstep of the Islamic Cultural Centre of Quebec City along with a note that said, "Bon appétit." Six months later university student Alexandre Bissonnette opened fire in the mosque, murdering six innocent people. They included immigrants, civil servants, academics and parents. Nineteen others were injured in the rampage. The police burst in and arrested a suspect—Mohamed Belkhadir, a bystander administering first aid. The killer, however, had already slipped away. Survivor Samir Djada later brought reporters to the scene. "I know who that was, and who that was," he said, pointing to bloodstains on the ground. "These were my friends, who I'd known for years. We wanted people to see how horrible it was. This wasn't a movie. There were lives lost and orphans created."

Bissonnette's online presence indicated an admiration for Trump and other right-wing political figures. Media asked Kellie Leitch if she could see any connection between hate crimes like the one in Quebec City and the rhetoric surrounding issues like her proposal to screen immigrants for anti-Canadian values. She dismissed the charge as ridiculous but her Conservative colleague, former cabinet minister and Ontario MP Michael Chong, directly linked the murders to the toxic dialogue over identity issues perpetuated by politicians. "This mosque attack is no accident: It's a direct result of demagogues and wannabe demagogues playing to fears and prejudices. Politicians talking division, not unity, help normalize hate. Not acceptable, enough is enough, stop. And yes, I'm angry. This is Canada. This was an attack on real Canadian values enshrined in the Charter: religious freedom," he stated.

Many others shared Chong's fury. They also felt empathy for the victims. Vigils were held across the country. Thousands gathered at the Maurice Richard Arena in Montreal for a memorial where Premier Philippe Couillard gave a heartfelt speech. "I want to tell Muslim Quebecers: you're at home here, we are all Quebecers," he said. "We feel your pain, we share your pain." According to Amira Elghawaby, the reaction to the murders was a watershed moment. "It really brought home, for many Canadians, that this is a problem, that we do have to address this." According to journalist Martin Patriquin, who spoke to the CBC, the enlightenment was only temporary: "There was a gigantic pause and everybody had a lot of empathy, rightfully so, for this group of human beings who were killed in cold blood. And that empathy lasted, I would say, probably two or three news cycles, and then it was back to the status quo."

One of the first opportunities for reconciliation was missed. No graveyard in the province, outside the greater Montreal area, had a dedicated ground for burials according to Islamic traditions (traditions which include, for example, orienting the body toward

Mecca). The cultural centre where the massacre had taken place had been trying to buy some land on the outskirts of Saint-Apollinaire, a small town near Quebec City, to build a Muslim cemetery to accommodate this need. However, forty local residents signed a petition calling for a referendum on whether the cemetery should be permitted. Under municipal rules, that was enough to trigger the referendum. Even with memories of the murders still fresh, locals voted against allowing the cemetery. The victims would need to be buried elsewhere. Opponents of the cemetery claimed they were simply secularists opposed to any kind of religious burial grounds, but cemeteries for a variety of religious denominations are common in Quebec and have not provoked resistance. Although the pool of eligible voters (those living in the vicinity of the proposed cemetery) was too small to be a representative sample of broader Quebec society, the message was profound: even as dead bodies, Muslims were to be feared.

The NCCM called for the anniversary of the attack to be officially commemorated as a day against Islamophobia. The Quebec Liberals, PQ and Coalition Avenir Québec (CAQ) all rejected the idea. In the year following the attack, hate crimes against Muslims in Quebec City doubled.

*   *   *

The next battle would take place on a grander stage than the ballot boxes in Saint-Apollinaire—the House of Commons itself. On February 15, 2017, a little more than two weeks after the Quebec City murders, Liberal MP Iqra Khalid moved a motion that would:

> recognize the need to quell the increasing public climate of hate and fear;

> condemn Islamophobia and all forms of systemic racism and religious discrimination; and

request that the Standing Committee on Canadian Heritage undertake a study on how the government could develop a whole-of-government approach to reducing or eliminating systemic racism and religious discrimination including Islamophobia in Canada.

Designated motion number 103, or M-103, as a parliamentary proceeding was fairly innocuous. It was moved by a backbencher, not by a member of the cabinet. Entirely non-binding if passed, it would merely advise the government that it should condemn Islamophobia and request that the Canadian Heritage committee study racism and religious discrimination and include Islamophobia in its study. It didn't force the government to do anything. It didn't even force the Canadian Heritage committee to do anything. But to hear opponents tell it, the rookie backbencher's motion was just short of Prime Minister Trudeau himself unilaterally declaring sharia law in Canada.

In parliament, the Conservatives were measured in their opposition. MP David Anderson argued that Islamophobia was undefined. Liberals contended that the definition was self-explanatory and straightforward. According to the Merriam-Webster dictionary, Islamophobia is "irrational fear of, aversion to, or discrimination against Islam or people who practice Islam." Anderson also suggested that the motion was an attack on free speech that could include any criticism of Islam. Since the motion covered all forms of racism and religious discrimination, he argued, why single out Islamophobia for special consideration? Khalid rejected that argument, noting that the current climate demanded that discrimination against Muslims be specifically acknowledged. "I have been asked by some to change the wording of my motion to remove 'Islamophobia' and other references. I will not do so any more than I would speak of the Holocaust and not mention that the overwhelming majority of victims were six million followers of the Jewish faith, and that anti-Semitism was the root cause of the

Holocaust. We cannot address a problem if we fail to call it by its true name," Khalid said.

Outside of parliament, the debate was not as civil. As the motion sat on the order paper waiting for its next turn to be debated, anti-M-103 protests were organized across the country, some drawing hundreds of people. In attendance were members of the far-right groups Soldiers of Odin, La Meute and Pegida. In Montreal there were violent clashes between protesters and counter-protesters. The Rebel Media, the far-right media outlet founded by Ezra Levant, organized a protest featuring four Conservative leadership candidates as speakers. In her speech, Kellie Leitch declared how pleased she was to be among "severely normal people." Her website, meanwhile, featured a photo of a woman with "M-103" taped across her mouth. The photo was set against a background photo of RCMP officers responding to the Parliament Hill shooting. The message was clear: Canadians should fear terrorism, and if Canadians feared terrorism, they should also fear condemning Islamophobia.

Despite the hysteria—or perhaps even more convinced of the need for her motion—Khalid pressed ahead. When it was put to a vote, the motion passed 201 to 91, with the Liberals and NDP in favour and Conservatives mostly opposed. After such a nasty and dramatic prologue, what happened next was underwhelming. The Canadian Heritage committee dutifully undertook its study and produced a sixty-eight-page report with thirty recommendations. Only two of those recommendations specifically referred to Islam: one urged the government to condemn racism and religious discrimination including Islamophobia, and the other recommended a national day of remembrance and action on Islamophobia and other forms of religious discrimination. There were no calls to limit freedom of speech or introduce sharia law.

There were other circumstances in which nasty rhetoric did become policy reality. Quebec in particular remains a distinct battleground in the fight against discrimination toward Muslims in Canada, but the news hasn't been all bad: after the local referendum prohibiting an Islamic cemetery from being built in Saint-Apollinaire, the Quebec Islamic Cultural Centre and the municipal government in Quebec City worked together to find another location. They found one close to the mosque. "For over four hundred years, Quebec has been a welcoming city for all cultures, languages and religions," said Mayor Régis Labeaume. After hearing the news, many at the mosque had tears in their eyes. "It's a historic day," said Mohamed Labidi, president of the Centre.

That moment of humanity contrasted starkly with October 18, 2017 when the Liberal government of Quebec passed Bill 62, a new law prohibiting anyone from wearing face coverings while giving or receiving public services. It applied to doctors, nurses, teachers, daycare employees and all their clients. It even included public transit. Although the PQ and their fellow opposition party CAQ argued it didn't go far enough, it went farther than any vaguely comparable law in North America, and it was strikingly similar to the former Charter of Quebec Values. "For reasons linked to communication, identification and safety, public services should be given and received with an open face," said Premier Philippe Couillard. "We are in a free and democratic society. You speak to me, I should see your face, and you should see mine."

Although technically the law applied to Halloween costumes as much as to niqabs or burqas, there was no doubt who would be most affected, and who was targeted. The government claimed that the bill would simply ensure the neutrality of the secular state, but that claim rang hollow, the bill having passed in a chamber in which a large crucifix still hung over the heads of the members. The three reasons cited by Couillard—communication, identification and safety—were hollow, too. The bearded Couillard's suggestion that he or anyone else had a right to see someone else's face is false; there is no such right, nor is there a reason for one. In this century, Canadians are becoming more and more comfortable interacting by email, text and other anonymous means. Identification is necessary in certain circumstances, but generally not when riding a bus. There is no safety reason for the law, either; a bomb or other weapon is easier to hide under a thick sweater or winter parka than under a niqab.

Once again, supporters of the ban have argued that Islam does not require head coverings, so a ban on them is no impediment to the practice of Islam. They have also argued that head coverings are inherently an attack on women's rights. As previously noted, the Supreme Court ruled that, since religious practice is not monolithic, it is only the individual's sincere belief that his or her action is a religious requirement that matters, not what anyone else says. If head coverings are an attack on equality, Bill 62 was a counter-productive measure. "If any of these women are oppressed, subject to such misogynistic control by their husbands or fathers, the effect of the law will not be to free them from their shackles, but instead will be to simply ban them from the bus," wrote University of Waterloo political science professor Emmett Macfarlane for the CBC. "The state cannot impose freedom by restricting it."

Before the bill passed, 87 percent of Quebecers approved of its objectives. Yet when it actually became law, it suddenly seemed too heavy-handed. Days after the law was announced, protesters lined a popular bus route in downtown Montreal during rush hour wearing surgical masks and scarves over their faces. Montreal Mayor Denis Coderre denounced the new law. Ottawa Mayor Jim Watson sent a letter to Couillard informing him that Ottawa bus drivers whose routes passed through nearby Gatineau, Quebec's third-largest city, would be instructed not to obey the new law.

In response to mounting condemnation, the Liberals backtracked on a few key provisions. On buses, for example, clients would only have to show their face if photo ID was required, such as for students claiming a reduced fare. Rather than being forced to leave their faces uncovered for the duration of the ride, as the government had initially dictated, riders could put their coverings back on again after satisfying the bus driver as to their identity. In libraries, clients would have to uncover their faces if speaking to an employee, but otherwise they were free to browse while covered. In emergency rooms as well, face coverings would not be allowed when speaking to staff, but would now be permitted in the waiting room.

Before the impact of the new law could be determined, in 2018 the Quebec Liberals were defeated by the further right-leaning CAQ, led by François Legault. With Legault's election, it quickly became apparent that the divisive identity debate in Quebec would continue. When Legault's deputy premier, Geneviève Guilbault, agreed to look into whether the government of Quebec should recognize a day dedicated to action against Islamophobia, Legault unequivocally quashed the notion only two days later. "We looked at it. There won't be one," Legault said bluntly. More concerning than his brusque refusal was the willful blindness inherent in his reasoning: "I don't think there is Islamophobia in Quebec, so I don't see why there would be a day dedicated to Islamophobia," he said.

Less than six months after being elected, Legault's government introduced Bill 21, something of a supercharged version of the Liberals' Bill 62. Like the former bill, this bill would require people to uncover their faces when giving or receiving public services. Promoted as a bill championing secularism, the new bill would prevent public authority figures, including police, teachers and judges, from wearing any religious garments at all, of any kind or size, whether or not they covered their faces. Interestingly, wildlife officers were also included, presumably to prevent the moose, caribou and white-tailed deer indigenous to Quebec from being offended by affronts to Quebec's secularism. Knowing that the bill would likely be struck down as unconstitutional, the government took the extraordinary step of invoking the notwithstanding clause. The complicated and controversial history of that clause has resulted in it being used more often in Quebec than elsewhere in Canada; nevertheless, the clause was designed to be used as a safeguard in truly exceptional circumstances when application of a Charter right would cause greater harm than good. In this case, it was being used to allow the government to violate the Charter right to freedom of religion simply to promote its own version of secularism.

Legault did promise that the crucifix in the legislative assembly could be moved to another room—if legislators passed the bill, which they did in June 2019. Certainly, the law has its proponents. Many Quebeckers have a sincere desire for a secular society, to move on from the stranglehold the Catholic Church once exerted over the province. As noted, the law targets all religious garments, including those worn by Christians or Jews, like crucifixes and kippahs. Time will tell if the law represents another step in the legacy of the Quiet Revolution that freed Quebec from Catholic domination, or if the effect of the law is simply to push Muslims into the fringes of Quebec society.

* * *

Every political party endures civil wars. Sometimes they are bids for power between competing personalities; other times, they are battles for the soul of the party itself. In the nineties, the Liberal Party sought to manage an endless feud between the then and future leaders of the party, Jean Chrétien and Paul Martin. In 2001, NDP Leader Alexa McDonough had to fend off a challenge from the more radical left wing of the party, which called for the NDP to be disbanded and re-formed as an amalgam of like-minded social movements. Today the conservative movement appears to be grappling with a similar existential question: how to manage the influence of the far right. To a large degree, the answer to that question will determine where they stand on issues of religious discrimination and social inclusion affecting Muslims.

Although there is an oft-recounted narrative that the Conservative Party is some sort of bastion of anti-Islamic sentiment, such an assertion must be challenged. Conservatives have led the charge in the House of Commons to raise awareness of the ethnic cleansing in Malaysia being perpetrated against the Rohingya people, the majority of whom are Muslim. Two prominent Conservatives voted in favour of Iqra Khalid's motion to have the Canadian Heritage committee study Islamophobia: former cabinet minister Michael Chong and MP Bruce Stanton, a man so respected by his colleagues that he was named deputy speaker. "Canadians have the right to the religion of their choice," Stanton told the *Orillia Packet and Times*. "That's a rock-solid part of our society. It's a principle I stand firmly with. It's part of the values of my party."

After failing to defeat Khalid's motion, Conservative MP David Anderson, the party's lead spokesman on the file, struck a conciliatory tone. "I think that many of us have wanted to have a mature discussion about this for a long time, and I think actually Ms. Khalid and I would be on the exact same wavelength on that issue," he said. "The committee can do a good job, and we can have a discussion about what this means for Canada, the role of Islam in Canada. It's time we had that discussion and did it on a different level than we have over the last month."

With that statement, the Conservatives seemed to be sending a signal that they intended the tone to change. Not long after, the card-carrying Conservative membership appeared to send the same message. In the 2017 Conservative leadership contest, despite a campaign that generated significant media attention and often portrayed her as a frontrunner, controversial candidate Kellie Leitch was trounced. She finished sixth behind centrist Michael Chong, and with less than 8 percent of the vote. During the campaign, fellow Conservatives had strongly criticized her proposals. Influential Conservative MP Lisa Raitt mocked her "anti-Canadian values" proposal. Stephen Harper's former director of policy Rachel Curran called it "Orwellian." Conservative strategist Chad Rogers even called on her to resign her candidacy. Clearly the Conservative Party of 2017 did not share Leitch's vision of Canada.

While the media spent much of the Conservative leadership campaign focused on Leitch and the aborted candidacy of businessman and reality TV star Kevin O'Leary, the actual horse race turned out to be between former cabinet minister Maxime Bernier and former Speaker Andrew Scheer. When Scheer eked out a narrow victory over Bernier after thirteen rounds of voting, pundits found him difficult to pigeonhole. He'd been elected to the House at age twenty-five and spent nearly his entire career in the Speaker's chair, acting as a neutral arbiter of debate and maintaining order in the Chamber. He was affable and had made a few procedurally significant decisions. But after winning the race, his platform was quickly removed from his website. The best some pundits could do was suggest he might be "Stephen Harper with a smile." To many Canadians, he remains an unknown.

Maxime Bernier is better known. Once a high-profile member of Stephen Harper's cabinet, Bernier has been called "Mad Max" for his sometimes-controversial, libertarian-leaning views. *The Globe and Mail*'s investigation of far-right online hate groups revealed enthusiasm for Bernier: "He was dog-whistling pretty hard," wrote one user of a far-right chat room who'd attended a Bernier leadership event. After a little over a year of Scheer's leadership, Bernier decided he no longer fit in with the Conservative Party. Declaring that the party had "all but abandoned its core conservative principles," he launched a new political party with himself as leader, which he called the People's Party of Canada. Where Bernier intends to take the new party might be revealed by a series of tweets he made days before quitting the Conservatives.

"Why should we promote ever more diversity? If anything and everything is Canadian, does being Canadian mean something?" Bernier asked. "People who refuse to integrate into our society and want to live apart in their ghetto don't make our society strong.... It's time we reverse this trend before the situation gets worse. More diversity will not be our strength, it will destroy what has made us such a great country."

By staking a position to the right of the Conservative Party, Bernier may represent a long-term threat to them. The dynamic stirs up memories of the late eighties when the socially and fiscally conservative Reform Party was created as an alternative to Brian Mulroney's more mainstream Progressive Conservatives (PCs). At first, Reform was a Western-based fringe movement, but they managed to access a voting block that felt abandoned by the centre-right PCs. Ten years later they were the Official Opposition, and the PCs were struggling to keep official party status in the House of Commons. A few years after that, the PCs were gone, subsumed into the Canadian Alliance, Reform's successor party. Scheer's delicate task is to compete with Bernier for votes on the right without alienating the votes in the centre that he needs to win.

This balancing act has resulted in an evolving relationship with the far right. At one time, Conservative MPs were regular guests on Ezra Levant's The Rebel Media. During the 2017 Conservative leadership race, Scheer himself appeared on Rebel-personality Faith Goldy's show and agreed to go duck hunting with her if he became Conservative leader. However, this relationship ended after the alt-right rally in Charlottesville, Virginia, in which counter-protester Heather Heyer was murdered by a member of a far-right group. Goldy's notoriously biased coverage of the rally so disgusted observers from across the political spectrum that Scheer announced the Conservatives would be boycotting The Rebel until its editorial direction changed. (Goldy would go on to further infamy: she was later fired from The Rebel after appearing on a neo-Nazi-affiliated podcast. She later appeared on another alt-right podcast where she recited what are called "The Fourteen Words," a mantra of white supremacists: "We must secure the existence of our people and a future for white children.")

Scheer acted decisively by boycotting The Rebel, but the potential threat from Bernier makes taking such strong stances more difficult. In February 2019 a convoy of trucks drove from Red Deer to Parliament Hill, ostensibly in support of oil and gas workers. Somewhere along the way, that message was hijacked. The United We Roll convoy was associated with Yellow Vests Canada, a movement that, according to the Canadian Anti-Hate Network, has become a magnet for anti-immigrant and racist rhetoric. "The hate is mostly directed at Muslims, left-leaning individuals, government, media, and, occasionally, law enforcement. They share conspiracy theories such as: Muslims are behind the Fort McMurray wildfire so they could build a super-mosque. Oil and economic concerns are an issue, but not their primary concern," the anti-hate organization stated.

Maxime Bernier spoke at the United We Roll Parliament Hill rally, and the Conservatives calculated that Scheer needed to speak too. He was criticized, though, for failing to offer a sufficiently strenuous condemnation of the racist and anti-immigration sentiment that was present at the rally. "With Maxime Bernier trying to make inroads with the further right areas of the party's base, Conservatives need to show unwavering support for western Canada, pipelines and the oil and gas industry. But Scheer ought to have made a distinction between his support for Canadian oil workers, and support for the racism and violence that has been associated with United We Roll," wrote the CBC's Angela Wright. If it had not been clear in advance what sort of politics had infiltrated the rally, it was certainly clear after the fact. During the rally, in which many protestors sported red "Make Canada Great Again" hats imitating the red hats worn by Donald Trump's disciples, Faith Goldy hopped up on an impromptu stage and gave an impassioned speech to her supporters.

Scheer faced further criticism for his response to the terrorist attacks in Christchurch, New Zealand, in March 2019. When an Australian white supremacist murdered fifty people at two mosques, Scheer's statement of condolence condemned the attack but didn't mention mosques or Muslims. According to the *Toronto Star*'s Emma Teitel, some pundits interpreted Scheer's choice of words as an attempt to appear to show solidarity to victims without offending Islamophobes. It is perhaps illustrative of the challenge Scheer faces that his statement satisfied no one.

Progressives were offended, although here Scheer may have fallen victim to a scrutiny which was not extended to every public figure; there were other notable public figures whose first statements after the attack also did not mention Muslims, and they were not similarly criticized. But there was also a backlash from his own party. "Delete and try again. Name the place of worship. Name their religion. Put your arms around them. Condemn the specific pathology that drove their killer(s)," tweeted Andrew MacDougall, a former spokesman for Stephen Harper. Scheer's deputy, Lisa Raitt, issued her own statement on Twitter, which she followed up with, "Anyone who comments on my previous posts with anti-Muslim statements will be blocked." Conversely, Maxime Bernier made no statement of condolence at all, despite having done so in the past when Muslims had been perpetrators of terrorist acts. Scheer chose to revise his statement, issuing a new one the next day that did make references to standing with "our Muslim brothers and sisters."

As the 2019 election approached, Scheer made his strongest statement yet to counter accusations that his party was soft on hate: "I find the notion that one's race, religion, gender, or sexual orientation would make them in any way superior to anybody else absolutely repugnant... and if there's anyone who disagrees with that, there's the door." That same day, one of his MPs, Michael Cooper, angrily confronted the president of the Alberta Muslim Public Affairs Council in a Justice committee meeting telling him he should be ashamed for suggesting there was a link between Conservative commentators and acts of extremist violence. In support of his argument, Cooper read from the Christchurch killer's manifesto, which has been banned in New Zealand.

In response, Scheer called Cooper's actions unacceptable and had him removed from the committee. Once again, Scheer had been put in a challenging position. Some were satisfied with his swift action, while others said he didn't go far enough, and that he should have fired Cooper from his position as deputy justice critic, or even kicked him out of caucus. In the media, though, Bernier defended Cooper: "Michael didn't do anything wrong. He was expressing his point of view, and we need people like that in our parliament," Bernier said.

Each such dilemma Scheer faces shows that whatever alchemy might unite the conservative movement without alienating the centre has yet to be discovered. Added to the landscape that Scheer must navigate are two powerful provincial Conservatives, Jason Kenney and Doug Ford. Each carries enormous clout in the Canadian conservative movement. How the ascendance of Jason Kenney as the new premier of Alberta will impact the relationship between Muslims and Conservatives remains to be seen. Kenney was widely known as the "Minister of Curry in a Hurry" when he was a member of Stephen Harper's cabinet. His belief that the values and aspirations of immigrant communities could make them natural allies of the federal Conservatives spurred tireless work establishing personal connections within those communities. He attended countless cultural events, learned greetings in multiple languages and built up an impressive knowledge of international issues. Under his watch, Citizenship and Immigration even spent $750,000 monitoring ethnic media, work which included making pie charts to gauge Kenney's popularity in those communities. His work paid off. Kenney is often credited with making significant inroads for the party in communities that had previously been Liberal strongholds.

But his relationship with Muslims is complicated. After the murders at the Islamic Cultural Centre of Quebec City, Kenney's words of condolence seemed heartfelt. When President Donald Trump instituted a ban on entry to the US for anyone coming from seven Muslim-majority countries, Kenney slammed it as a "brutal, ham-fisted act of demagogic political theatre." It wasn't quite what some observers expected from Kenney. After all, this was the same man whom Reform Party founder Preston Manning referred to as part of a "Catholic mafia" of MPs in his caucus pushing religious conservatism. "Is this the same Jason Kenney?" asked the Huffington Post. His relentless efforts to ban niqabs during citizenship ceremonies have not been forgotten, nor has his support of other related policies of the Harper government. Critics suggest Kenney is manipulating immigrant communities he thinks might vote for him, while supporters maintain he has a genuine belief that immigrant communities deserve a prominent role in setting the direction of the Conservative Party. As leader of the United Conservative Party of Alberta, Kenney turfed candidates who had claimed Muslims were "worshipping Satan" or who had posed for pictures with known white supremacists. He unequivocally condemned their actions, yet the question remains: why have these candidates been drawn to his party?

The same question might need to be asked of Doug Ford, the populist former Toronto city councillor who was elected PC premier of Ontario in 2018. When Faith Goldy ran for mayor of Toronto that year (in a campaign in which she pledged to "launch a Special Research Desk on Islamic Extremism to monitor finances in and out of Toronto Islamic centres" and ultimately received over twenty-five thousand votes), she sent out robocalls that stated she was "the only candidate who stands with Doug Ford." In September she posed for a photo with him at his family's annual "Ford Fest" barbeque. It took Ford three days to disavow her, despite repeated requests from opposition politicians, and even then, his response was tepid, stating that he condemned hate speech, "be it from Faith Goldy or anyone else." It may be fair to suggest that if Ford condemns Faith Goldy, he may need to take a hard look at why Faith Goldy doesn't condemn him.

It's the same question that plagues the movement at large. It's difficult to say what will happen in the relationship between the moderate and far-right ranks of Canadian conservatives. In the three by-elections held after the formation of the People's Party of Canada, Bernier's team has made little impact in two of them. Clearly, the party has a long way to go. Surprisingly, though, the one riding in which they did make an impact, garnering nearly 11 percent of the vote, was Burnaby South—a part of BC sometimes called the "People's Republic of Burnaby" for its traditionally left-wing politics. In a close election, where dozens of ridings can be won or lost by just a few percentage points, the People's Party of Canada may well prove a difference maker. If they are, or if some successor party proves to be, pragmatic Conservatives will face ever greater pressure to make room for the far right in mainstream discourse.

* * *

Of course, histrionic commentary from the likes of Faith Goldy is easy to monitor and condemn. It's much harder to find what's buried in a 392-page budget bill. That's where, in 2019, Justin Trudeau's government backtracked on its "Welcome to Canada" promise, which prompted asylum seekers to abandon claims in the US to trek on foot across the border. The budget bill proposed making people with open or accepted refugee claims in other countries ineligible for asylum in Canada. According to former Conservative spokesman Andrew MacDougall in *Maclean's*, "#WelcomeToCanada was #OnlyAMarketingSlogan."

The Gifts: The Message We're Sending

To CONFRONT THE bigotry and discrimination that has been directed toward Muslims in Canada in recent years, non-Muslims must carefully and humbly examine their own behaviour. They also need to hear from Muslims to understand the impact Islamophobia is having on them. Of course, Muslim communities do not speak with one voice. For example, although they appear to be outliers, there are prominent Muslims who have called for a niqab ban themselves and are supportive of efforts to institute one. More broadly, some Muslims have argued eloquently that undue focus on discrimination against Muslims instills a sense of victimhood, which is an impediment to inclusion. However, when speaking with Muslim individuals and organizations generally, an overarching theme becomes clear. "It's not an easy time to be a Muslim in Canada," says Amira Elghawaby, former spokesperson of the NCCM.

Often people are afraid to talk to one another, evidence that the fundamental right to freedom of association is under threat. Because people fear being connected with someone who might be an intelligence target, they unintentionally ostracize that person. "No one wants to be 'Arared,'" wrote Sheema Khan in *The Globe and Mail*, recalling what happened to Maher Arar after a lunch with a casual acquaintance who happened to be under surveillance. Muslim communities have been pitted against each other. Some Arab Muslims report hostility from non-Arab Muslims who believe that Arabs are responsible for drawing negative attention to Islam.

The relationship between Muslims and non-Muslims has been badly damaged, too. Once that process begins, it's hard to stop.

Sociologist Gerard Bouchard stated that minorities that are pushed away eventually stop trying to integrate, and they ultimately reject mainstream society. This only deepens the cycle of alienation and mistrust. Other analysts concur. "When people are constantly reminded that they are inferior Others—whether by crude far-right rhetoric, media stereotyping, day-to-day discrimination, or government indifference to their concerns and needs—it is only a matter of time before they will feel alienated and lose the desire to belong," wrote Dr. Zijad Delic.

It's important to keep the damage to the relationship in perspective. Polls show that most Muslims in Canada are pretty satisfied about life here. The cold is still their biggest complaint, as it is for the many non-Muslims who complain about snow from December to March. The polls also tell a more complex story. In 2016, an Environics poll showed that a strong majority—61 percent—of Muslim youth defined themselves as Muslim first and Canadian second. To some that's alarming, at least at face value. They feel the respondents' loyalty to Canada should be called into question.

Upon closer inspection, it's not only permissible for someone to feel Canadian second and something else first, but also normal. Every Canadian's identity is constructed according to their own personal hierarchy of subsidiary identities: any one of us might define ourselves first by sex, gender, marital or family status rather than by nationality. Would any parent define themselves as a Canadian first and a parent second? Would it be so strange for a Christian to feel that their primary loyalty is to God and not to a man-made institution like the Canadian state? It is not for anyone to say where another person's religious beliefs should rank among the components of their identity. The same poll also showed that over 80 percent of Muslims felt very proud to be Canadian, a clear indication of how the two identities—Muslim and Canadian—can be deeply held simultaneously.

However, the Environics poll also showed that 35 percent of Canadian Muslims had been the victims of discrimination or unfair treatment. Clearly the relationship requires careful, mature attention from both sides. Among the most popular comments on the CBC web article reporting on the 2016 Environics poll were "Promoting White Guilt is Canada's newest and largest industry," and "Welcome to Canada, how can we change to make you happier?" To stop discriminating was apparently too much of a change for some Canadians to stomach without a snarky comment.

Some Muslims, particularly visibly Muslim women (women in hijabs, niqabs or burkas) fear for their physical safety. Given the rash of hate crimes targeting them, it's understandable. Some feel that law enforcement is unwilling or unable to protect them, and worse, that they themselves are suspects in the eyes of the state. It's no wonder some feel that their Canadian citizenship isn't worth as much as that of non-Muslim Canadians.

For former *Toronto Star* editor Haroon Siddiqui, what is happening to Muslims in Canada harkens back to the worst episodes of Canada's past. "Of course Muslim Canadians are not being interned as the Japanese Canadians were, but most Muslims feel psychologically interned," he said. The unjustified cloud of suspicion hovering over them becomes a kind of prison, preventing them from fully accessing Canadian culture and citizenship. He says that many Muslim communities are in shock. They believed that Canada in the twenty-first century stood for something better.

* * *

Canada has learned much from its past mistakes. The internment of Japanese Canadians and other persecuted groups during the Second World War is universally seen as an injustice. Canadians react with shame to such stories today. Although there is work to be done to reconcile with Indigenous peoples, and the election of US President Donald Trump has emboldened racist buffoonery from fringe groups in Canada too, in many ways the Canada of today is a more inclusive and welcoming place than it has ever been. So why does this problem between Muslims and non-Muslims persist, and what solutions do experts propose?

The particularly tense atmosphere in Quebec likely has its origins in history. Before the Quiet Revolution of the sixties, the Catholic Church controlled almost everything in Quebec. "Many in Quebec have what they see as wounds and scars from the Catholic period and the Catholic hegemony, and the last thing they want to see, whether they are on the right or the left, is some opening up of the public space for Islam," says religious studies expert Dr. David Goa of the University of Alberta.

Another factor contributing to fear of Muslims may be self-interested advocacy from weapons manufacturers and security agencies. Both are powerful entities with the ear of the government. They may have nothing against Islam, but they probably know that the more fearful the population is, the more resources and powers will be allocated to them. "They're not all anti-Muslim. They're just doing it for the buck," sasy Haroon Siddiqui.

Such broad societal issues are difficult to resolve. Other impediments to inclusion have more ready solutions. Some have argued that some responsibility for the current environment falls on Muslims themselves for not communicating to non-Muslim Canadians in a way that resonates. Communication is a two-way street. "They have not been able to explain clearly the ethical and humanistic content of Islam; they have also, by default, often allowed militant Islamists to become the spokespersons for all Muslims," wrote Karim H. Karim. Some will see that criticism as unfair; many people have worked hard to explain the true nature of Islam, and they have found it difficult to get non-Muslim Canadians to listen. Their methods of communication may need to become more strategic. In Canada, the best way for a community to make their voice heard is to vote and traditionally, voter turnout has been low in Muslim communities. That changed in 2015, but their previously low level of interest in the electoral process meant that politicians spent too little time listening to Muslim voices and too little time chasing Muslim votes. By contrast, voters who were either disinterested in or hostile to the concerns of Muslim communities were highly engaged in the electoral process. If people want change, they have to vote for it.

Muslim communities cannot retreat into silos. Despite the challenges in their relationship with non-Muslims, they must continue to be engaged members of the community at large and interact with non-Muslims as much as possible. This will not always be easy. Liberal MP Omar Alghabra has an interesting, if perhaps controversial, take on it. He suggests that for a while, Muslims may need to tolerate the discomfort of non-Muslims. "We should not really call people who are expressing that discomfort racist or Islamophobic. We need to understand that it's a natural thing to ask such questions about something you're not familiar with. We need to welcome this conversation," he says. He knows that advice might be tough to swallow. "I know some activists would say, 'Why would I need to explain myself? My rights are my rights, and they're protected by law. Why would I need to explain myself?' But I disagree with that. I think it's the right thing to do, to acknowledge human frailties and fears. You need to find a way to reach out and showcase who you are, and what your values are. It may appear on paper that that's not fair, but it's the healthy thing to do."

One reason this is necessary is that there is widespread ignorance of Islam in non-Muslim Canada, ignorance that is fertile ground for misconceptions to take hold. Baby Boomers, Generation x and Millennials were taught very little about Islam in the public school system. For David Goa, the problem goes deeper than that. In his view, that ignorance is rooted in an ignorance of religion in general and a paper-thin commitment to multiculturalism. "I think there is, in our country, a deep, deep immaturity about genuine pluralism. Our multiculturalism policy has tended to be one of food and dance, and about commonalities," he says. This analysis rings true to Canadians who grew up in multicultural environments, who learned to dance basic bhangra moves but know nothing about the rich and ancient histories of Punjabi religious beliefs, or who learned to say Happy New Year in Cantonese, but know nothing about the religious and philosophical underpinnings of Chinese culture. Certainly the multicultural population of Canada offers an opportunity to examine the divergent ways that cultures perceive the world, an opportunity we're not taking as seriously as we could. Goa believes that educators have a crucial role to play in correcting this: "What about me? What about my colleagues in the professoriate? What about the high school teachers and the grade school teachers? What have we done in our country to actually bring forward healthy knowledge about the contributions of Islam to human civilization? And of Christianity to human civilization? What have we done about that? Well, my sense is we've done a piss-poor job."

Clearly Canadians in general and policy-makers in particular need to know more about Islam. Evidence shows that the more non-Muslim Canadians come into contact with Muslims, the more stereotypes are dispelled and the more favourable impressions of Islam are developed. Confronting prejudice and discrimination is only the first step. "It's not good enough to just critique Islamophobia. Of course. Of course," Goa emphasizes. "But what's the antidote? The antidote is actually learning something about the gifts of Islam, and why it is precious to so many people.... Of course, do critique. But also do the gifts. And we haven't done the gifts."

Developing a greater respect for religion could also be a powerful tool in making Canada more attractive to immigrants in general. Canada should be known as a place where you can integrate into a safe, multicultural community while retaining your most cherished beliefs. To truly embrace religious pluralism and the fascinating, divergent viewpoints and philosophies pluralism would bring into the Canadian mainstream, a fundamental mindset has to shift. Once, tolerance was the epitome of progressive values.

Over time we moved toward multiculturalism, an appreciation that went beyond the mere absence of discrimination.

Now our commitment to multiculturalism needs to mature into a commitment to honour more than just ethnic foods and dances. When we understand and respect each other's fundamental worldviews, we may find that we work and live much better together. True social and economic inclusion has to be the goal, not just communities living side by side in peace, but not really together. On the ground there are people already working to make that shift happen. When Sergeant David Zackrias of the Ottawa Police Service describes the changes he sees taking place, the passion in his voice is evident. "I want to shift from diversity to inclusion. Diversity, multiculturalism—that was great at one time. But we're past that," he says.

There are a number of specific policy changes that might go a long way. Promotion of a more substantive multiculturalism in schools would help. So would a national anti-hate strategy, perhaps bolstering police hate-crime units and offering more avenues to report harassment and discrimination from security services as well. Police need to be more transparent about what is reported to them, what is being investigated and what is being prosecuted. Only a few police services publish annual reports on hate-crime data, but more of them could. Security agencies also need to hire more Muslim officers who better understand Muslim communities. Better training needs to be provided to show non-Muslim officers what Muslims in Canada are experiencing. Gaps in the law regarding hate expression online need to be addressed.

Fortunately, many potential solutions are being vigorously pursued. Following the toxic atmosphere of the 2015 federal election, the Ottawa Police Service became the first police force in Canada to let people report hate crimes online. Now Ottawa residents can make a complaint without neighbours seeing a police car pull up to their house. Non-Muslim religious leaders have made efforts to confront and defuse Islamophobic elements in their communities.

Muslims in Canada, too, should be given credit for the ways they've approached the challenge of inclusion. Many Muslim organizations are working hard at outreach to non-Muslims. Mosques are generous contributors to non-Muslim charities, particularly during Ramadan. Muslims have responded calmly to attacks questioning their loyalty. "The expression of their dissent has been very Canadian," says Haroon Siddiqui. The urge to retreat into tribalism has been resisted, even when Muslims encounter tribalism themselves. The image of Canada among younger Muslims in particular is one in which they feel they belong. As Baljit Nagra's study confirmed, it is in fact the tribalism displayed by some non-Muslims that younger Muslims see as profoundly un-Canadian.

There are a lot of reasons to believe they're right.

After September 11, 2001, many Muslims genuinely feared a backlash. As noted, many experienced just that. Many, though, were touched by the kindness of individual Canadians who wanted to reassure them that they weren't hated or feared because of what had happened in New York and Washington, and that they understood that the terrorists didn't represent them or Islam. Other encouraging signs followed. CBC had a hit with *Little Mosque on the Prairie*, a comedy that depicted ordinary Muslims and non-Muslims interacting. The massively popular Naheed Nenshi became the first Muslim mayor of a major city in Canada when he was elected mayor of Calgary in 2010. To Sheema Khan, the public support shown to Monia Mazigh as she fought to rescue her husband, Maher Arar, clearly showed where Canadians stood. "The fact that a Muslim woman can engage in and win a public campaign to have her husband's wrongful deportation overturned; that her effort wins national respect; that alleged police wrongdoing in the deportation becomes the subject of a government inquiry; and that she becomes a bona fide candidate in a national election [Mazigh ran for the NDP in Ottawa South]—all these speak volumes about the fundamental nature of Canada as a place where an individual, regardless of gender, creed, or ethnic origin can strive for justice, a claim few nations can make," Khan wrote in *The Globe and Mail*.

Shortly after Michael Zehaf-Bibeau murdered Corporal Nathan Cirillo and attacked Parliament Hill, vandals smashed windows and spray-painted "Go home" and "CANADA" on a mosque in Cold Lake, Alberta. Within hours, dozens of concerned citizens showed up to help clean and repaint the wall. They taped their own messages to the wall, messages like, "You Are Home" and "Love Your Neighbour." Some brought flowers. It was a message from the community to their Muslim neighbours, but also to the vandals who apparently saw no irony in using the word "CANADA" to adorn their crime. If they saw themselves as defenders of Canadian values, they were about to get a shock. "I just want to say that the Muslim community is at home in Cold Lake, so maybe [the vandals] need to evaluate whether or not they belong in Cold Lake," said Mayor Craig Copeland. When the same mosque was defaced with nearly the same graffiti a year later, the community did it all over again.

In October 2014, university student Omar Albach staged a social experiment in Hamilton where Corporal Cirillo's funeral had recently been held. The goal was to test how ordinary Canadians would react to an obvious display of Islamophobia. He asked two friends to wait at a busy bus stop. One, Zakaria Ghanem, wore traditional Muslim dress and the other, Devin Giamou, wore stereotypically western clothes. Giamou began by remarking to other bus riders that Ghanem shouldn't be allowed on the bus because he might have explosives. Christian Cotroneo of the Huffington Post explained what happened next: "Over and over again, the young man's efforts to get bystanders on the hate train met with failure. At every turn, the 'hater' was scolded, yelled at, shamed... Canadians appeared to have no taste for the Islamophobia he was peddling." Eventually Giamou pretended to shove Ghanem. A bystander leapt in and walloped Giamou with an old-fashioned Canadian haymaker straight out of a game of pond hockey.

The social experiment proved instructive, if a little heavy-handed. In Toronto in January 2015, a more touching experiment took place. Mustafa Mawla stood on a busy street corner, blind-folded and with a sign reading, *I am a Muslim. I am labeled as a terrorist. I trust you. Do you trust me? Give me a hug.* Dark skinned and heavily bearded, he looked every inch the kind of man Islamo-phobes fear, but over and over, Canadians of every age, gender and race came up to hug him. Assma Galuta, Mawla's friend whose idea it was, said, "It is a first step in helping educate people that not all Muslims are bad people, and a reminder for radical Mus-lims as well that if we want to defend Islam, we should do so in a way Islam teaches, not with acts of violence forbidden in Islam." It was a lovely demonstration of common humanity—an act of outreach by one Muslim to non-Muslims, literally met with open arms.

Afterword

POLITICIANS ARE CAREFUL about what they say but step away from Parliament Hill and speak to people who support measures that target Muslims in Canada. Some mount interesting arguments to support their beliefs, but many speak with emotion, not reason. At the root of their frustration is a belief that what they call "Canadian culture" has been under attack for a long time. Restrictions on an encroaching Islam are a way of standing up for something that matters to them, of fighting back on behalf of their traditional values. These beliefs aren't necessarily based on a thoughtful analysis of reality; witness, for example, the widespread belief that people "aren't allowed to say Merry Christmas anymore." It's not true, but the central idea that European, Christian-based ideals are somehow in peril in Canada is fervently believed. Perhaps it isn't technically racism. Most of the people described above would be aghast at such a label being applied to them. Still they clearly resent seeing Muslims taking up space that used to belong exclusively to them. They don't feel they should have to accommodate to create a welcoming space for others. It's the others who should accommodate, they say. While not necessarily racist, these notions nevertheless often appear to be based on the idea that there is a certain "us" who are legitimate standard-bearers of Canadian culture and a "them" who must adapt.

Culture wars are nothing new in Canada. French Canadians had to fight long and hard to have their rights and contributions to Canada recognized by the British cultural and political hegemony. Eventually the idea of a bicultural Canada, with two founding nations instead of one, became firmly entrenched. In time, that notion would be challenged by the idea of a multicultural Canada, a recognition of the non-British, non-French contributions to our country: Chinese Canadians who built railroads, Italian Canadians who built roads and sewers, Ukrainian Canadians who cleared land and started farms, and immigrants from every other culture who have made Canada home.

If there is an "us" and a "them," who are we and who are they? What is Canadian culture? The emergence of multiculturalism as our central identity has given rise to accusations that if Canadian culture is defined by such a principle, then in fact there is no definable Canadian culture. Others have lamented that Canadian culture can only be expressed in comparison to American culture: we're like them but quieter, more polite, more tolerant, more able to identify our hometown on an unmarked map. But for the younger Canadians for whom multiculturalism is a given, and for the older Canadians who have chosen to embrace it, a more confident sense of Canadian identity is possible within that framework. It is a sense of Canadian culture that is unencumbered by its contradictory elements.

Canadian culture is paradoxical. Our culture is intertwined with hockey, not cricket, and yet there is something very Canadian about the teams of cricket players who gather to play on the grounds of Rideau Hall in Ottawa during the summer. The Tragically Hip are Canada's band; their hit "Wheat Kings" even opens with the haunting call of a loon. But Drake, a rapper with no similarity to the Hip, sprinkles references to Canada throughout his work and must be a part of any discussion of modern Canadian music. Nothing is more Canadian than winter, snow and sub-zero temperatures, but people wore shorts and T-shirts as the Olympic torch passed through the Lower Mainland of BC en route to the 2010 Winter Olympics in Vancouver.

Our culture encompasses everything Canada produces and everything Canada adopts. William Shatner became famous in the US and the rest of the world probably believes he's American, but here, he's a Canadian icon. He's from here. Conversely, Arthur

Lismer and Frederick Varley were grown men before they ever set foot in Canada and became members of the Group of Seven, the landscape painters who—despite painting in widely diverse styles—have been synonymous with Canadian art ever since. They weren't from here, but they painted here, and they painted the images that resonate in our core.

So who are we? Canadians. Who are they? Everybody else, for now.

This inclusive notion of Canadian culture is what allows new-comers to take on past glories, from years before their families immigrated. First-generation Canadian kids today will still feel butterflies when shown Paul Henderson's winning goal against the Soviets in 1972. Even if their parents were still in their countries of origin when the goal was scored, that goal belongs to those kids, too. Adopting a Canadian identity also requires new Canadians to bear the dishonour of the less-glorious stories of our past. It is not new Canadians whose ancestors spawned the tragic legacy of residential schools, but it is their shame to bear, as much as it is for all Canadians. As new Canadians accept these legacies, both good and bad, they also share the cultures of their countries of origin. Witness the diversity in the throngs of onlookers and participants at Toronto's Caribana, Vancouver's Dragon Boat Festival or in any Canadian bar on St. Patrick's Day.

Canadians can hyphenate if they want to, but they should never be compelled to. Far from having no identity or culture, Canada has every identity, every culture. This doesn't mean that every set of values is acceptable. Some clearly aren't. But so-called Canadian values are aspirational anyway. We may pride ourselves on being polite, laugh at how often we say sorry, and believe in the core values of the Charter of Rights and Freedoms, but we've all met Canadians who don't fit those descriptions, and those who don't cannot be identified by their language, skin colour or religion. The idea of "us" and "them" in Canada—when defined by language, skin colour, religion or cultural trait—is offensive and wrong.

We've done this before. As Sheema Khan writes in *Of Hockey and Hijab: Reflections of a Canadian Muslim Woman*, "In looking back through Canadian history, we see that dark episodes of ethnic profiling have been punctuated by the enlightened efforts of those who fought back, leading to the evolution of social justice and law for the benefit of future generations. In the process, each discriminated group became further entrenched within the Canadian mosaic." It happened to the French, the Irish, the Chinese, the Indians, the Japanese, the Italians, the Germans and many others. Now, it's happening again to Muslims and to people we assume might be Muslims.

It's time to stop forcing people to run the gauntlet.

* * *

In 2015 in Peterborough, an arsonist attacked the local mosque an hour after community members had been inside celebrating the birth of a baby boy. It wasn't the first time the mosque had been targeted; after 9/11 the windows had been smashed and local churches had raised money to help replace them. This time, though, the fire caused over eighty thousand dollars in damage. That was a lot to expect people to donate. Within a couple of days, the full amount had been raised and donations kept coming in. After the total had reached over one hundred thousand dollars, the mosque had to ask the public to stop.

Let us prove that this openhearted generosity is the real Canada. Let us ensure that our response to fear and hate always embodies that spirit. Some shameful and crass responses to tragedies have been banged out anonymously on keyboards across the country, but the most-liked comment on the CBC web article reporting on the fire at the Peterborough mosque was different. The five simple words are penitent, yet imbued with a steely determination:

"We are better than this."

Notes

BELOW IS A SELECTION of sources used in this book, organized by chapter, topic and general chronology in the text. In addition to citations from books, newspapers, magazines, web articles and parliamentary records, this book also includes content from original interviews with representatives of Muslim organizations, politicians, lawyers, academics, law enforcement professionals and experts in a variety of fields. In all cases, quotes from interviews conducted by the author are attributed in the text in present tense; all other quotes are cited in past tense.

1. Introduction:

John A. Macdonald: Aaron Wherry, "Was John A. Macdonald a white supremacist?" *Maclean's* (August 2012): http://www.macleans.ca/politics/ottawa/was-john-a-macdonald-a-white-supremacist/.

Italians as "non-preferred" immigrants: Doug Saunders, *The Myth of the Muslim Tide: Do Immigrants Threaten the West?* (Toronto: Knopf Canada, 2012).

"Japanese Internment: British Columbia wages war against Japanese Canadians," CBC: http://www.cbc.ca/history/EPIS CONTENTSE1EP14CH3PA3LE.html.

All-black segregated schools: "End of Segregation in Canada," *Historica Canada*: http://blackhistorycanada.ca/events.php? themeid=7&id=9.

Slaves fleeing south: Natasha L. Henry, "Black Enslavement in Canada," *The Canadian Encyclopedia* (June 2016): https://www. thecanadianencyclopedia.ca/en/article/black-enslavement.

Polls about Islamophobia: Janice Williamson, *Omar Khadr, Oh Canada* (Montreal: McGill-Queen's University Press, 2012).

2. Welcome to Canada:

Early Muslim immigration: "A New Life in a New Land: The Muslim Experience in Canada," http://www.anewlife.ca; Daood Hassan Hamdani, "Canada's Muslims," (May 1996): http:// muslimcanada.org/cdnmuslm.htm; Sarah Mushtaq, "Islam's 144-year History in Canada," *Windsor Star* (October 2015): http:// windsorstar.com/opinion/columnists/mushtaq-islams-144-year-history-in-canada; Zuhair Kashmeri, *The Gulf Within: Canadian Arabs, Racism and the Gulf War* (Toronto: James Lorimer & Company, 1991); Dr. Zijad Delic, *Canadian Islam: Belonging and Loyalty* (Ottawa: Kirtas Publishing, 2014); Abdolmohammad Kazemipur, *The Muslim Question in Canada: A Story of Segmented Integration* (Vancouver: UBC Press, 2014); Hassan Munir, "The History of Muslims in Canada, *The Link Canada* (November 2015): http://thelinkcanada.ca/history-muslims-canada/; Janice Williamson, *Omar Khadr, Oh Canada* (Montreal: McGill-Queen's University Press, 2012).

Muslims and churches: Daood Hassan Hamdani, "Canada's Muslims," (May 1996): http://muslimcanada.org/cdnmuslm.htm; "brain drain": Dr. Zijad Delic, *Canadian Islam: Belonging and Loyalty* (Ottawa: Kirtas Publishing, 2014).

Positive data: Doug Saunders, *The Myth of the Muslim Tide: Do Immigrants Threaten the West?* (Toronto: Knopf Canada, 2012); Edward M. Iacobucci and Stephen J. Toope, *After the Paris Attacks: Responses in Canada, Europe, and around the Globe* (Toronto: University of Toronto Press, 2015)

"The true universality of Islam": Dr. Zijad Delic, *Canadian Islam: Belonging and Loyalty* (Ottawa: Kirtas Publishing, 2014).

"Fear of stereotyping": Dr. Imam Zijad Delic, *Canadian Islam: Belonging and Loyalty* (Ottawa: Kirtas Publishing, 2014).

Discouraging data: Abdolmohammad Kazemipur, *The Muslim Question in Canada: A Story of Segmented Integration* (Vancouver: UBC Press, 2014).

"Muslims are generally satisfied": Abdolmohammad Kazemipur, *The Muslim Question in Canada: A Story of Segmented Integration* (Vancouver: UBC Press, 2014).

Kidnappings in Lebanon: Karim H. Karim, *Islamic Peril: Media and Global Violence* (Black Rose Books, 2003).

"A militant, Marxist, Islamic Middle East": Karim H. Karim, *Islamic Peril: Media and Global Violence* (Black Rose Books, 2003).

Gulf War: Zuhair Kashmeri, *The Gulf Within: Canadian Arabs, Racism and the Gulf War* (Toronto: James Lorimer & Company, 1991); Sheema Khan, *Of Hockey and Hijab: Reflections of a Canadian Muslim Woman* (Toronto: TSAR Publications, 2009).

Canadian media: Karim H. Karim, *Islamic Peril: Media and Global Violence* (Black Rose Books, 2003).

3. Sticks and Stones:

Christian war: Christina Lamb, *Farewell Kabul: From Afghanistan to a More Dangerous World* (Toronto: HarperCollins, 2015); Dennis Gruending, *Pulpit and Politics: Competing Religious Ideologies in Canadian Public Life* (London: Kingsley Publishing, 2011).

"We are not the Public Service of Canada": Bruce Campion-Smith and Les Whittington, "Hillier brought candour to role," *Toronto Star* (April 2008): https://www.thestar.com/news/canada/2008/04/16/hillier_brought_candour_to_role.html.

Afghan presidency: Christina Lamb, *Farewell Kabul: From Afghanistan to a More Dangerous World* (Toronto: HarperCollins, 2015).

Polls: Sheema Khan, *Of Hockey and Hijab: Reflections of a Canadian Muslim Woman* (Toronto: TSAR Publications, 2009); Janice Williamson, *Omar Khadr, Oh Canada* (Montreal: McGill-Queen's University Press, 2012).

"A few media commentators brazenly": Sheema Khan, *Of Hockey and Hijab: Reflections of a Canadian Muslim Woman* (Toronto: TSAR Publications, 2009).

Mark Steyn: Natasha Bakht, *Belonging and Banishment: Being Muslim in Canada* (Toronto: TSAR Publications, 2008); Doug Saunders, *The Myth of the Muslim Tide: Do Immigrants Threaten the West?* (Toronto: Knopf Canada, 2012).

Soldiers in "brownface": "Military investigates video of racially charged skit," CBC (November 2012): http://www.cbc.ca/news/canada/nova-scotia/military-investigates-video-of-racially-charged-skit-1.1283193; Chris Selley, "Is Canada the least funny nation on Earth?" *National Post* (November

2012): http://news.nationalpost.com/full-comment/
chris-selley-is-canada-the-least-funny-nation-on-earth.

Cartoons: "Western Canadian magazine published
Muhammad cartoons," CBC (February 2006): http://www.
cbc.ca/news/canada/western-canadian-magazine-publishes-
muhammad-cartoons-1.591923; Mark Gollom, "Charlie
Hebdo shooting: Debate over publishing the Muhammad
cartoons," CBC (January 2015): http://www.cbc.ca/news/
world/charlie-hebdo-shooting-debate-over-publishing-the-
muhammad-cartoons-1.2894097; Edward M. Iacobucci and
Stephen J. Toope, *After the Paris Attacks: Responses in Canada,
Europe, and around the Globe* (Toronto: University of Toronto
Press, 2015).

Use of language: Sheema Khan, *Of Hockey and Hijab: Reflections
of a Canadian Muslim Woman* (Toronto: TSAR Publications,
2009); "Survey shows Muslim population is fastest growing
religion in Canada," *National Post*, http://news.nationalpost.
com/news/canada/survey-shows-muslim-population-is-fastest-
growing-religion-in-canada; Felicia Schwartz, "One More Name
for Islamic State: Daesh," *The Wall Street Journal* (December
2014): http://blogs.wsj.com/washwire/2014/12/23/one-more-
name-for-islamic-state-daesh; Maria Vultaggio, "ISIL, ISIS,
Islamic State, Daesh: What's The Difference?" *International
Business Times* (November 2015): http://www.ibtimes.com/
isil-isis-islamic-state-daesh-whats-difference-2187131.

Muslims losing their jobs: Baljit Nagra, "Unequal Citizenship:
Being Muslim and Canadian in the Post 9/11 Era," (Ph.D. diss.,
University of Toronto, 2011).

Hate crimes: "Aftermath of the 9/11 terrorist attack," Religious
Tolerance, http://www.religioustolerance.org/reac_ter1.htm;

Kerry Pither, *Dark Days: The Story of Four Canadians Tortured in the Name of Fighting Terror* (Toronto: Penguin, 2008); Keith Gilligan, "Shot fired through door of Pickering Islamic Centre," *Durham Region News* (September 2014): http://www.durhamregion.com/news-story/4883018-shot-fired-through-door-of-pickering-islamic-centre/; "NCCM denounces attack on Quebec Muslim woman," National Council of Canadian Muslims (April 2015): http://www.nccm.ca/eng-fr-nccm-denounces-attack-on-quebec-muslim-woman-le-cnmc-denonce-lagression-dont-a-ete-victime-une-musulmane-du-quebec/; "NCCM condemns recent anti-Muslim incidents," (September 2014): http://www.nccm.ca/nccm-condemns-recent-anti-muslim-incidents/; Erika Stark, "Calgary Imam allegedly attacked in city's northeast," *Calgary Herald* (September 2014): http://www.calgaryherald.com/news/calgary/Imam+allegedly+attacked+northeast+Calgary/10200077/story.html; Baljit Nagra, "Unequal Citizenship: Being Muslim and Canadian in the Post 9/11 Era," (Ph.D. diss., University of Toronto, 2011).

Victimizing non-Muslims: Evidence of the Standing Committee on Justice, November 6, 2001; "Aftermath of the 9/11 terrorist attack," Religious Tolerance, http://www.religioustolerance.org/reac_ter1.htm; Ritu Bhasin, "Sikhs have been living in fear of hate crimes since 9/11," *The Globe and Mail* (April 2018): http://www.theglobeandmail.com/opinion/columnists/sikhs-have-been-living-in-fear-of-hate-crimes-since-911/article4468643/.

Hate crime statistics: Baljit Nagra, "Unequal Citizenship: Being Muslim and Canadian in the Post 9/11 Era," (Ph.D. diss., University of Toronto, 2011).

Community safety kit: "National Muslim Advocacy Organization Denounces Attack on Muslim Students," National Council of

Canadian Muslims (October 2013): http://www.nccm.ca/national-muslim-advocacy-organization-denounces-attack-on-muslim-students/.

4. Let's Keep Talking About Niqabs:

Avoiding anti-Muslim sentiment: Hassan Munir, "The History of Muslims in Canada," The Link Canada (November 2015): http://thelinkcanada.ca/history-muslims-canada/; Caroline Plante, "Quebec solidaire motion condemning 'islamophobia' passes unanimously in National Assembly," *Montreal Gazette* (October 2015): http://montrealgazette.com/news/quebec/quebec-solidaire-calls-for-calm-as-use-of-term-islamophobia-debated; "Alexa McDonough Visits the Arab Community," Canadian Arab Federation (October 2001): http://www.caf.ca/2001/10/alexa-mcdonough-visits-the-arab-community/; "Aftermath of the 9/11 terrorist attack," Religious Tolerance, http://www.religioustolerance.org/reac_ter1.htm.

Herouxville Code of Conduct: Abdolmohammad Kazemipur, *The Muslim Question in Canada: A Story of Segmented Integration* (Vancouver: UBC Press, 2014); Sheema Khan, *Of Hockey and Hijab: Reflections of a Canadian Muslim Woman* (Toronto: TSAR Publications, 2009).

Bouchard-Taylor commission: Natasha Bakht, *Belonging and Banishment: Being Muslim in Canada* (Toronto: TSAR Publications, 2008); "This kind of 'reasonable accommodation police'," *Montreal Gazette*: http://www.canada.com/montrealgazette/news/story.html?id=006205d2-dc3b-491a-8839-b59562ba52d1&k=58807; Sheema Khan, *Of Hockey and Hijab: Reflections of a Canadian Muslim Woman* (Toronto: TSAR Publications, 2009); Jonathan Montpetit, "Religious garb OK for cops, judges, says Bouchard-Taylor report's co-author,"

CBC, February 14, 2017, https://www.cbc.ca/news/canada/
montreal/charles-taylor-hijab-reasonable-accommodation-
reversal-1.3982082.

Voting without removing veils: Natasha Bakht, *Belonging
and Banishment: Being Muslim in Canada* (Toronto: TSAR
Publications, 2008); "Muslim women will have to lift veils to vote
in Quebec election," CBC (March 2007): http://www.cbc.ca/news/
canada/montreal/muslim-women-will-have-to-lift-veils-to-vote-
in-quebec-election-1.688602.

Daniel Leblanc, "Elections Canada blasted for allowing
Muslim women to vote with faces covered," *The Globe and
Mail* (September 2007): http://www.theglobeandmail.
com/news/national/elections-canada-blasted-for-
allowing-muslim-women-to-vote-with-faces-covered/
article1082104/.

Charter of Quebec Values: "Charter of Quebec values would
ban religious symbols for public workers," CBC (September
2013): http://www.cbc.ca/news/canada/montreal/charter-
of-quebec-values-would-ban-religious-symbols-for-public-
workers-1.1699315.

PQ's slide in the polls: Tu Thanh Ha, "Three reasons the PQ
lost and Couillard's biggest challenge," *The Globe and Mail*
(April 2014): http://www.theglobeandmail.com/news/politics/
three-reasons-the-pq-lost-and-couillards-biggest-challenge/
article17872997/.

Nussbaum's analysis: Dennis Gruending, *Pulpit and Politics:
Competing Religious Ideologies in Canadian Public Life* (London:
Kingsley Publishing, 2011).

Discomfort with niqabs: "Niqabs: the election's weapon of mass distraction," *The Globe and Mail* (September 2015): http://www.theglobeandmail.com/globe-debate/editorials/niqabs-the-elections-weapon-of-mass-distraction/article26551328/.

Supreme Court ruling: Natasha Bakht, *Belonging and Banishment: Being Muslim in Canada* (Toronto: TSAR Publications, 2008).

Niqab ban during citizenship ceremonies: Ken MacQueen, "Who Gets to Be Canadian?" *Maclean's* (October 2015): https://www.macleans.ca/politics/ottawa/who-gets-to-be-canadian/.

"To segregate one group of Canadians": Lee -Anne Goodman, "Jason Kenney defends niqab ban at citizenship ceremonies on Twitter," CBC (October 2014): http://www.cbc.ca/news/politics/jason-kenney-defends-niqab-ban-at-citizenship-ceremonies-on-twitter-1.2803642.

Verifying identities and court challenge: Joan Bryden, "Baloney Meter: Is niqab ban needed to prove citizenship applicant's ID?" CBC (March 2015): http://www.cbc.ca/news/politics/baloney-meter-is-niqab-ban-needed-to-prove-citizenship-applicant-s-id-1.2994562.

"I believe, and I think most Canadians believe": "Niqab-citizenship ceremony ruling will be appealed," CBC (February 2015): http://www.cbc.ca/news/politics/niqab-citizenship-ceremony-ruling-will-be-appealed-pm-says-1.2955418.

"Whatever else the election of 2015 will be remembered for": Andrew Coyne, "To uncover or not to uncover – why the niqab issue is ridiculous," *National Post* (September 2015): http://news.

nationalpost.com/full-comment/andrew-coyne-to-uncover-or-not-to-uncover-why-the-niqab-issue-is-ridiculous.

Government poll: "Niqabs: the election's weapon of mass distraction," *The Globe and Mail* (September 2015): http://www.theglobeandmail.com/globe-debate/editorials/niqabs-the-elections-weapon-of-mass-distraction/article26551328/.

Conservative promises: Donovan Vincent, "Conservatives out in front, new poll finds," *Toronto Star* (October 2015): http://www.thestar.com/news/federal-election/2015/10/01/conservatives-out-in-front-new-poll-finds.html.

"Harper understood and embraced": John Duffy, "Quebec Rises Again," *Maclean's* (October 2015): https://archive.macleans.ca/article/2015/10/26/quebec-rises-again.

Bloc campaign ad: Benjamin Shingler, "Bloc Québécois targets NDP over niqabs, pipelines in controversial new ad," CBC (September 2015): http://www.cbc.ca/news/canada/montreal/canada-election-2015-bloc-quebecois-niqab-pipeline-1.3234830.

"These are troubling times": "Justin Trudeau: Tories threaten liberty by fostering prejudice against Muslims," CBC (March 2015): http://www.cbc.ca/news/politics/justin-trudeau-tories-threaten-liberty-by-fostering-prejudice-against-muslims-1.2988155.

"The overwhelming majority of Canadians": Justin Ling, "Political Spat over Niqab Comment Ends with Conservative Minister Calling Liberal Party 'Racist'," *Vice* (June 2015): http://www.vice.com/en_ca/read/political-spat-over-niqab-comment-ends-with-conservative-minister-calling-liberal-party-racist-152.

Harper's comments: Debates, March 10, 2015; "Will Stephen Harper regret remark on niqabs?" CBC (March 2015): http://www.cbc.ca/news/canada/manitoba/will-stephen-harper-regret-remark-on-niqabs-1.2991721.

"They're playing to Islamophobia": Ken MacQueen, "Who Gets to Be Canadian?" *Maclean's* (October 2015): https://www.macleans.ca/politics/ottawa/who-gets-to-be-canadian/.

French-language leaders' debate: Robin Levinson King, "French language debate erupts in heated exchange over niqab," *Toronto Star* (September 2015): http://www.thestar.com/news/canada/2015/09/24/why-you-should-watch-the-french-language-debate-tonight.html.

Coderre and Mulcair: Andy Blatchford, "Mulcair holds firm on allowing niqabs during citizenship oath, even if vote slides," *The Globe and Mail* (September 2015): http://www.theglobeandmail.com/news/politics/mulcair-clarifies-stance-on-niqab-at-citizenship-ceremonies/article26540126/.

"In the 60 days since the start of the campaign": *Maclean's*, October 12, 2005.

"The day a government imposes": "Niqabs: the election's weapon of mass distraction," *The Globe and Mail* (September 2015): http://www.theglobeandmail.com/globe-debate/editorials/niqabs-the-elections-weapon-of-mass-distraction/article26551328/.

"When the head of the Islamic Supreme Council": Evan Solomon, "Harper didn't have to run on a culture war," *Maclean's* (October 2015): https://www.macleans.ca/politics/ottawa/harper-didnt-have-to-run-on-a-culture-war/.

RCMP tip line: Ken MacQueen, "Who Gets to Be Canadian?" *Maclean's* (October 2015): https://www.macleans.ca/ politics/ottawa/who-gets-to-be-canadian/; Terry Milewski, "Conservatives crank up values clash by taking aim at 'barbaric cultural practices'," CBC (October 2015): http://www.cbc.ca/news/ politics/canada-election-2015-conservatives-barbaric-cultural-practices-1.3254886.

Syrian refugees: John Geddes, "Ultimate issue primer cheat sheet," *Maclean's* (October 2015): https://archive.macleans.ca/ article/2015/10/26/ultimate-issue-primer-cheat-sheet; Aaron Wherry, "Life, death and politics," *Maclean's* (September 2015): https://www.macleans.ca/politics/life-death-and-politics/.

Controversy from NDP and Liberals: Benjamin Shingler, "Bloc Québécois targets NDP over niqabs, pipelines in controversial new ad," CBC (September 2015): http://www.cbc.ca/news/ canada/montreal/canada-election-2015-bloc-quebecois-niqab-pipeline-1.3234830; "'Santa has to be white': BC Liberal candidate quits over Facebook posts," *Toronto Star* (September 2015): http:// www.thestar.com/news/canada/2015/09/30/liberal-candidate-in-bc-resigns-over-facebook-posts.html.

Hate crime statistics: Kathleen Harris, "Hate crimes against Muslims in Canada up 60%, StatsCan reports," CBC (June 2017): http://www.cbc.ca/news/politics/ hate-crimes-muslims-statscan-1.4158042.

"Priorities going forward in this Parliament": "Full text of Rosemary Barton's interview with Stephen Harper," CBC (October 2015): http://www.cbc.ca/news/politics/canada-election-2105-full-text-of-rosemary-barton-interview-with-stephen-harper-1.3259045.

NDP polling: "A single niqab eclipses all," *Maclean's* (November 2015): https://archive.macleans.ca/article/2015/11/2/a-single-niqab-eclipses-all; Martin Patriquin, "The orange wave crashes," *Maclean's* (October 2015): https://archive.macleans.ca/article/2015/10/12/the-orange-wave-crashes; Martin Patriquin, "Tours de force," *Maclean's*, August 24, 2015; Aaron Wherry, "Greater expectations,"

Maclean's (October 2015): https://archive.macleans.ca/article/2015/10/26/greater-expectations; "Secretly ready," *Maclean's*, November 2, 2015.

5. The Veneer of Justice:

Reactions to 9/11: Kerry Pither, *Dark Days: The Story of Four Canadians Tortured in the Name of Fighting Terror* (Toronto: Penguin, 2008).

Bill C-36: Janice Williamson, *Omar Khadr, Oh Canada* (Montreal: McGill-Queen's University Press, 2012); Kerry Pither, *Dark Days: The Story of Four Canadians Tortured in the Name of Fighting Terror* (Toronto: Penguin, 2008); Dennis Gruending, *Pulpit and Politics: Competing Religious Ideologies in Canadian Public Life* (London: Kingsley Publishing, 2011); Debates, October 16, 2001; Evidence of the Standing Committee on Justice, November 6, 2001; "Another Liberal breaks ranks over anti-terror bill," CBC (November 2001): https://www.cbc.ca/news/canada/another-liberal-breaks-ranks-over-anti-terror-bill-1.282480.

Security certificate process: Janice Williamson, *Omar Khadr, Oh Canada* (Montreal: McGill-Queen's University Press, 2012); "Security certificates and secret evidence," CBC (August 2009): http://www.cbc.ca/news/canada/security-certificates-and-secret-evidence-1.777624; Andrew Duffy, "2006 to be year of high

drama for Harkat", *Ottawa Citizen* (January 2006): http://www.
justiceforharkat.com/news.php?extend.1321.

James Hugessen: Sheema Khan, *Of Hockey and Hijab: Reflections
of a Canadian Muslim Woman* (Toronto: TSAR Publications, 2009).

CSIS: Andrew Duffy, "Terror suspect's lawyer says CSIS work
'sometimes shoddy'," *Ottawa Citizen* (October 2004): http://
www.justiceforharkat.com/news.php?extend.425; Richard Foot,
"Terror law revision still violates Charter, lawyer says," *Ottawa
Citizen* (February 2008): http://www.justiceforharkat.com/
news.php?extend.2551; "CSIS selects facts to match its theories,
Harkat hearing told," CBC (December 2004): http://www.
justiceforharkat.com/data2/cbc_dec7_2004.php.

"Before the state can detain people": "Canada court rejects terror
law," *BBC News* (February 2007): http://www.justiceforharkat.
com/news.php?extend.2029.

Special advocate system: Janice Williamson, *Omar Khadr, Oh
Canada* (Montreal: McGill-Queen's University Press, 2012);
"Mohamed's Story," Justice for Harkat (November 2015): http://
www.justiceforharkat.com/e107_plugins/content/content.
php?content.408; "New Legislation another blockade towards
full civil liberties," Canadian Arab Federation (October 2007):
http://www.justiceforharkat.com/news.php?extend.2368; Michael
Valpy, "Detention solution found wanting in Britain," *The Globe
and Mail* (February 2007): http://www.justiceforharkat.com/
news.php?extend.2053; Cristin Schmitz, "Bar deeply divided
about legitimacy of 'special advocate'," *Lawyers Weekly* (February
2008): http://www.justiceforharkat.com/news.php?extend.2579.

"I regard this case to be as serious as a capital punishment case":
Andrew Duffy, "The fight for the soul of Canada's justice system,"

Ottawa Citizen (December 2004): http://www.justiceforharkat.
com/news.php?extend.522.

Deportations despite risk of torture: Andrew Duffy, "2006 to be
year of high drama for Harkat, *Ottawa Citizen* (January 2006):
http://www.justiceforharkat.com/news.php?extend.1321.

Adil Charkaoui and Mohamed Harkat testifying before
committee: Thomas Walkom, "Not enough time for civil rights,"
Toronto Star (December 2007): http://www.justiceforharkat.com/
news.php?extend.2438; Evidence of the Standing Committee on
Public Safety and National Security, December 6, 2007.

Mohamed Harkat: Lisa Lisle, "It's not right," *Ottawa Sun* (July
2004): http://www.justiceforharkat.com/Lisle_July31_2004.php;
Lisa Lisle, "Wife's lonely vigil is her obsession," *Ottawa Sun* (July
2004): http://www.justiceforharkat.com/news.php?extend.333.

Questionable evidence: Lisa Lisle, "Wife's lonely vigil is her
obsession," *Ottawa Sun* (July 2004): http://www.justiceforharkat.
com/news.php?extend.333; Mohammed Adam, "Harkat gets
bombshell help from declassified U.S. documents," *Ottawa
Citizen* (April 2010): http://www.justiceforharkat.com/news.
php?extend.3536; Andrew Duffy, "Information on Harkat
not 'credible'," *Ottawa Citizen* (October 2004): http://www.
justiceforharkat.com/news.php?extend.417; Ian MacLeod,
"Harkat informant called 'insane'," *Ottawa Citizen* (June 2006):
http://www.justiceforharkat.com/news.php?extend.1654; Ian
MacLeod, "Harkat informant at centre of CIA tape controversy,"

Ottawa Citizen (December 2007): http://www.justiceforharkat.
com/news.php?extend.2468; Tonda MacCharles, "Key
polygraph tests withheld," *Toronto Star* (June 2009): http://
www.justiceforharkat.com/news.php?extend.3239; Michelle

Shephard, "Did spy's affair taint case against terror suspect?" *Toronto Star* (March 2009): https://www.thestar.com/news/canada/2009/03/07/did_spys_affair_taint_case_against_terror_suspect.html.

Sophie Harkat: Maha Zimmo, "One thousand and one nights: A tale from Canada's security certificates," Media Monitors (July 21, 2005): http://www.justiceforharkat.com/news.php?extend.916; Sophie Harkat, "Life without my husband, best friend and HERO," Socialist.ca (January 2005): http://www.justiceforharkat.com/news.php?extend.674.

Security certificate reasonable: Andrew Duffy, "We both had faith in the system," *Ottawa Citizen* (March 2005): http://www.justiceforharkat.com/news.php?extend.734.

Harkat's incarceration: Maha Zimmo, "One thousand and one nights: A tale from Canada's security certificates," MediaMonitors (July 2005): http://www.justiceforharkat.com/news.php?extend.916; Andrew Duffy, "Harkat suffers visions of torture," *Ottawa Citizen* (October 2005): http://www.justiceforharkat.com/news.php?extend.1153; Jeffrey L. Metzner and Jamie Fellner, "Solitary Confinement and Mental Illness in U.S. Prisons: A Challenge for Medical Ethics," *The Journal of the American Academy of Psychiatry and the Law* (March 2010): http://jaapl.org/content/38/1/104.

Harkat's supporters: Andrew Duffy, "Harkat suffers visions of torture," *Ottawa Citizen* (October 2005): http://www.justiceforharkat.com/news.php?extend.1153; Jim Bronskill, "Federal questioning of accused terrorist 'offensive'," Justice for Harkat (October 2005): http://www.justiceforharkat.com/news.php?extend.1155.

"We've built a special jail for Muslims": Catherine Solyom, "Protest groups seek abolition of controversial security certificates," *Montreal Gazette* (February 2007): http://www. justiceforharkat.com/news.php?extend.2010.

Harkat's bail restrictions: "Mohamed's Story," Justice for Harkat (November 2015): http://www.justiceforharkat.com/e107_plugins/ content/content.php?content.408; Michelle Shephard, "Terror suspect Harkat gets bail," *Toronto Star* (May 24, 2006): http:// www.justiceforharkat.com/news.php?extend.1580.

Harkat's fortieth birthday: Jennifer Campbell, "Birthday party turns into rally for Harkat," *Ottawa Citizen* (September 7, 2008):, http://www.justiceforharkat.com/news.php?extend.2938.

New security certificate: Sophie Lamarche Harkat, "One day it could be you. The persecution of Mohamed Harkat," Peace Alliance Winnipeg (March 2011): http://www.justiceforharkat. com/news.php?extend.3883.

"You can't have human beings": Andrew Duffy, "Jail Harkat, seize $95,000, lawyer urges," *Ottawa Citizen* (February 2008): http:// www.justiceforharkat.com/news.php?extend.2595.

Harkat's new bail conditions: Andrew Duffy, "Federal Court judge softens Harkat restrictions," *Ottawa Citizen* (March 2009): http://www.justiceforharkat.com/news.php?extend.3162; "Harkat lawyers accuse officials of conducting illegal raid," CBC (June 2009): http://www.justiceforharkat.com/news.php?extend.3224.

"My husband and I married": Tonda MacCharles, "Terror suspect vows to appeal ruling," *Toronto Star* (December 2010): http://www.justiceforharkat.com/news.php?extend.3682.

Peter Mansbridge: Peter Mansbridge, "Prime-time killers" *Maclean's* (July 2005): http://www.justiceforharkat.com/data2/Mansbridge_July21_2005.php.

Mohammad Mahjoub returns to jail: Zoe Chong, "God Willing: The Story of Sophie Harkat," Journalists for Human Rights (February 2016): http://www.justiceforharkat.com/news.php?extend.3972.

"That's the real root": Debra Black, "Mohamed Harkat girds himself for another fight to stay," *Toronto Star* (August 2016): http://www.justiceforharkat.com/news.php?extend.3985.

"I blame the certificate": Zoe Chong, "God Willing: The Story of Sophie Harkat," Journalists for Human Rights (February 2016): http://www.justiceforharkat.com/news.php?extend.3972.

Bill C-24: "Bill C-24 is wrong: There is only one kind of Canadian citizen," *The Globe and Mail* (June 2014): http://www.theglobeandmail.com/opinion/editorials/bill-c-24-is-wrong-there-is-only-one-kind-of-canadian-citizen/article19400982/; Michelle McQuigge, "Civil rights groups launch constitutional challenge against Bill C-24," Global News (August 2015): http://globalnews.ca/news/2176204/civil-rights-groups-launch-constitutional-challenge-against-bill-c-24/; Ken MacQueen, "Who Gets to Be Canadian?" *Maclean's* (October 2015): https://www.macleans.ca/politics/ottawa/who-gets-to-be-canadian/.

Michael Zehaf-Bibeau: Michael Friscolanti, "A Mom's worst nightmare," *Maclean's* (February 2015): https://archive.macleans.ca/article/2015/2/23/a-moms-worst-nightmare.

Michelle Rempel: Michelle Rempel, Twitter post, October 22, 2014, https://twitter.com/MichelleRempel/

status/524924161526104064; Kady O'Malley, "Michelle Rempel responds to ISIS threat with #SecureBedroomSelfie," CBC (September 2014): https://www.cbc.ca/news/ politics/michelle-rempel-responds-to-isis-threat-with-securebedroomselfie-1.2774238.

Bill C-51: Edward M. Iacobucci and Stephen J. Toope, *After the Paris Attacks: Responses in Canada, Europe, and around the Globe* (Toronto: University of Toronto Press, 2015); Evidence of the Standing Committee on Public Safety and National Security, March 12, 2015.

6. Names Like Mohamed:

Hassan Almrei: Matthew Behrens, "40 Days Gone: Hassan Almrei on Day 40 of Hunger Strike," Justice for Harkat (August 2005): http://www.justiceforharkat.com/news.php?extend.928; Alexandre Trudeau, "Without charge, without trial, without hope," *Maclean's* (June 2006): http://www.justiceforharkat.com/ news.php?extend.1617.

Mahmoud Jaballah: "Security certificates and secret evidence," CBC (August 2009): http://www.cbc.ca/news/canada/ security-certificates-and-secret-evidence-1.777624; Matthew Behrens, "Victory: Jaballah secret trial security certificate found unreasonable," Rabble.ca (May 2016): http://www. justiceforharkat.com/news.php?extend.3984.

Adil Charkaoui: Dennis Bueckert, "UN group condemns Canada's detention of suspected terrorists without trial," *Maclean's* (June 2005): http://www.justiceforharkat.com/news. php?extend.861; Christian Legeais, "Our Security Lies in Our Fight!" The Marxist-Leninist Daily (December 2007): http:// www.justiceforharkat.com/news.php?extend.2451.

"If we had the threshold belief": Jim Bronskill, "Future top Mountie Paulson declared security certificate process 'off the rails'," *Ottawa Citizen* (June 2013): http://www.justiceforharkat. com/news.php?extend.3910.

Project Thread: Stewart Bell, "Possible al-Qaeda cell: Some detainees may have been in U.S. on 9/11," *National Post* (September 2003): http://britishexpats.com/forum/immigration-citizenship-canada-33/21st-mohammad-arrested-toronto-176286/; Canada: Immigration and Refugee Board of Canada, Pakistan: Whether Pakistani citizens who were arrested in Toronto by Citizenship and Immigration Canada officials in August 2003 under "Project Thread" and who were deported to Pakistan in December 2003, held a press conference in Islamabad where they announced their intention to sue the government of Canada; whether details of their treatment in Canada are known to the Human Rights Commission of Pakistan, including its conclusion in this regard; whether these citizens have filed an official complaint against the government of Canada; whether the government of Pakistan has filed an official diplomatic complaint against the government of Canada; whether these deported individuals were investigated by Pakistani officials for possible links to terrorist organizations upon their return to Pakistan including details of their treatment upon their return (March 2004): http://www.refworld.org/docid/41501c46e.html; Felix Odartey-Wellington, "Racial Profiling and Moral Panic: Operation Thread and the Al-Qaeda Sleeper Cell that Never Was," Global Media Journal: Canadian Edition (2009): https:// bit.ly/2JPHKYm.

Laya Behbahani: Shanifa Nasser, "How Islamophobia is driving young Canadian Muslims to reclaim their identity," CBC (April 2016): https://www.cbc.ca/news/canada/ environics-muslim-canadian-survey-1.3551465.

Men taking photos at Pacific Centre in Vancouver: "Mohammed Sharaz reveals why his group took photos that aroused Vancouver suspicions," CBC (January 2016): http://www.cbc.ca/news/canada/british-columbia/vancouver-police-say-men-in-mall-mystery-completely-innocent-1.3406619.

Secret CSIS brief: Sikander Hashmi, "CSIS visits can be chilling," *Montreal Gazette* (August 2007): http://www.justiceforharkat.com/news.php?extend.2259.

Far-right hate groups and violent extremism: Dakshana Bascaramurty, Joe Friesen and Les Perreaux, "Extremism does not stop at the border," *The Globe and Mail* (August 2017): https://www.theglobeandmail.com/news/national/extremism-does-not-stop-at-the-us-canadaborder/article36036046/; Shannon Carranco and Jon Milton, "Decoding Canada's far right," *The Globe and Mail* (April 2019).

Toronto 18: Janice Williamson, *Omar Khadr, Oh Canada* (Montreal: McGill-Queen's University Press, 2012); "Informant says militant training camp was 'potty training' exercise," CBC (June 2008): http://www.cbc.ca/news/canada/toronto/informant-says-militant-training-camp-was-potty-training-exercise-1.764918; Sheema Khan, *Of Hockey and Hijab: Reflections of a Canadian Muslim Woman* (Toronto: TSAR Publications, 2009); Heather Mallick, "The subtlety of words: Are you Canadian or Canadian-born?" CBC (June 2006): http://www.justiceforharkat.com/news.php?extend.1643; "Toronto 18: Key events in the case," CBC (June 2008): http://www.cbc.ca/news/canada/toronto-18-key-events-in-the-case-1.715266.

Halifax mall plot: Thomas Walkom, "Halifax murder plot shows absurdity of anti-terror laws," *Toronto Star* (February 2015): https://www.thestar.com/news/canada/2015/02/17/

halifax-murder-plot-shows-absurdity-of-anti-terror-laws-walkom.html; "Many would deny killers the notoriety they seem to crave, but is that possible – or even desirable?" *National Post* (February 2015): http://news.nationalpost.com/news/canada/many-would-deny-killers-the-notoriety-they-seem-to-crave-but-is-that-possible-or-even-desirable; "Six stories in Canada we're watching," *Maclean's* (April 2015): http://www.macleans.ca/news/canada/six-stories-in-canada-were-watching-4/.

Michael Zehaf-Bibeau: Michael Friscolanti, "A Mom's worst nightmare," *Maclean's* (February 2015): https://archive.macleans.ca/article/2015/2/23/a-moms-worst-nightmare; "Ottawa shooting suspect Michael Zehaf-Bibeau had 'very developed criminality,'" CTV (October 2014): http://www.ctvnews.ca/canada/ottawa-shooting-suspect-michael-zehaf-bibeau-had-very-developed-criminality-1.2067255.

Bill C-51: "Garbled radio call delayed police response to Parliament Hill attacker: RCMP," CTV (June 2015): http://www.ctvnews.ca/canada/garbled-radio-call-delayed-police-response-to-parliament-hill-attacker-rcmp-1.2403906; Evan Solomon, "Ottawa gunman Michael Zehaf-Bibeau was shot 31 times, police report to reveal," CBC (June 2015): http://www.cbc.ca/news/politics/ottawa-gunman-michael-zehaf-bibeau-was-shot-31-times-police-report-to-reveal-1.3096073; Lee Berthiaume, "Mounties now toting submachine guns for Hill security," *Ottawa Citizen* (June 2015): http://ottawacitizen.com/news/politics/rcmp-brings-out-the-big-guns-to-the-dismay-of-some; Emer O'Toole, "Canada won't be cowed by terrorism, or by a draconian response to its threat," *The Guardian* (October 2004): https://www.theguardian.com/commentisfree/2014/oct/23/ottawa-shooting-canada-terrorism-draconian-response; Andrew Seymour, "Police investigate vandalism at mosque," *Ottawa Citizen* (November 2014): http://ottawacitizen.com/

news/local-news/police-investigate-vandalism-at-mosque; Nancy MacDonald and Ken MacQueen, "Unrequited love," *Maclean's* (August 2015): https://archive.macleans.ca/article/2015/8/17/ unrequited-love.

Justin Bourque: Michael MacDonald, "Justin Bourque targeted mounties, wanted to start rebellion, court told," CTV (October 2014): http://atlantic.ctvnews.ca/justin-bourque-targeted-mounties-wanted-to-start-rebellion-court-told-1.2072588; "Justin Bourque: latest revelations about man charged in Moncton shooting," CBC (June 2014): http://www.cbc.ca/news/canada/ new-brunswick/justin-bourque-latest-revelations-about-man-charged-in-moncton-shooting-1.2665900); "The manhunt is over alleged Moncton RCMP killer Justin Bourque captured," *Ottawa Citizen*, formerly available at: http://ottawacitizen.com/storyline/ the-manhunt-is-over-alleged-moncton-rcmp-killer-justin-bourque-captured.

Attacks in Paris: Edward M. Iacobucci and Stephen J. Toope, *After the Paris Attacks: Responses in Canada, Europe, and around the Globe* (Toronto: University of Toronto Press, 2015).

7. O Canada:

"We pick up a suspect": Kerry Pither, *Dark Days: The Story of Four Canadians Tortured in the Name of Fighting Terror* (Toronto: Penguin, 2008).

Torture: Janice Williamson, *Omar Khadr, Oh Canada* (Montreal: McGill-Queen's University Press, 2012).

Brenda Martin: "Ottawa pays Brenda Martin's fine to speed up transfer," CBC (April 2008): http://www.cbc.ca/news/ world/ottawa-pays-brenda-martin-s-fine-to-speed-up-transfer-1.768039; Maureen Brosnahan, "Brenda Martin in and out of prison since parole," CBC (May 2010): http://www.cbc.ca/news/canada/brenda-martin-in-and-out-of-prison-since-parole-1.875529; Janice Williamson, *Omar Khadr, Oh Canada* (Montreal: McGill-Queen's University Press, 2012).

"Security officials engaged in their own game": Sheema Khan, *Of Hockey and Hijab: Reflections of a Canadian Muslim Woman* (Toronto: TSAR Publications, 2009).

El-Maati, Almalki, Arar, Nureddin: Kerry Pither, *Dark Days: The Story of Four Canadians Tortured in the Name of Fighting Terror* (Toronto: Penguin, 2008); interview with Kerry Pither; interview with Barbara Jackman; Janice Williamson, *Omar Khadr, Oh Canada* (Montreal: McGill-Queen's University Press, 2012); Sheema Khan, *Of Hockey and Hijab: Reflections of a Canadian Muslim Woman* (Toronto: TSAR Publications, 2009); Third Report of the Standing Committee on Public Safety and National Security, June 2009; Government Response to the Third Report of the Standing Committee on Public Safety and National Security; Monique Scotti, "Trudeau: Canadians rightfully angry after Ottawa pays $31.25M to men falsely imprisoned in Syria," *Global News* (October 2017): https://globalnews.ca/news/3826253/ottawa-pays-settlement-of-31-25m-to-3-men-falsely-imprisoned-in-syria/; "The Arar inquiry: recommendations and documents," CBC (August 2007): http://www.cbc.ca/new/background/arar/arar_inquiry.html; Debates, November 18, 2002; Evidence of the Standing Committee on Foreign Affairs and International Trade, October 7, 2003; Paul Koring, "Canada feared U.S. backlash over man trapped in Sudan," *The Globe and Mail* (July 2008): http://www.theglobeandmail.com/news/world/canada-feared-us-backlash-over-man-trapped-in-sudan/article4222201/.

Abousfian Abdelrazik: Janice Williamson, *Omar Khadr, Oh Canada* (Montreal: McGill-Queen's University Press, 2012); Paul Koring, "Canada feared U.S. backlash over man trapped in Sudan," *The Globe and Mail* (July 2008): http://www. theglobeandmail.com/news/world/canada-feared-us-backlash-over-man-trapped-in-sudan/article4222201/; Paul Koring, "Abdelrazik deserves no compensation, Ottawa argues, *The Globe and Mail* (October 2010): http://www.theglobeandmail. com/news/politics/abdelrazik-deserves-no-compensation-ottawa-argues/article1214877/?from=4179856; "Abdelrazik brings requests to Harper's office," CBC (November 2010): http://www. cbc.ca/news/canada/calgary/abdelrazik-brings-requests-to-harper-s-office-1.945881; "Abdelrazik begins journey back to Canada," CBC (June 2009): http://www.cbc.ca/news/world/ abdelrazik-begins-journey-back-to-canada-1.815244.

Toews' directives on sharing information: Jim Bronskill, "Letter to Minister Toews on the Use of Torture-tainted information," *Ottawa Citizen* (November 2012): http://www.justiceforharkat. com/news.php?default.0.120.

8. The Head of the Spear:

Childhood: Michelle Shephard, *Guantanamo's Child: The Untold Story of Omar Khadr* (Mississauga: John Wiley & Sons Canada Ltd, 2008); Janice Williamson, *Omar Khadr, Oh Canada* (Montreal: McGill-Queen's University Press, 2012).

Abu Laith al-Libi: Michelle Shephard, *Guantanamo's Child: The Untold Story of Omar Khadr* (Mississauga: John Wiley & Sons Canada Ltd, 2008); Charles Rusnell and Jennie Russell, "Omar Khadr poses 'low-moderate' risk to commit future crimes: psychological report," CBC (May 2016): http://www.cbc.ca/news/canada/edmonton/

omar-khadr-poses-low-moderate-risk-to-commit-future-crimes-psychological-report-1.3062957.

Account of the battle: Michelle Shephard, *Guantanamo's Child: The Untold Story of Omar Khadr* (Mississauga: John Wiley & Sons Canada Ltd, 2008), Janice Williamson, *Omar Khadr, Oh Canada* (Montreal: McGill-Queen's University Press, 2012); "Khadr interrogator convicted in prisoner's torture death," *The Toronto Star* (March 2008): http://www.thestar.com/news/world/2008/03/14/khadr_interrogator_convicted_in_prisoners_torture_death.html.

"They do not serve warrants": Michelle Shephard, *Guantanamo's Child: The Untold Story of Omar Khadr* (Mississauga: John Wiley & Sons Canada Ltd, 2008).

Bagram Air Base: Christina Lamb, *Farewell Kabul: From Afghanistan to a More Dangerous World* (Toronto: HarperCollins 2015); Michelle Shephard, *Guantanamo's Child: The Untold Story of Omar Khadr* (Mississauga: John Wiley & Sons Canada Ltd, 2008); "Khadr interrogator convicted in prisoner's torture death," *The Toronto Star* (March 2008): http://www.thestar.com/news/world/2008/03/14/khadr_interrogator_convicted_in_prisoners_torture_death.html; Janice Williamson, *Omar Khadr, Oh Canada* (Montreal: McGill-Queen's University Press, 2012).

Guantanamo Bay: Michelle Shephard, *Guantanamo's Child: The Untold Story of Omar Khadr* (Mississauga: John Wiley & Sons Canada Ltd, 2008).

Field reports of the battle: Janice Williamson, *Omar Khadr, Oh Canada* (Montreal: McGill-Queen's University Press, 2012).

"Many witnesses are dead": Conservative Dissenting Opinion to the Seventh Report of the Standing Committee on Foreign Affairs and International Development, June 2008.

US *Military Commissions Act*: Janice Williamson, *Omar Khadr, Oh Canada* (Montreal: McGill-Queen's University Press, 2012).

Child soldiers: Janice Williamson, *Omar Khadr, Oh Canada* (Montreal: McGill-Queen's University Press, 2012).

Foreign Affairs listing US as torturer: Janice Williamson, *Omar Khadr, Oh Canada* (Montreal: McGill-Queen's University Press, 2012).

Trial in a reasonable time: Janice Williamson, *Omar Khadr, Oh Canada* (Montreal: McGill-Queen's University Press, 2012).

Canada's requests to the US: Michelle Shephard, *Guantanamo's Child: The Untold Story of Omar Khadr* (Mississauga: John Wiley & Sons Canada Ltd, 2008); Janice Williamson, *Omar Khadr, Oh Canada* (Montreal: McGill-Queen's University Press, 2012).

Omar in the news: Aaron Wherry, "'This young man in an unfortunate situation'," *Maclean's* (September 2012): http://www.macleans.ca/politics/ottawa/this-young-man-in-an-unfortunate-situation/.

"Claw back": Michelle Shephard, *Guantanamo's Child: The Untold Story of Omar Khadr* (Mississauga: John Wiley & Sons Canada Ltd, 2008).

"Canada cannot be seen": Janice Williamson, *Omar Khadr, Oh Canada* (Montreal: McGill-Queen's University Press, 2012).

"What we knew then": Janice Williamson, *Omar Khadr, Oh Canada* (Montreal: McGill-Queen's University Press, 2012).

CSIS interrogations: Janice Williamson, *Omar Khadr, Oh Canada* (Montreal: McGill-Queen's University Press, 2012).

Foreign Affairs statement on Omar: Janice Williamson, *Omar Khadr, Oh Canada* (Montreal: McGill-Queen's University Press, 2012).

"If one state is engaged in violations": Janice Williamson, *Omar Khadr, Oh Canada* (Montreal: McGill-Queen's University Press, 2012).

Guantanamo Bay after the interrogations: Janice Williamson, *Omar Khadr, Oh Canada* (Montreal: McGill-Queen's University Press, 2012).

Combatant Status Review Tribunals: Michelle Shephard, *Guantanamo's Child: The Untold Story of Omar Khadr* (Mississauga: John Wiley & Sons Canada Ltd, 2008).

"He grew up before our eyes": Michelle Shephard, *Guantanamo's Child: The Untold Story of Omar Khadr* (Mississauga: John Wiley & Sons Canada Ltd, 2008).

Hunger strike: Janice Williamson, *Omar Khadr, Oh Canada* (Montreal: McGill-Queen's University Press, 2012); Michelle Shephard, *Guantanamo's Child: The Untold Story of Omar Khadr* (Mississauga: John Wiley & Sons Canada Ltd, 2008).

Military Commissions: Michelle Shephard, *Guantanamo's Child: The Untold Story of Omar Khadr* (Mississauga: John Wiley & Sons Canada Ltd, 2008); Janice Williamson, *Omar Khadr, Oh Canada* (Montreal: McGill-Queen's University Press, 2012).

Clean team interrogations: Janice Williamson, *Omar Khadr, Oh Canada* (Montreal: McGill-Queen's University Press, 2012).

"You always say that I have an obligation": Janice Williamson, *Omar Khadr, Oh Canada* (Montreal: McGill-Queen's University Press, 2012).

Comments in Canada: Janice Williamson, *Omar Khadr, Oh Canada* (Montreal: McGill-Queen's University Press, 2012).

Foreign Affairs committee: Seventh Report of the Standing Committee on Foreign Affairs and International Development, June 2008.

Advocacy from other countries: Janice Williamson, *Omar Khadr, Oh Canada* (Montreal: McGill-Queen's University Press, 2012); Michelle Shephard, *Guantanamo's Child: The Untold Story of Omar Khadr* (Mississauga: John Wiley & Sons Canada Ltd, 2008).

In court: Michelle Shephard, *Guantanamo's Child: The Untold Story of Omar Khadr* (Mississauga: John Wiley & Sons Canada Ltd, 2008); Janice Williamson, *Omar Khadr, Oh Canada* (Montreal: McGill-Queen's University Press, 2012).

Bureaucratic delays: Janice Williamson, *Omar Khadr, Oh Canada* (Montreal: McGill-Queen's University Press, 2012).

In Canadian custody: "What Omar Khadr's lawyer said: 'Mr. Harper is a bigot'," *Toronto Star* (May 2015): http://www.thestar.com/news/world/2015/05/07/what-omar-khadrs-lawyer-said-mr-harper-is-a-bigot.html.

Bail: "Omar Khadr granted bail, but federal government to appeal," CBC (April 2015): http://www.cbc.ca/news/canada/edmonton/omar-khadr-granted-bail-but-federal-government-to-appeal-1.3046775; Rick McConnell, "Omar Khadr continues to divide Canadians," CBC (May 2015): http://www.cbc.ca/news/canada/edmonton/omar-khadr-continues-to-divide-canadians-1.3067505; "Omar Khadr's release on bail 'disappointing,' says public safety minister," CBC (May 2015): http://www.cbc.ca/news/canada/edmonton/omar-khadr-s-release-on-bail-disappointing-says-public-safety-minister-1.3064945; "What Omar Khadr's lawyer said: 'Mr. Harper is a bigot'," *Toronto Star* (May 2015): http://www.thestar.com/news/world/2015/05/07/what-omar-khadrs-lawyer-said-mr-harper-is-a-bigot.html; Debates, May 7, 2015; "Omar Khadr, free on bail, vows to prove he is 'a good person'," CBC (May 2015): http://www.cbc.ca/news/canada/edmonton/omar-khadr-free-on-bail-vows-to-prove-he-is-a-good-person-1.3065692; "Stephen Harper showing his vindictive side with attitude toward Omar Khadr," *Calgary Sun*, formerly available at: http://www.calgarysun.com/2015/05/10/prime-minister-stephen-harper-showing-his-vindictive-side-with-attitude-toward-omar-khadr.

Settlement: John Paul Tasker, "Government formally apologizes to Omar Khadr as Andrew Scheer condemns 'disgusting' payout," CBC (July 2017): https://www.cbc.ca/news/politics/cabinet-explain-omar-khadr-settlement-1.4194467.

9. A Canadian Is...:

Election results: John Paul Tasker, "Paul Calandra says it was a 'mistake' to focus on niqab, barbaric practices," CBC (October 2015): http://www.cbc.ca/news/politics/paul-calandra-niqab-c24-conservative-mistakes-1.3291271; interview with Haroon Siddiqui; "Justin Trudeau, for the record: 'We beat fear with hope'," *Maclean's* (October 2015): http://www.macleans.ca/politics/ottawa/justin-trudeau-for-the-record-we-beat-fear-with-hope/; Noor Javed, "'Unprecedented' surge in Muslim vote

in federal election: poll," *Toronto Star*, November 19, 2015, https://
www.thestar.com/news/gta/2015/11/19/unprecedented-surge-in-
muslim-vote-in-federal-election-poll.html.

Syrian refugees: "Timeline: Canada and the Syrian refugee
crisis," *Maclean's* (November 2015): http://www.macleans.ca/
politics/ottawa/timeline-canada-and-the-syrian-refugee-crisis/;
Stephanie Levitz, "Canada's ever-changing response to Syrian
refugee crisis," *Toronto Star* (January 2016): https://www.thestar.
com/news/canada/2016/01/01/canadas-ever-changing-response-
to-syrian-refugee-crisis.html.

"A terrorist is a terrorist is a terrorist": Evidence of the Standing
Committee on Citizenship and Immigration, April 12, 2016.

Omar Khadr: Marion Warnica, "Omar Khadr engaged to
Edmonton woman who tried to get him freed," CBC (April
2016): https://www.cbc.ca/news/canada/edmonton/omar-
khadr-engaged-to-edmonton-woman-who-tried-to-get-him-
freed-1.3542706; "Omar Khadr to stay out on bail after federal
government drops appeal," CBC (February 2016): http://www.cbc.
ca/news/politics/omar-khadr-bail-fight-1.3454278.

Mohamed Harkat: Debra Black, "Mohamed Harkat girds
himself for another fight to stay," *Toronto Star* (August 2016):
https://www.thestar.com/news/immigration/2016/08/02/
mohamed-harkat-girds-himself-for-another-fight-to-stay.html.

Donald Trump: Jenna Johnson and Abigail Hauslohner, "'I
think Islam hates us': A timeline of Trump's comments about
Islam and Muslims," *Washington Post* (May 2017): https://www.
washingtonpost.com/news/post-politics/wp/2017/05/20/i-think-
islam-hates-us-a-timeline-of-trumps-comments-about-islam-
and-muslims/?noredirect=on&utm_term=.b49049ae4189.

Refugee claimants arriving in Canada: Laura Glowacki, "Asylum seekers taking advantage of Canadian generosity, MP Ted Falk says," CBC (March 2017): http://www.cbc.ca/news/canada/manitoba/ted-falk-refugees-emerson-1.4011441.

Maryam Monsef: Robert Fife, "Heralded as Canada's first Afghan-born MP Maryam Monsef shocked to discover truth of roots," *The Globe and Mail* (September 2016): http://www.theglobeandmail.com/news/politics/mp-maryam-monsef-was-born-in-iran-not-afghanistan/article31995873/; Katie Simpson, "PM's top adviser compares Maryam Monsef criticism to U.S. 'birther' movement," CBC (September 2016): http://www.cbc.ca/news/politics/gerald-butts-likens-monsef-questions-to-us-birthers-1.3784793; "Maryam Monsef confirms she was born in Iran, not Afghanistan," CBC (September 2016): http://www.cbc.ca/news/politics/maryam-monsef-iran-afghanistan-1.3773930; "A question for Maryam Monsef about her birthplace," *The Globe and Mail* (September 2016): http://www.theglobeandmail.com/opinion/editorials/a-question-for-maryam-monsef-about-her-birthplace/article32113079/.

Jagmeet Singh: Kayla Goodfield, "'I'm not racist': Jagmeet Singh's heckler posts video defending herself," CTV (September 2017) http://toronto.ctvnews.ca/i-m-not-racist-jagmeet-singh-s-heckler-posts-video-defending-herself-1.3584886; Andray Domise, "Get real. Jagmeet Singh has been dealing with racist hecklers for months," *Maclean's* (September 2017): http://www.macleans.ca/news/canada/get-real-jagmeet-singh-has-been-dealing-with-racist-hecklers-for-months/.

Kellie Leitch: Angus Reid, "Canadians aren't as accepting as we think – and we can't ignore it, writes Angus Reid," CBC (October 2016): http://www.cbc.ca/news/canada/

angus-reid-poll-canadian-values-immigration-1.3789223;
Dara Lind, "Donald Trump's plan to subject immigrants to
'ideological tests' explained," *Vox* (August 2016): http://www.
vox.com/2016/8/16/12491000/trump-extreme-vetting-test-
immigrant; Aaron Wherry, "How do you screen beliefs? The
troublesome task of testing for 'anti-Canadian values'," CBC
(September 2016): http://www.cbc.ca/news/politics/wherry-
leitch-values-1.3746846; Aaron Wherry, "How Kellie Leitch
and Justin Trudeau are defining themselves on immigration,"
CBC (September 2016): http://www.cbc.ca/news/politics/
wherry-leitch-trudeau-immigration-1.3763951.

Hate crimes: Sheena Goodyear, "Paris attacks spark anti-Muslim
backlash, but Canadians are fighting back," CBC (November
 ͻ15): http://www.nccm.ca/anti-muslim-backlash-canadians-
fighting-back/; "Brother of alleged hate crime victim says
sister 'scarred for life'," CBC (November 2015): http://www.cbc.
ca/news/canada/toronto/muslim-woman-allegedly-attacked-
toronto-1.3322298; "Muslim student allegedly spat on, insulted by
stranger," CBC (November 2015): http://www.cbc.ca/news/canada/
toronto/muslim-student-spat-on-1.3326765; "Ottawa police
investigate hate crime after Muslim school targeted with graffiti,"
CBC (April 2016): http://www.cbc.ca/news/canada/ottawa/
ottawa-muslim-school-graffiti-1.3530626; *Calgary Sun*, formerly
available at: http://www.calgarysun.com/2016/02/20/hateful-
graffiti-scrawled-on-calgary-school-targets-syrian-newcomers-
prime-minister-justin-trudeau.

Alexandre Bisonnette: "The Quebec City Mosque attack: what
we know so far," *The Globe and Mail* (January 2017): http://www.
theglobeandmail.com/news/national/quebec-city-mosque-
shooting-what-we-know-so-far/article33826078/; "Leaving fear
behind," *The Globe and Mail* (February 2017).

Muslim cemetery: Elysha Enos, "19 voters quash Muslim-run cemetery in Saint-Apollinaire, Que," CBC (July 2017): http://www.cbc.ca/news/canada/montreal/muslim-cemetery-referendum-saint-apollinaire-1.4207923; "Muslim cemetery opponents collect 40 signatures in effort to block project in Saint-Apollinaire," CBC (April 2017): http://www.cbc.ca/news/canada/montreal/muslim-cemetery-opponents-referendum-1.4086423; Angelica Montgomery and Kim Garritty, "Quebec City mayor vows to give Muslims a place to bury dead," CBC (February 2017): http://www.cbc.ca/news/canada/montreal/muslim-burial-ground-quebec-1.3963553; Brent Bambury, "Quebec is split over Islamophobia one year after the mosque attack," CBC (January 2018): http://www.cbc.ca/radio/day6/episode-374-mosque-attack-anniversary-defending-horror-films-thrift-shops-vs-waste-shehacks-and-more-1.4500139/quebec-is-split-over-islamophobia-one-year-after-the-mosque-attack-1.4500153.

M-103: Debates, February 15, 2017; Jonathan Montpetit, "What we learned about the far right over the weekend," CBC (March 2017): http://www.cbc.ca/news/canada/montreal/far-right-m-103-protest-what-we-learned-1.4010710; Jonathan Montpetit and Stephen Smith, "Supporters, critics clash at Montreal protest over federal Islamophobia motion," CBC (March 2017): http://www.cbc.ca/news/canada/montreal/far-right-groups-opponents-clash-at-montreal-protest-against-federal-islamophobia-motion-1.4010179; Elizabeth Renzetti, "A motion to quell anti-Muslim hate shouldn't be up for debate, but here we are," *The Globe and Mail* (February 2017): https://www.theglobeandmail.com/opinion/a-motion-to-quell-anti-muslim-hate-shouldnt-be-up-for-debate-but-here-we-are/article34067397/; Laura Stone, "Kouvalis still on campaign team for Conservative leadership, Leitch says," *The Globe and Mail*, (February 2017): https://www.theglobeandmail.com/news/politics/

kouvalis-still-on-campaign-team-for-conservative-leadership-leitch-says/article34068481/; "House of Commons passes anti-Islamophobia motion," CBC (March 2017): http://www.cbc.ca/news/politics/m-103-islamophobia-motion-vote-1.4038016.

Bill 62: Benjamin Shingler, "'I should see your face, and you should see mine,' Quebec premier says of new religious neutrality law," CBC (October 2017): https://www.cbc.ca/news/canada/montreal/quebec-niqab-burka-bill-62-1.4360121; "OC Transpo won't enforce 'regressive' niqab law, mayor says," CBC (October 2017): https://www.cbc.ca/news/canada/ottawa/ottawa-mayor-quebec-bill-face-covering-1.4370994; Marilla Steuter-Martin, "Breaking down Bill 62: What you can and can't do while wearing a niqab in Quebec," CBC (October 2017): https://www.cbc.ca/news/canada/montreal/bill-62-examples-ministry-release-1.4369347; "Quebec doesn't have a problem with Islamophobia, Premier Legault says," CBC (January 2019): https://www.cbc.ca/news/canada/montreal/quebec-mosque-shooting-islamophobia-1.5000950; Emmett Macfarlane, "Quebec law banning face coverings is neither neutral nor constitutional," CBC (October 2017): https://www.cbc.ca/news/opinion/quebec-neutrality-law-1.4360942.

Bill 21: Benjamin Shingler, "What's in Quebec's secularism bill: Religious symbols, uncovered faces and a charter workaround," CBC (March 2019): https://www.cbc.ca/news/canada/montreal/quebec-laicity-secularism-bill-1.5075547.

Conservative Party: *Orillia Packet*, "The motion targeting islamophobia passed," previously available at: http://www.orilliapacket.com/2017/03/24/the-motion-targeting-islamophobia-passed-201-91; "House of Commons passes anti-Islamophobia motion," CBC (March 2017): http://www.cbc.ca/news/politics/m-103-islamophobia-motion-vote-1.4038016;

Ryan Maloney, "Kellie Leitch: American cousins threw out elites by electing Trump," Huffington Post (November 2016): http://www.huffingtonpost.ca/2016/11/09/kellie-leitch-donald-trump-fundraising-lisa-raitt_n_12878078.html; Laura Stone, "Immigrant-screening proposal about promoting tolerance, Leitch says," *The Globe and Mail* (September 2016): https://beta.theglobeandmail.com/news/politics/immigrant-screening-proposal-about-promoting-tolerance-leitch-says/article31737206/?ref=http://www.theglobeandmail.com&; Joanna Smith, "Should we screen immigrants for 'anti-Canadian values?' Kellie Leitch's campaign wants to know," CBC (September 2016): http://www.cbc.ca/beta/news/politics/kellie-leitch-survey-question-1.3744948.

Andrew Scheer: John Ibbitson, "In Andrew Scheer, Conservatives elect Stephen Harper 2.0 – with a smile," *The Globe and Mail* (May 2017): https://www.theglobeandmail.com/news/politics/andrew-scheer-conservatives-elect-stephen-harper-20-with-a-smile/article35138917/; Elizabeth Thompson, "Critics accuse Andrew Scheer of hiding policies after campaign win," CBC (May 2017): https://www.cbc.ca/news/politics/scheer-conservative-leadership-policies-1.4136911.

Maxime Bernier: Shannon Carranco and Jon Milton, "Decoding Canada's far right," *The Globe and Mail* (April 2019); "Bernier quits Conservatives to start new party," CTV (August 2018): https://www.ctvnews.ca/politics/bernier-quits-conservatives-to-start-new-party-1.4064855; "Maxime Bernier slams Justin Trudeau's 'cult of diversity' in Twitter rant," Global News (August 2018): https://globalnews.ca/news/4385065/maxime-bernier-twitter-diversity-justin-trudeau/.

The Rebel Media: Sean Craig, "New Tory leader Andrew Scheer campaign linked with controversial Rebel Media," Global

News (May 2017): https://globalnews.ca/news/3485784/andrew-scheer-rebel-media/; Stephanie Levitz, "Scheer says he'll reject interviews with The Rebel until it changes editorial direction," *Toronto Star* (August 2017): https://www.thestar.com/news/canada/2017/08/17/scheer-says-anything-that-gives-platform-to-obnoxious-groups-is-worth-condemning.html.

"United We Roll" convoy: Alex Boutilier, "Scheer defends speech to 'yellow vest'-associated protest," *Toronto Star* (February 2019): https://www.thestar.com/politics/federal/2019/02/26/scheer-defends-speech-to-yellow-vest-associated-protest.html; Angela Wright, "United We Roll wasn't just about oil and gas. Scheer knew that and worked the crowd anyway,"

CBC (February 2019): https://www.cbc.ca/news/opinion/united-we-roll-1.5030419; "Important context about the Yellow Vests Canada (YVC) convoy, aka 'United We Roll,'" Canadian Anti-Hate Network (February 2019): https://www.antihate.ca/important_context_about_the_yellow_vests_canada_yvc_convoy_aka_united_we_roll; John Geddes and Jason Markusoff, "Andrew Scheer has a problem," *Maclean's* (May 2019): https://www.macleans.ca/politics/andrew-scheer-has-a-problem/.

Terrorist attacks in Christchurch: Janice Dickson, "After New Zealand, Tory cancels event with anti-Muslim speaker; Scheer ripped by Harper aide for weak response," *The Globe and Mail* (March 2019): https://www.theglobeandmail.com/politics/article-tory-mp-cancels-event-with-controversial-speaker-out-of-respect-for/; Fatima Syed, "Hours after New Zealand terror attack, Andrew Scheer offers olive branch to Muslims," National Observer (March 2019): https://www.nationalobserver.com/2019/03/15/news/andrew-scheer-just-responded-new-zealand-terror-attack-without-mentioning-muslims; Emma Teitel, "Andrew Scheer can't be tough on crime if he is soft on

hate," *Toronto Star* (March 2019): https://www.msn.com/en-ca/
news/politics/emma-teitel-andrew-scheer-cant-be-tough-on-
crime-if-he-is-soft-on-hate/ar-BBVdQUK?ocid=spartanntp;
Stephen Maher, "Why won't Maxime Bernier denounce the
terror attack in Christchurch?" *Maclean's* (March 2019): https://
www.macleans.ca/opinion/why-wont-maxime-bernier-
denounce-the-terror-attack-in-christchurch/.

Michael Cooper: Elise von Scheel, "Muslim witness calls for
MP to be booted from caucus after 'you should be ashamed'
outburst," CBC (June 2019): https://www.cbc.ca/news/politics/
muslim-witness-calls-for-mp-to-be-booted-from-caucus-
after-you-should-be-ashamed-outburst-1.5159346; Cosmin
Dzsurdzsa, "'They are rewriting history': Maxime Bernier
defends Michael Cooper on CTV while Conservatives curiously
absent," The Post Millennial (June 2019): https://www.
thepostmillennial.com/they-are-rewriting-history-maxime-
bernier-defends-michael-cooper-on-ctv-while-conservatives-
curiously-absent/.

Jason Kenney: Lisa MacGregor and Karen Bartko, "UCP
candidate for Calgary-South East resigns, says she's 'tired of
being bullied for her beliefs'," Global News (March 2019):
https://globalnews.ca/news/5091982/alberta-election-ucp-
candidate-calgary-south-east-resigns/; Adam Toy, "Todd Beasley
defends anti-Muslim Facebook posts after removal from Brooks-
Medicine Hate UCP

nomination," Global News (July 2018): https://globalnews.ca/
news/4334292/todd-beasley-anti-muslim-posts-removal-from-
ucp-nomination/.

Doug Ford: Emma Paling, "White nationalist Faith Goldy is
now campaigning as the Doug Ford candidate," Huffington Post

(September 2018): https://www.huffingtonpost.ca/2018/09/26/
white-nationalist-faith-goldy-is-now-campaigning-as-the-doug-
ford-candidate_a_23542808/.

Trudeau budget bill: Andrew MacDougall, "The new Liberal
strategy: turn into Conservatives," *Maclean's* (April 2019): https://
www.msn.com/en-ca/news/politics/the-new-liberal-strategy-
turn-into-conservatives/ar-BBVQqK7?ocid=spartandhp.

10. "The Gifts":

Freedom of association: Sheema Khan, *Of Hockey and Hijab:
Reflections of a Canadian Muslim Woman* (Toronto: TSAR
Publications, 2009); Baljit Nagra, "Unequal Citizenship: Being
Muslim and Canadian in the Post 9/11 Era" (Ph.D. diss.,
University of Toronto, 2011).

Relationship between Muslims and non-Muslims: Chris Selly,
"Tories might have a crass political agenda, but it's not an
anti-Muslim one," *National Post* (March 2015): http://news.
nationalpost.com/full-comment/chris-selley-tories-might-have-
a-crass-political-agenda-but-its-not-an-anti-muslim-one;
Dr. Zijad Delic, *Canadian Islam: Belonging and Loyalty* (Ottawa:
Kirtas Publishing, 2014).

Polls: Dr. Zijad Delic, *Canadian Islam: Belonging and Loyalty*
(Ottawa: Kirtas Publishing, 2014); Shanifa Nasser, "How
Islamophobia is driving young Canadian Muslims to reclaim
their identity," CBC (April 2016): http://www.cbc.ca/news/
canada/environics-muslim-canadian-survey-1.3551465; "They
have not been able to explain clearly": Karim H. Karim, *Islamic
Peril: Media and Global Violence* (Montreal: Black Rose Books,
2003).

Policy changes: National Council of Canadian Muslims, www. nccm.ca; interview with Amira Elghawaby; interview with David Zackrias; interview with Alia Hogben.

Baljit Nagra's study: Baljit Nagra, "Unequal Citizenship: Being Muslim and Canadian in the Post 9/11 Era" (Ph.D. diss., University of Toronto, 2011).

"The fact that a Muslim woman can engage": Sheema Khan, *Of Hockey and Hijab: Reflections of a Canadian Muslim Woman* (Toronto: TSAR Publications, 2009).

Cold Lake: "Town rallies around vandalized Cold Lake Mosque," CBC (October 2014): http://www.cbc.ca/news/canada/edmonton/town-rallies-around-vandalized-cold-lake-mosque-1.2811968; "Cold Lake Mosque hit by vandals, again," CBC (November 2015): http://www.cbc.ca/news/canada/calgary/cold-lake-mosque-vandalized-again-1.3342228; Sarah Rieger, "Cold Lake Mosque vandalized for the second time," Huffington Post (November 2015): http://www.huffingtonpost.ca/2015/11/30/cold-lake-mosque_n_8683138.html.

Hamilton social experiment: "Hamilton racism 'social experiment' ends with a punch," *Toronto Star* (October 2014): http://www.thestar.com/news/gta/2014/10/29/hamilton_racism_social_experiment_ends_with_a_punch.html; Adam Carter, "Nathan Cirillo-inspired racism 'experiment' ends with sucker punch," CBC (October 2014): http://www.cbc.ca/news/canada/hamilton/news/nathan-cirillo-inspired-racism-experiment-ends-with-sucker-punch-1.2816837; Christian Cotroneo, "Omar Albach video 'Canadians react to Ottawa shooting,' ends with punch in face," Huffington Post (October 2014): http://www.huffingtonpost.ca/2014/10/29/omar-albach-islam-video-canada_n_6066622.html.

Toronto social experiment: Rachel Jones, "Blindfolded Muslim takes to the street for hugging experiment," *The Telegraph* (February 2015): http://www.telegraph.co.uk/news/worldnews/ northamerica/canada/11406213/Blindfolded-Muslim-takes-to-the-street-for-hugging-experiment.html; May Warren, "From Yonge and Dundas Square to Paris, with love," *Toronto Star* (November 2015): http://www.thestar.com/news/gta/2015/11/25/ from-yonge-and-dundas-square-to-paris-with-love.html; Steven D'Souza, "New Yorker re-creates Canadian Hug-a-Muslim experiment," CBC (March 2015): http://www.cbc.ca/ news/world/new-yorker-re-creates-canadian-hug-a-muslim-experiment-1.2990717.

11. Afterword:

"In looking back through Canadian history": Sheema Khan, *Of Hockey and Hijab: Reflections of a Canadian Muslim Woman* (Toronto: TSAR Publications, 2009).

Peterborough mosque: "Peterborough mosque arson is suspected hate crime," CBC (November 2015): http://www.cbc. ca/news/canada/toronto/mosque-peterborough-fire-1.3320013; "Peterborough mosque hit by arson reaches $80k crowdfunding goal," CBC (November 2015): http://www.cbc.ca/news/ canada/toronto/peterborugh-mosque-fire-1.3320488; Selena Ross, "'Motivated by Hate': Muslim girls told not to walk alone in Toronto at night," *The Globe and Mail* (November 2015): http://www.theglobeandmail.com/news/toronto/ assault-of-toronto-woman-being-treated-as-a-hate-crime/ article27291302/.

Graeme Truelove

The views expressed in this work are solely those of the author in his private capacity. While all due care was taken, the responsibility for any errors, omissions or views expressed herein remains with the author and cannot and should not be attributed to the House of Commons, its employees, officers and agents, or the Board of Internal Economy.

Acknowledgements

MY WIFE JANINE and I were driving somewhere along Highway 7 in southern Ontario when she suggested the idea for this book. I had been unsure of what to write next, and without her insight and instinct, I might still be wondering. The book was written in Ottawa, Delta, Orillia and Phoenix between 2014 and 2019. I hope the final product is worthy of the vision we discussed on that long drive.

There is a long list of people and organizations to whom I have become indebted since I last wrote a list like this including: Jordan Abel; Omar Alghabra; the BC Book Prizes; Pamela Bean; the Bill Reid Gallery of Northwest Coast Art; Books on Beechwood; Caitlin Jesson and Book Warehouse; Marie Paul and the Burnaby Public Library; Alia Hogben and the Canadian Council of Muslim Women; Leslie Clark and Chapters; Jeff O'Reilly and D'Arcy McGee's; Michelle Douglas; Dennis Edney; Noah Evanchuk; Ron Fisher; Mary Choy, Phil Fernandez, Casey Sabawi, Vanessa Wong and Frontier College; Jim Schmidt, Lee Trentadue, Mary Trentadue and the Galiano Literary Festival; Scott Dagostino and Glad Day Bookshop; Ihsaan Gardee; David Goa; Bill Graham; Marisa Alps at Harbour Publishing, Meagan and Michael Hatch; Jason Herda; David Hoskin; the genius photographers at Intuition Photography; Barbara Jackman; Peter Julian; Brett and Maria Kenworthy; Sheema Khan; Ijab Khanafer; Bob Kimberley; Arno Kopecky; Walter Lanz; Philippe Larocque; Stephanie Lawson; Dave LeDrew; Megan Leslie; Catherine Leggett; Stephen Lewis; Brian Lim; David McGrane; Amber McMillan; Grant McLaughlin; Linda McQuaig; Tracey Mitchell; Amira

Elghawaby and the National Council of Canadian Muslims; Mike Leyne, Rolf Maurer and New Star Books; Zarqa Nawaz; Alexis Normand; Elise Normand; Peter O'Neil; Staff Sergeant David Zackrias and the Ottawa Police Service; Jennifer Pedersen; Sarah Pendlebury; John Taylor and the People's Co-op Bookstore; Lynda Grace Philippsen; Kerry Pither; Sarah Polley; Peter Prebble; James Rajotte; Sheila Schroeder; Michelle Shephard; Haroon Siddiqui; Alan Zisman and Spartacus Books; David Suzuki; Kevin Williams and Talonbooks; Manon Tremblay; Sean Tucker and his lovely family; Peter Garden and Turning the Tide Bookstore; University of British Columbia Press; the University of Saskatchewan; the University of Regina; Sergeant Jason Robillard and the Vancouver Police Department; Raili Haapalainen and the Vancouver Public Library; Gillian Wigmore; Carleton Wilson; Norman Zepp; and Rebecca Peng at ZG Communications. To all of you, thank you from the bottom of my heart.

I would particularly like to thank Silas White and Nightwood Editions for their professionalism and dedication and, most of all, for believing in this project. I met Silas in 2014 and carried his business card around in my wallet for years after because I had a feeling we would work together someday. I'm glad I did.

I would also like to thank my family, especially: my always-supportive in-laws, Brian and Gaye Bell, who told Kevin O'Leary's family I was as famous as him; my brother-in-law John Muggleton and my sister Dana Truelove, whose dedication to the arts continues to inspire me; my father, Patrick Truelove, who taught me everything I needed to know about politics; and my mother, Judy Truelove, whose sharp, careful work helped fine-tune the many clumsy sentences in earlier versions of this book. It is thanks to her guidance, support and love of language that I became a writer.

Finally, I would like to thank my wife, Janine Truelove, not only for coming up with the idea, but also for reading and offering comments on the manuscript. Her suggestions turned a somewhat-dense collection of facts and quotes into something readable

and engaging, and I am thankful for the support and encourage-
ment she has always shown for my writing. She is a talented artist,
a wonderful wife and mother, and has my undying love. This book
would not exist without her, and so it is to her, and to our extraordinary daughter Abigail, that it is dedicated.

About the Author

GRAEME TRUELOVE IS the author of the critically acclaimed biography *Svend Robinson: A Life in Politics* (New Star Books, 2013) which was shortlisted for a 2014 BC Book Prize and listed on the *BC Bookworld* Bestseller List. He has worked on Parliament Hill since 2001. He lives in Ottawa with his wife Janine and daughter Abigail.

Index